Enterprise Agile®

Practical Insight and Methods for Successful IT Delivery

Innovations in technology and commerce have combined to disrupt traditional business models and drive an increased pace of change.

Organisations are looking to employ new working methods and technologies to increase their Agility, whilst remaining efficient and without introducing significant risk.

BJSS has developed the Enterprise Agile® approach to help organisations realise greater value through increased flexibility to meet user needs. The approach has been developed by expert practitioners and draws on nearly 30 years' experience of successful delivery for public and private sector clients.

This book presents key concepts of the BJSS Enterprise Agile® approach and offers practical guidance for anyone involved in the delivery and support of technology-led products and services.

bjss.com/enterprise-agile

First edition published in 2008 in Great Britain by

BJSS Limited
1 Whitehall Quay
Leeds
LS1 4HR
United Kingdom

Ninth edition ('Norma Jean'), 17th January 2022.

ISBN: 978-0-9565371-9-5

This book is a FSC® Carbon Balanced Product.

About BJSS

BJSS is the UK's leading privately-owned technology and engineering consultancy for business. Trusted by its clients, BJSS collaborates to deliver complex, innovative technology, engineering, and industry solutions that millions of people use every day.

Renowned for technical excellence, cost-effective delivery, and its award-winning Enterprise Agile approach, BJSS works with some of the world's largest public and private sector organisations to design, deliver and support large-scale digital transformation.

With locations across the UK, Europe, the USA, and Australia, BJSS is an end-to-end transformation partner covering everything from strategy and service design through to technology delivery and managed services.

The Queen's Award for Enterprise

The Enterprise Agile approach is a distillation of years of our learnings from delivering industrial-strength software for clients in some of the most complex environments, and has been recognised with a Queen's Award for Enterprise in the Innovation category.

Foreword

When our company was founded in 1993, one of our core principles was a total focus on delivery. In our constant search to deliver on that vision, we have dedicated a great deal of effort to discover what works and what doesn't when designing, delivering, and maintaining enterprise-scale systems.

One of our core values as a business is the pride we take in sharing our knowledge and expertise with clients. We first published this book in 2008 to distill thousands of work years of real-world experience of creating industrial-strength software in some of the most demanding public and private sector environments. And we've regularly updated the book to document how our thinking has changed with the constantly changing trends in technology and business.

Enterprise Agile is now in its ninth edition, and we have evolved our approach as global pressures drive our clients to implement new business models, and as innovations in technology redefine the way organisations operate. This latest updated includes a new chapter about how enterprise-level organisations can drive value through data-led programmes, outlining Agile approaches to the data challenge that our clients have found useful.

I hope you find something of value here and that we have helped encourage you to put into practice some of the techniques we describe.

Stuart Bullock
Managing Director, BJSS

Contents

Chapter 01

The Agility Challenge

Irrespective of the nature of your organisation, the chances are you are grappling with the same challenge - how to more rapidly and reliably adapt to the changing demands of clients, consumers or citizens within a shifting global marketplace.

While the drive to do things faster, cheaper and better is not new, the number of sectors being disrupted by innovative commercial models powered by digital technologies is unprecedented. These inventive new offerings further increase the expectations of customers, driving organisations to quickly adapt their services, or risk becoming irrelevant.

Introduction

In the first edition of Enterprise Agile, published in 2008, we focused on the use of Agile techniques to deliver software projects. Since then, we have delivered many more projects using our Enterprise Agile method.

In the light of the Covid-19 pandemic, these techniques, as well as the values and principles that underpin them, have been demonstrated to be relevant beyond just software delivery. During a period of unprecedented disruption, some previously successful organisations have tragically failed to survive. Others, however, have been able to respond quickly and effectively to the changes thrust upon them, their customers and their employees. These organisations have been able to survive, and in some cases thrive, in a radically different world.

At a time of rapid upheaval, Agility is no longer the preserve of Software Development Teams in isolation from the rest of the enterprise. It is increasingly important that the entire organisation follows Agile values and principles and is capable of rapid change.

In response to these changes, we have updated our approach once again. In this revised edition, we look not only at the software delivery lifecycle but also at the wider subject of building and running technology-led products and services in an Agile organisation. This expanded scope includes areas such as remote and hybrid working, enterprise data, integrating business change, Design Thinking, service management, Cloud and software-defined infrastructure.

We have significantly expanded the scope of our method, but the underlying principles remain:

1. **An absolute focus on high-quality delivery**
2. **A risk-first approach to prioritising delivery and change**
3. **Strong architecture and engineering principles at the core**
4. **Using only 'Necessary and Sufficient' processes and artefacts**
5. **Delivering change with a 'No surprises endgame'.**

As in previous editions of this book, we explore current concepts, outline our views and experience, and present our approach for successful delivery. We aim to help all organisations address the Agility challenge with a focus on the delivery of high-quality, technology-led products and services.

Concepts

The Drivers for Agility

The events of the previous 18 months have taught us just how unpredictable the future can be and the critical importance of being able to respond rapidly to the changes to market conditions and consumer behaviours.

Amid an unprecedented level of global upheaval, digital technologies continue to be a key catalyst for increased Agility. Digital adoption has skyrocketed across virtually every industry and customer segment, prompting many organisations to reconsider their entire business model. Social media enables near-instant feedback, making or breaking products and services overnight. As economic pressures have intensified, consumers have become increasingly fickle, and the abundance of aggregators such as price comparison engines makes shopping around easier than ever before. Long term brand loyalty is much less prevalent when consumer purchasing decisions are driven by price.

As a result, organisations are seeking to transform themselves and embed the ability to change to meet customer needs into the fabric of who they are. By reorganising themselves to rapidly deliver business and technological change, businesses can respond to the challenges of:

- **Global events that transform customer needs, invalidate business models, and necessitate new and different operating models**
- **Disruption of a whole industry sector by innovative commercial models delivered by digital technologies**
- **Reduced customer loyalty and the ease of switching to new service providers**
- **Demand from a technologically savvy customer base that is increasingly seeking better digital experiences.**

Delivering More with Less

Not only do organisations now face unprecedented pressure to rapidly change and deliver new services, but they must also increase efficiency and minimise expenditure while doing so. Doing more with less is a common theme across all industry sectors, and achieving it means not only delivering change effectively but also becoming more efficient at running existing products and services.

Success is no longer measured by delivering a pre-defined scope on time and to budget. The success of a product is defined by its ability to deliver business value by meeting customer needs. The challenge organisations face is delivering this value with the minimum expenditure possible and then, once delivered, gathering feedback from customers to build the next iteration as rapidly and cost-effectively as possible.

Considerable work has been done over the years on Lean thinking in manufacturing, and Agile delivery in technology. At BJSS we talk about efficiency in terms of lightweight processes supporting the 'Necessary and Sufficient' tasks for predictable and efficient delivery.

Managing Risk

A desire for predictability in project and technology delivery is common to all our conversations with clients. Organisations are driven to plan and budget in annual cycles, often as a result of the need to meet short-term shareholder or stakeholder expectations. Corporate governance often drives risk avoidance behaviours that are counter to the need to evolve and innovate for long term survival.

Every organisation must innovate and embrace Agility to survive in markets that are being disrupted with greater frequency than ever before. Innovation and Agility are the essential ingredients of a modern successful organisation, but embracing Agility cannot result in a loss of control or governance. Over many years we have adapted Agile techniques to harness the benefits of incremental delivery and the flexibility to change whilst providing a degree of predictability and linkage to good governance practices.

The key to predictability is not to try and know everything up front before committing to something, but to know just enough that the risk profile is understood. Key risks can then be managed and surprises during delivery avoided. This requires properly configured and experienced teams, supported by sufficient, lightweight processes.

A Brief Overview of Agile

The set of principles and practices that the industry has come to know as Agile ways of working have been around for some time. The underlying concepts can be traced back to software development methodologies such as XP, RUP and Scrum that originated in the 1990s.

We can look even further back to parallels in manufacturing, research and development practices such as Toyota's Lean manufacturing or Lockheed Martin's Skunk Works.

Written in 2001, the Agile Manifesto has come to codify and act as a rallying point for similar philosophies and ways of working.

Figure 1-1: The Agile Manifesto

We are uncovering better ways of developing software by doing it and helping others do it.

Through this work we have come to value:

Individuals and interactions over processes and tools

Working software over comprehensive documentation

Customer collaboration over contract negotiation

Responding to change over following a plan

That is, while there is value in the items on the right, we value the items on the left more.

A common misconception is that Agile working supports extremes of behaviour, such as the abandonment of processes, plans and documentation. The Manifesto itself states that this is not the case (as it attributes value to the items on the right) and some of the authors of the Manifesto have gone on record to suggest that it primarily indicates a weighting or preference to guide behaviour when constrained or operating at edge cases.

Agile is not a process or methodology in itself, but rather a philosophy and an umbrella term for an expanding number of frameworks and practices that share common principles and values. Irrespective of the methodologies adopted, organisations or teams that succeed in embracing Agile working share many traits, including:

- **A focus on satisfying the customer's needs**
- **Value derived through end deliverables rather than intermediate artefacts**
- **Iterative working with tight feedback loops**
- **'Necessary and Sufficient' ceremonies and documentation**
- **Anticipation and acceptance of change**
- **Elimination of overheads/waste**
- **Concurrent working over consecutive working**
- **Early (and continuous) focus on quality**
- **Minimisation of independent silos of practice, knowledge or control**
- **Introspection and continuous improvement.**

Although Agility may not necessarily directly improve straight-line delivery speed, the elimination of unnecessary work, focus on small deliveries, maximisation of concurrency and emphasis on delivery of customer value will often yield a significant performance improvement for many teams.

As mentioned previously, a number of these concepts originate from outside of software development, and as a result, many of them are relevant to the wider organisation. Agile is no longer a term that can be applied exclusively to software.

BJSS Opinion

The Value Triangle

In earlier editions of this book, we discussed the concept of the iron triangle for a software development project. This considers the triple constraint of scope, time and cost, and the challenge of meeting all three simultaneously to create a quality outcome.

We recently updated this diagram to address a broader triple constraint facing organisations, particularly the technology function - the Value Triangle. This challenges CIOs to deliver technology predictably, with low risk, whilst retaining organisational flexibility and Agility, reducing costs and delivering value for money.

This updated Value Triangle is shown in **Figure 1-2** and is something we address throughout this book.

Figure 1-2: The Value Triangle for the Agile Organisation

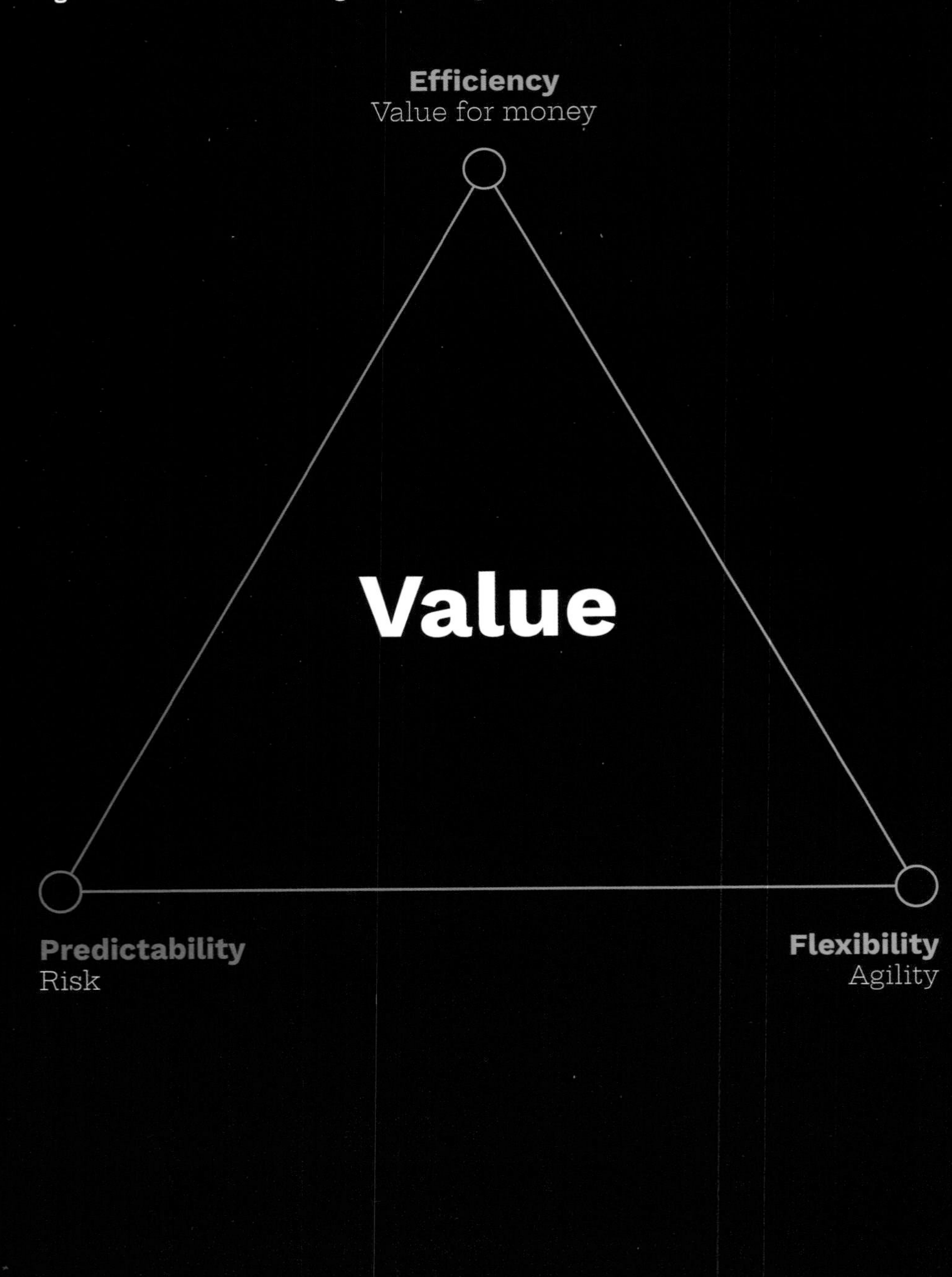

Becoming a More Agile Organisation

Organisations must become more Agile - to embrace change, innovate and be more responsive to user needs.

This book offers practical insights into organisation, processes, and techniques to deliver change and technology-led products. It is worth noting that becoming a more Agile organisation is an ongoing journey, not a one-off activity, and so we do not offer a prescriptive target operating model for the organisation.

Embracing change requires good working practices, with feedback loops for continuous improvement, and a supportive culture and values system for the people involved. Organisations that combine these essential ingredients will thrive.

Change Often

Becoming a flexible organisation involves becoming comfortable with change as a routine activity. This is good for the organisation as it enables it to be responsive to customer needs and more readily realise value from those relationships.

Change can be unsettling for the people involved, but we believe it is worth learning to embrace this and using a culture and values system to support individuals in feeling secure in an organisation that regularly innovates and adapts.

Another barrier to frequent change is often an aversion to the 'risk' of technology change. This generally becomes a self-fulfilling prophecy. Due to the perceived risk of technology changes, rigorous approval gates and associated process overhead are mandated in an attempt to reduce the risk of failure. This high 'release tax' ensures change is less frequent and, as a consequence, more changes are put into each release.

Bigger changes of course carry a greater risk of failure. Modern DevOps and Continuous Delivery techniques can help break this cycle.

Overcoming Potential Barriers to Agility

Moving towards a more Agile organisation, one able to rapidly embrace change, isn't without challenges, but the benefits are worthwhile. Recent innovations in technology and delivery approaches have provided mechanisms for surmounting many of the traditional barriers to organisational Agility. Throughout this book, we offer some insights into how to overcome some of the typical challenges.

The Enterprise Agile Approach

Built on Experience

As a supplier that values long term client relationships and organic growth, we recognise the importance of delivering on our commitments. To do this, we have developed the approach described in this book. Enterprise Agile is what we believe 'good looks like' in terms of implementing technology change and running technology services. The ideas, processes and philosophy outlined here are embodied in the work we do for us to be successful as a supplier and for our clients to realise the value of their investment.

A focus on delivery is embedded in our psyche. Many evangelists theorise about how to deliver change and technology initiatives. We have written this book based on practical experience and insights and lessons learned from delivering hundreds of projects over more than 28 years to a broad range of clients in sectors as diverse as Public Sector, Health and Social Care, Retail and Consumer Markets, Financial Services, and Energy, Commodities and Utilities.

This perspective is an important dimension that is often missed from other texts on Agility. If your vendor model is not aligned to enterprise architecture and the delivery model, significant issues are likely. Organisational tensions and politics arising from misaligned goals will adversely impact the delivery of effective change.

Most organisations of any scale work with multiple suppliers to deliver all or part of their operational business processes, customer engagement and technology. It is only when supplier incentives and vendor management are consistent with the organisational goals, architecture and delivery model, that true Agility is possible.

Founding Principles

Successfully delivering change is first and foremost about people. Whatever the change initiative, the outcome will be determined by bringing people on the journey and engaging high-ability teams to deliver.

Supporting the teams delivering services are the lightweight patterns, processes, technology and tooling that we describe.

To guide any change initiative, we focus closely on two key components:

- **Insight** - Into the needs of the user and the marketplace
- **High-Quality Deliverables** - To underpin and de-risk the delivery.

Ultimately the goal of any change initiative is to create value for the organisation. Delivering business and technological change must be guided by insight and sound discipline. Supporting this are several essential principles:

- **Risk-First** - Prioritising change based on risk profile
- **Sustainability** – Building resilient solutions that can easily support change well into the future
- **Quality Built-in** – Embedding quality from the outset
- **Transparency** – Clarity throughout the delivery process
- **Innovation** – Thinking beyond the usual solution
- **'Necessary and Sufficient'** – Doing just enough of the right things.

Where to go Next

This book recommends good practice in the areas of People, Process and Tools - the three ingredients required for organisational Agility. If you are new to some of the concepts here you may wish to read from start to finish. Readers looking to pursue specific topics might want to choose from those listed below.

Within each chapter, we provide a consistent structure that introduces key concepts, offers our opinion and experience and outlines the Enterprise Agile method for achieving success.

Chapter 2 – Organisational Agility

Introduces some of the principles important in achieving greater Agility in both organisations and product delivery whilst managing risk.

Chapter 3 - A Pattern for Delivering Value

Provides a map of the approaches to delivering products to customers and introduces the Enterprise Agile product lifecycle.

Chapter 4 - The Optimal Team

Discusses how to structure people around the process and the human factors to be considered in creating productive teams.

Chapter 5 - Effective Leadership

Identifies the leadership skills and practices essential to building and running quality products.

Chapter 6 - Understanding Human-Centred Design

Outlines a structured approach to capturing user needs and focusing on achieving organisational outcomes.

Chapter 7 - Crafting the Product Increment

Describes the anatomy of the Sprint as the unit of delivery and the daily operating rhythm of Delivery Teams.

Chapter 8 - Engineering Quality Outcomes

Explores the delivery pipeline and engineering practices used in changing and running products to a high standard.

Chapter 9 - Service Agility

Describes how Enterprise Agile combines traditional structured service management approaches with Agile delivery.

Chapter 10 - The Journey to Agility

Suggests where to start with implementing greater Agility in the organisation and making it work in a client and supplier relationship.

Chapter 11 – Enterprise Data

Applying some of the principles and values of Enterprise Agile to data projects in order to deliver meaningful business results.

Afterword

Provides a link to more practical details of how to implement Enterprise Agile in your organisation.

Appendix A - Engineering Successful Change

Presents some 'golden rules' for achieving a 'No surprises endgame'.

Appendix B - Glossary

Defines some of the key terms used throughout the book.

Key Points

1. Rapid change is essential if organisations are to survive disruption.
2. Organisations are looking to create value through change and are grappling with the triple constraint of flexibility, effectiveness, and predictability.
3. Many of the historic barriers to greater Agility have been dissolved by new approaches and technologies. The global Covid-19 pandemic has also accelerated the need for businesses to be more rapidly responsive to change.
4. The Enterprise Agile approach focuses on insight into user needs and high-quality delivery principles.
5. This book describes a method for building and running technology-led products based on nearly 30 years of practical experience.

Chapter 02

Organisational Agility

Organisations are seeking greater Agility to thrive in a rapidly changing world where delivering value to customers is key. Meeting this challenge requires updated thinking on how to build and run technology, and how to weave this new approach into the organisational fabric.

Greater Agility requires a combination of the right people, supported by the organisational culture and values, lightweight processes, and appropriate tools. We start by exploring some of these key components and the essential things that enable Agility.

Concepts

Technology at the Heart of the Organisation

Organisations have historically imposed functional divides within their internal structure. There is, of course, a need to group people and processes in an organisation of any reasonable scale. The challenge as organisations grow is that people can develop an affinity to their job function at the expense of the delivery of business value through the product or service they provide.

Enabling true organisation-wide Agility requires a rethink of what organisations look and feel like. The established view of IT as an internal service provider, separate from 'the business' requires re-examination. Technologies can no longer be seen as merely useful tools provided by the IT department to help businesses execute their processes. To deliver innovative digital services, all modern organisations need technology at their core. The successful modern organisation is, fundamentally, a technology organisation operating in a particular domain.

Figure 2-1: Organisational Convergence

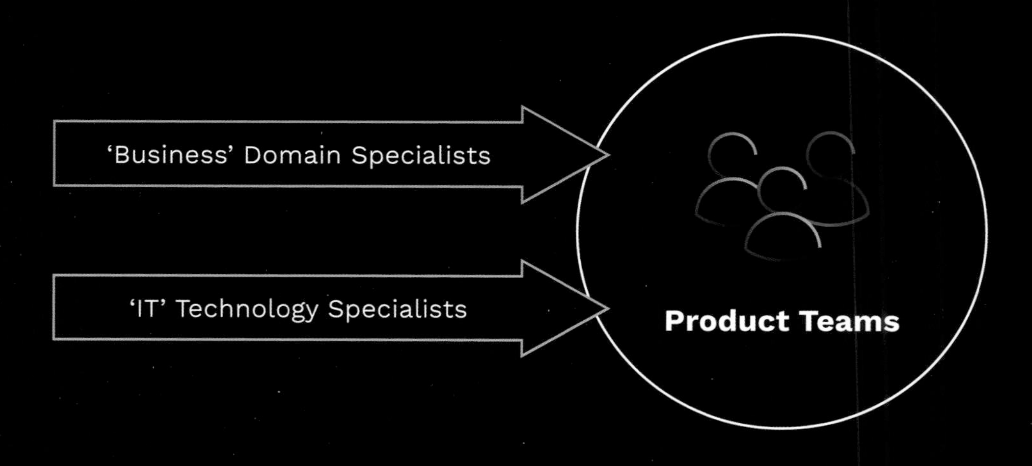

Now more than ever, CIOs need to understand how technology can add value to the organisation while CMOs need to understand what it can offer customers. In a rush to meet these challenges, many organisations have appointed a CDO (Chief Digital Officer). This move may help to get to a digital strategy more quickly, but to be able to transform into a truly Agile organisation that can rapidly deliver change, a deeper cultural and structural shift is required.

We explore culture and organisation in more detail in **Chapter 4**.

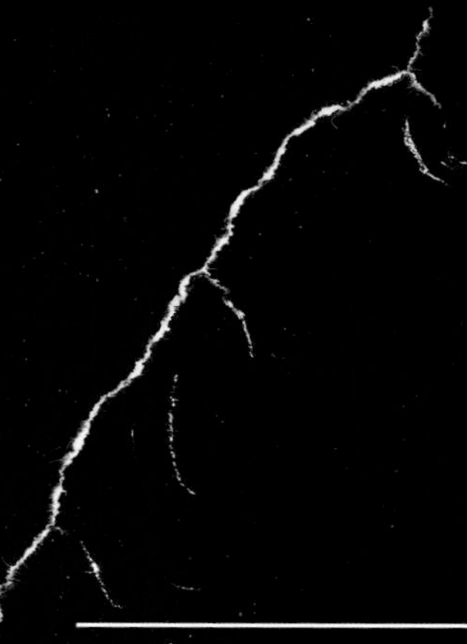

Multi-Speed IT

Delivering new and innovative digital services will not typically be a greenfield adventure. Unless you are a start-up or a relatively young organisation, you will already have mature back-office systems, legacy technology, and a wealth of experience around your customer needs and business processes. The challenge is to leverage existing knowledge and systems to change rapidly - without being constrained by a lack of elasticity in the legacy world.

Many people have already considered this dilemma and produced a variety of models to allow for varying rates of change. Much of this thinking is based on the concept of shearing layers - the different refresh rates of the components of a building: 'site, structure, skin, services, space and stuff'. The site on which a building is placed is fixed forever. The structure of a building is expected to last tens of years, whilst the services, layout and décor will change more frequently.

The use of shearing layers is adopted by the architectural principle of pace layering that designs buildings with future adaptability in mind.

Figure 2-2: Gartner Pace Layering

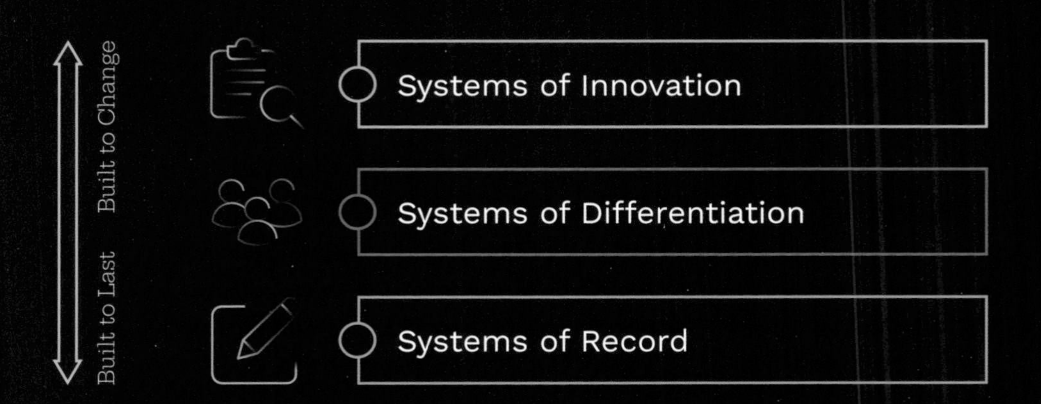

Pace layering was introduced into the technology domain by Gartner. Within the technology model, it is acknowledged that different systems can evolve at different speeds based on their proximity to the end-customer and the need for innovation.

The idea of multi-speed technology change was also popularised by Geoffrey Moore, who proposed that rapidly changing systems of engagement could be used to fuel innovation and develop new services with more stable systems of record as foundations.

Figure 2-3: Bimodal Technology Change

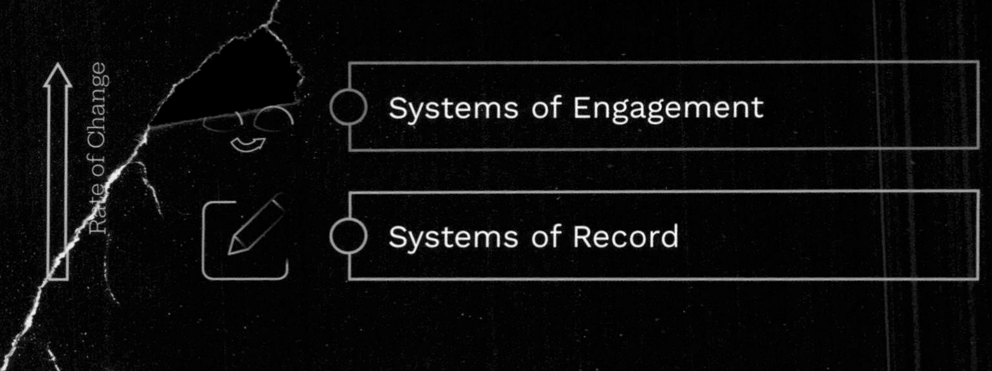

These models can be thought of as multi-lane highways with a different velocity of change in each lane. Both models highlight two key points that we will return to several times throughout this book:

1. **There is no 'one size fits all' delivery approach**
2. **Appropriate architecture is essential.**

The point on architecture is important - it is a critical ingredient in supporting one of the core values of Enterprise Agile - sustainability and the ability to easily support change well into the future. You can only achieve this proposed separation of layers if your technology stack supports it.

This is where well-defined APIs and service layers become essential. The use of these interfaces allows work to start while decisions on UI, database, and inter-service communication are yet to be made – which, in turn, demonstrates business value to customers early. Delivering value to the customer at the earliest opportunity can mean the difference between a customer-led success story and a technology-centric project that failed to deliver.

The Product Portfolio

The concept of portfolio management dates back to the 1970s. Whereas projects and programmes are temporary structures that deliver change, a portfolio is an enduring model of the applications in the organisation and is used to direct investment.

The product portfolio thus represents the work that the [illegible] is undertaking to deliver its strategy. Combining the produc[illegible] with a tool such as the McFarlan Matrix allows an organisation [illegible] track how individual initiatives contribute to each strategic goal.

Figure 2-4: McFarlan's Portfolio Matrix

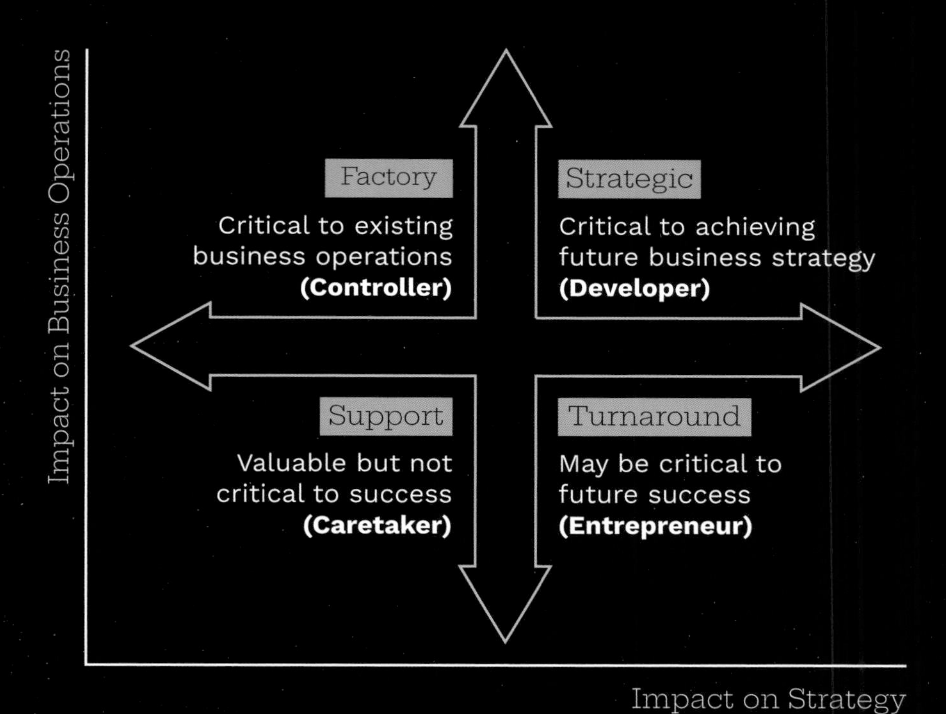

Figure 2-4 shows an example of the McFarlan Matrix of Portfolio Categorisation, which provides four basic classifications of application.

Complementing a portfolio view of applications is the ITIL (information technology infrastructure library) service portfolio or catalogue. Similarly, this describes the services provided by a technology function often related to the support of the application portfolio. Within the modern organisation, a portfolio management approach is still relevant, although separation of applications and services is likely to be replaced by a common view of the technology-led products provided to internal and external user communities.

Innovation as a Catalyst for Agility

All organisations are looking to change at an increasing pace to meet the Agility challenge set out in **Chapter 1**. Whilst start-ups have a perceived advantage over established organisations with significant legacy technology and processes, this perception may not always hold true. Whilst it is often true that being small can make change easier, the key factor is not size, or being new - it is **innovation**.

Many established organisations can find it hard to innovate, having spent considerable time and effort optimising their organisations for operational efficiency. This optimisation does not create an environment, nor encourage the behaviours required, for innovation. Nobody could argue against the need for innovation - just look at the fall of Blockbuster and the rise of Netflix, or the decline of Blackberry and Nokia as dominant forces in the mobile phone market, and the success of Apple and Samsung.

But what is innovation, and how can all organisations embrace it?

Some organisations embrace the concept of innovation labs, which are deliberately distanced from the core organisation, as a mechanism to generate new ideas for products and services. For others, innovation is built into the fabric of the firm.

To foster innovation, the critical ingredients are the right behaviours and skills combined with Lean thinking and a culture that supports risk-taking.

One model that describes the characteristics of innovation is the Harvard definition of the Innovator's DNA, as illustrated in **Figure 2-5**. Adopting these behaviours is an essential part of making innovation work in any organisation.

Figure 2-5: Harvard Definition of the Innovator's DNA

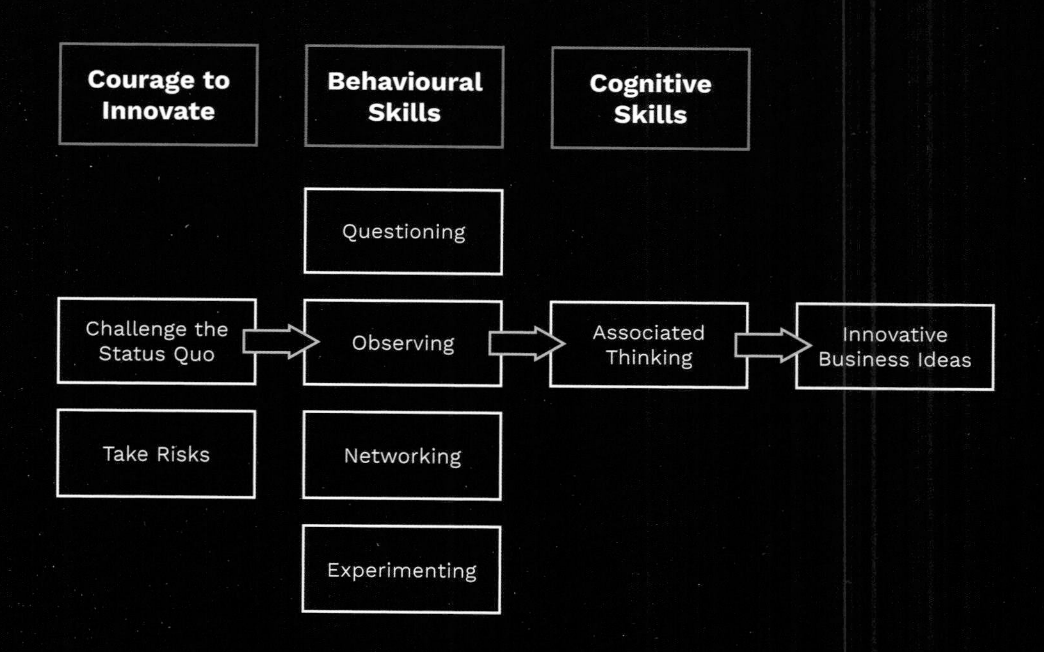

Taking a Product or Project Perspective

How an organisation delivers change is largely driven by the perspective of the products provided. Where 'run' the organisation and 'change' the organisation are distinct activities, full organisational Agility cannot be achieved. In this traditional model, the vehicle for delivering change is the project. Some organisations can take a product perspective and see both operating and enhancing a product as 'business as usual' activities. Within this model, the capacity of the Product Team dictates the speed at which change is delivered.

Key to whether an organisation takes a product or project perspective is often governance and funding. Run activities are typically funded from operational expenditure, while change is usually a capital investment.

Using projects and programmes as containers for change is not necessarily a bad thing. It can be useful for getting to an initial product launch, for example. Nonetheless, there are significant benefits to breaking down barriers between 'change' and 'run' teams, and having a combined, retained Product Team.

The most obvious downside to projects is that they are temporary structures. Considerable energy (and associated expense) is required to form a team that becomes a productive, coherent unit. This time-consuming and expensive process is then repeated for the next project.

Organisations should start thinking about change as business as usual rather than as a discrete project activity. In a product-led organisation, once the investment in creating a team has been made, the organisation is in a position to reap the long-term benefits from that investment.

BJSS Opinion

The Hierarchy of Concerns

To build a model of what 'good' looks like, it is useful to dimension the solution space in several ways. A good starting point is to consider the hierarchy of responsibilities and activities in product delivery. Progressing through successive levels reveals further detail and a lower level of granularity.

Figure 2-6 identifies four key layers: the organisation, the portfolio, the product, and the Delivery Team. Our model is constructed on the premise that organisations operate one or more portfolios of products they wish to build upon. The focus at the organisation level is on strategy, funding and governance.

Beneath the organisation layer sits the portfolio(s) containing the individual products that serve users and customers. Each of these products is typically technology-enabled and requires focused leadership to ensure they operate and change in a way that delivers value to the organisation.

Finally, the lowest layer deals with the day-to-day work of the Delivery Team and the implementation and support of technology and business change.

Figure 2-6: Hierarchy of Concerns

Organisation-Level Activities

The organisation needs to lay out the context and framework within which Product Teams can deliver value. Ultimately, the organisation needs to establish a strategy, and set goals and a roadmap. This process will be most effective when there is a feedback loop. This insight will come from Product Teams and will always be guided by information relating to the success of current products, user needs, and general movement in the market.

A complete discussion of business strategy and marketing is beyond the scope of this book. It is important to reflect on the attributes of strategy and organisational-level constraints that influence the work of Product Teams in delivering change and operating effectively.

Strategy and Roadmap

We expect there to be a forward vision for the direction of the organisation and its implications for the products and services offered. The organisation's strategy will address the markets it is targeting, and the range of products and services on offer.

Product Teams should be empowered to deliver against this strategy by maximising value through evolving their product to meet ever-changing user needs. A broad roadmap for the organisation should highlight the introduction of new products into the portfolio, or the retirement and replacement of legacy ones.

Culture and Values

The adoption of Agile is frequently misinterpreted as simply the adoption of a new set of practices and events. However, to truly evolve from a 'traditional' organisation to an Agile one, a fundamental change in the entire mindset of the organisation is often required.

The organisation's culture and values should support the work of the Product Teams and enable them to operate as autonomously as possible. The tone and behaviours of the team and its ability to collaborate effectively towards delivery should be reinforced by the organisation.

A challenge we often see is when multiple suppliers are engaged in support of a Product Team, or parts of the organisation are outsourced. Ideally, you would want all suppliers collaborating towards the common goal of delivering the most advantageous change for the customer. This requires not only the correct sourcing strategy, but we also recommend that all supplier staff are aligned to the culture and values of the host organisation.

Sourcing and Supplier Strategy

The approach taken to the use of suppliers by an organisation and the strategy for the use of internal and external teams plays a pivotal role in the success of any product. We believe that good delivery is ability-led and relies on having strong people in key roles. The procurement and utilisation of the right people for the job is a critical success factor.

All too often, procurement functions have been given objectives by the organisation that do not align with the objectives of the Product Teams. Ultimately, all functions in the organisation should be focused on the common goal of delivering customer value. Collaboration and effective working across the supply chain are the keys to Agility, and a balance is required such that the commercial interests of all parties are preserved.

Where a Product Team wishes to make use of external products or services, it is recommended that support from procurement or vendor management is embedded within the team. By including the vendor management function within the Product Team, supplier performance management can be more relevant within the context of the work being undertaken.

Cloud Migration

Moving to the Cloud can be a key enabler for business Agility. However, many organisations fail to unlock the full value, allowing Cloud migration to become a technical activity, and not considering the impact on the full operating model in advance.

The best starting point is to understand the current maturity of the business with Cloud, followed by a design phase to drive the optimum operating model that suits this competence. We have found the following patterns to be extremely useful for building Cloud readiness, as shown in **Table 2-1.**

Table 2-1: Cloud Migration Patterns

Pattern	Description	Best use
Strangler	o Build separate facade between old and new environments o Educate teams o Same team to run with resource augmentation o Gradual migration from old to new	o Large scale data centre exit, or gradual reduction o Typical lift and shift rehost
Side car	o Build small ops model and separate team o Deploy some shared services. Major focus on automation	o New business unit o Demand for app refractor or replatform
All in	o Straight switch from old to new operations model o No time constraints	o Start up o New business acquisition
Rotten apple	o Replacement of old tech stack driven by need to replace and reduce costs and/or add new features	o Replacement of expensive technology, such as WebSphere, WebLogic, Oracle, to Cloud system
Combination	o Combination of two approaches o Useful when time on side o Often an intermediate step before full pattern or when no clear strategy is available	o Start up o New business acquisition

Enterprise Architecture

In an organisation of any reasonable scale, we expect to see some form of enterprise architecture function. This group needs to provide a clear set of lightweight constraints and guidance that enable Product Teams to operate and deliver change. There is a clear balance to be struck. We are not in favour of ivory towers and overly prescriptive corporate standards that get in the way of Agility.

The enterprise architecture function operates best as a two-way dialogue and as a group that coaches and supports Product Teams, rather than simply passing down standards. The key reason for this function is to help the organisation move forward at pace rather than hold it back. To this end, enterprise architecture should primarily be about providing guidance. This will enable the experience from past lessons learned to benefit the team, rather than simply enforcing standards.

Certain strategic goals in the organisation may require support from the enterprise architecture function. It may be necessary, for example, to re-platform technology to introduce new levels of interoperability across a range of products. This type of broader organisation initiative will require overarching architectural support.

Several enterprise architecture models exist, and their coverage is beyond the scope of this book. It is useful to draw attention to the core elements that we expect the function to cover. The four key components are business architecture, information architecture, application architecture, and technology architecture as shown in **Figure 2-7**.

Figure 2-7: Four-layer Architecture

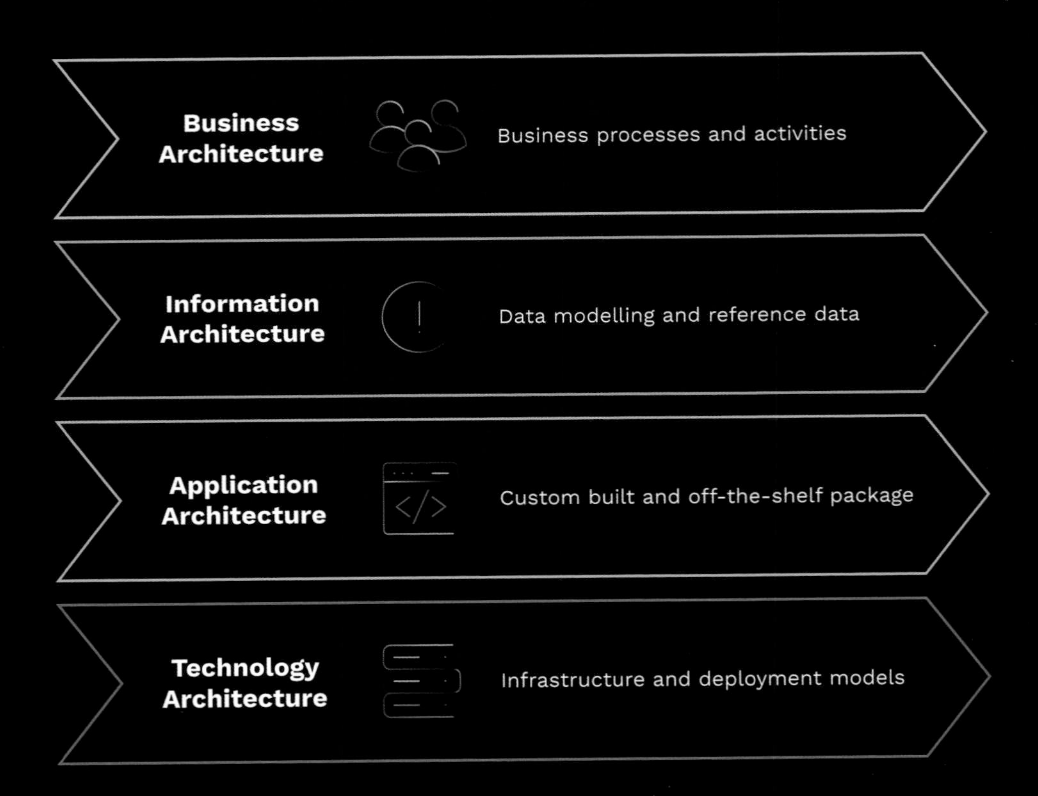

The enterprise architecture function will only cover the lightweight standards around these areas. Most of the specific detail will come from the solution architecture for specific products.

Governance and Funding

Funding the initiatives described in the product portfolio will be decided by how they contribute to the overall strategic aims of the organisation.

Funding will normally be allocated through an annual planning process. While this does not support a fully Agile model, it corresponds to a related need to report financial results to shareholders. This is often a real-world constraint that cannot be changed.

Through an appropriate governance process, it is possible that funding across the portfolio may be allocated more dynamically. However, this is unlikely to work for large-scale capital investment projects. A common route to funding change is allocating a budget to individual products. This effectively sets a resource capacity that product owners are empowered to use as they see fit to maximise value for the organisation.

A lightweight but effective governance process should sit between the broader organisation and the Product Teams. Governance should effectively draw together stakeholders from architecture, delivery management and product ownership to ensure proper alignment and decision making. Where relevant, it is likely vendor management or suppliers would also be represented. We cover governance in more detail in **Chapter 5**.

Figure 2-8: Technological Evolutions

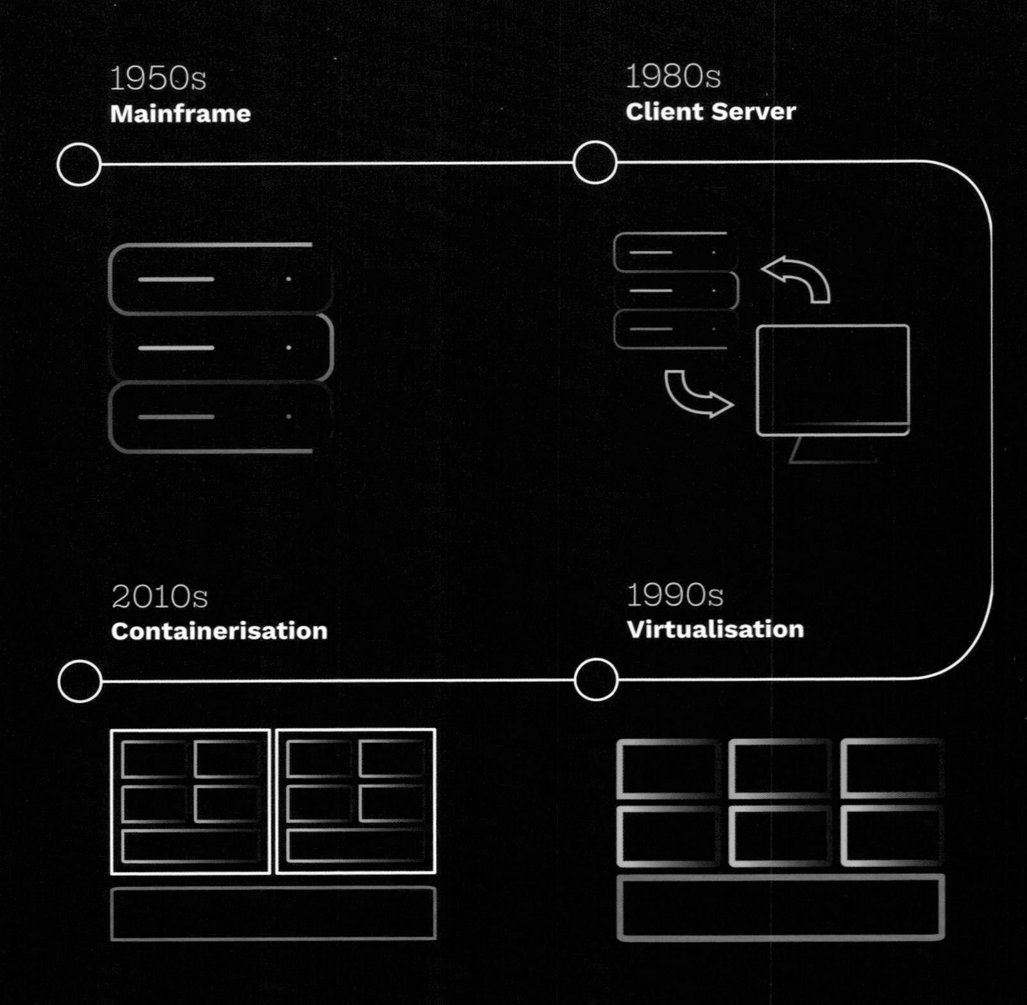

Cloud Governance

Enterprise IT has undergone several technological evolutions over the last 60 years: mainframe, client server, virtualisation, and containerisation have all driven architectural change.

In each case, technological change has enabled organisations to drive efficiencies and enable innovation but not without some significant internal changes. Cloud has been no different.

To fully realise the benefits of Cloud computing, organisations need to change their approach to people, processes, and culture.

Some of the key changes that are introduced by Cloud include:

1. **Cloud computing transforms spending from a capital expense for on-premises and co-located IT infrastructure to a pay-as-you-go utility billing model for Cloud resources and services.** This has not been an issue for Agile 'born-in-the-Cloud' organisations but has a significant impact on more traditional enterprises with legacy estates and existing investment in data centres

2. **On-demand Cloud computing offers scope for huge reductions. In the time it takes to provision infrastructure, engineers can deploy entire enterprise stacks across multiple environments at the push of a button.** For the first time, engineers have access to seemingly limitless resources and the associated potential for uncontrolled expenditure. Establishing deployment controls and the visibility of costs is imperative

3. **To fully realise the benefits of Cloud services, organisations must instill infrastructure change management processes to align with Agile software development practices such as continuous monitoring and continuous delivery**

4. **Cloud TCO requires a more nuanced analysis than previous models. The impact of a Cloud implementation on the business requires consideration of the 'soft' benefits of Cloud adoption as well as the spend.** These benefits are often hidden and include increased developer productivity, reuse of services, and architectural patterns which, in turn, lead to increased throughput of delivery and improved quality.

Mapping the Portfolio

The system landscape in many organisations is often quite complex. Mapping the portfolio can be undertaken in many ways depending on the view required. The decision as to the appropriate approach is informed by the desired rate of change and the criticality of the system, as illustrated in **Figure 2-9**.

Figure 2-9: Mapping System Changes

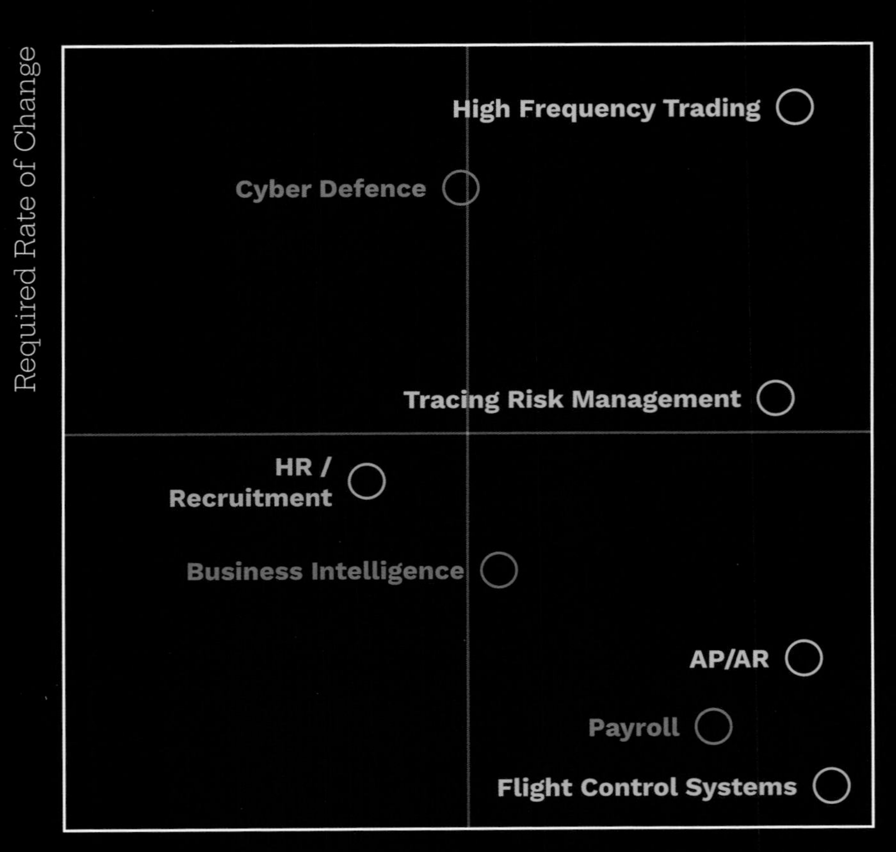

Mapping out the organisation's portfolio of products and services in this way can be very helpful. It allows the organisation to take a view on where investment should go, and also advise as to the types of teams and suppliers to apply. **Figure 2-10** introduces some broad categories of approach.

Figure 2-10: Technical Implementation Based on System Mapping

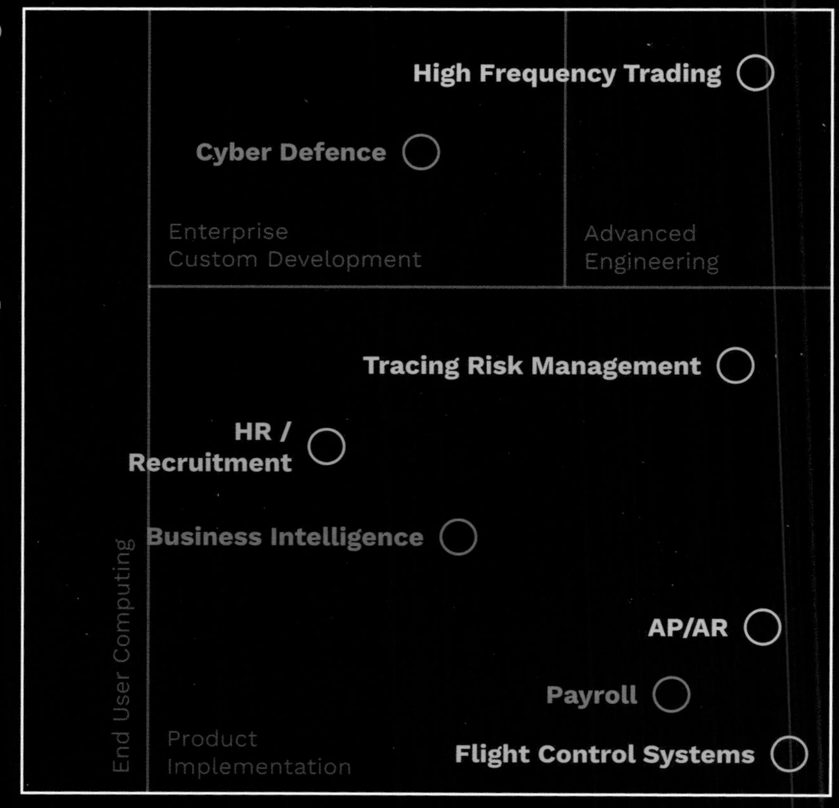

The Enterprise Agile Approach

Components of the Technology Landscape

In our approach, we recommend that modern organisations embrace several concepts within the technology space. The underlying culture and values of the organisation support these components and guide all behaviours and decision making.

Figure 2-11: Components of the Technology Landscape

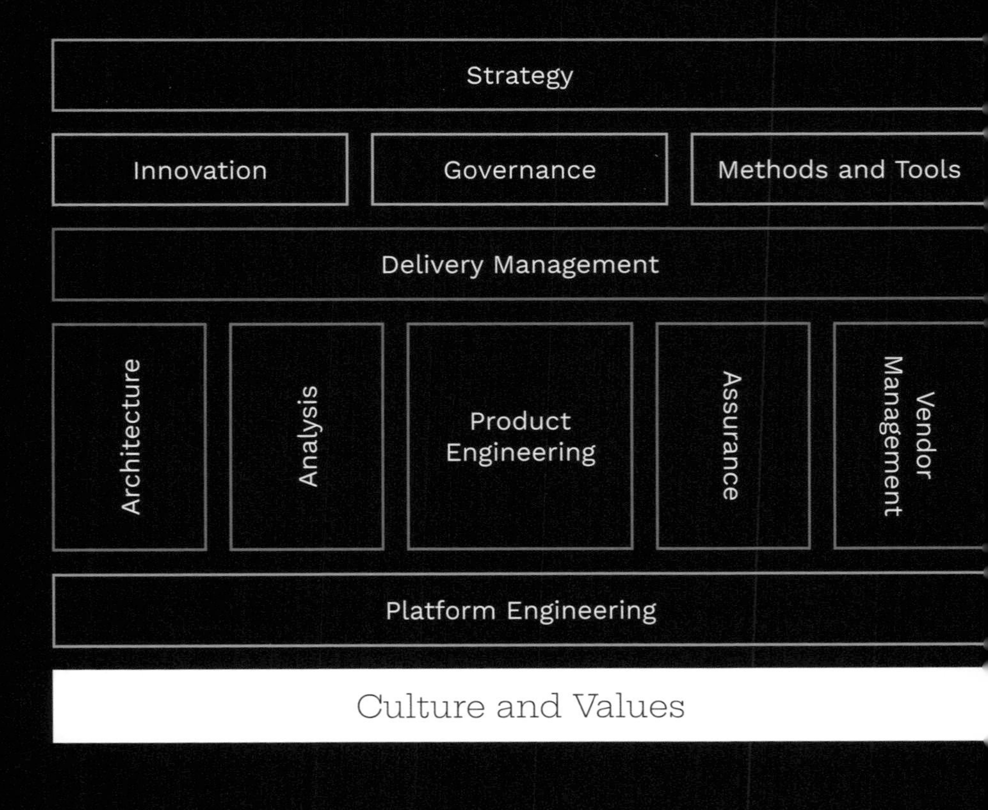

At the core of technology delivery are the strategic and supporting functions of Innovation, Governance, Methods, and Tooling. These functions serve to determine the direction and provide oversight on delivery and are often combined into the 'Office of the CIO'.

Delivering change and supporting the technology products of the organisation is the remit of Product Engineering Teams. These teams are aligned to particular products, and are principally concerned with the delivery and maintenance of software.

Platform engineering provides the underlying infrastructure on which products are run. For many organisations, this will be a public or private Cloud solution. The platform will usually be presented to Product Teams as Infrastructure as a Service (IaaS) or Platform as a Service (PaaS), allowing them to code against APIs and self-provision infrastructure, removing a traditional blocker to Agility - long infrastructure lead times.

The Innovation Lab

An Innovation Lab is useful for facilitating Agility in the organisation. Some organisations may have dedicated Innovation Labs, others may spin one up for a short period, or bring in a third party to facilitate one for them.

Either way, the key point is that the lab has a Lean process for generating innovative technology-led business ideas. Its purpose is to create a business idea that may be developed further into a product within the organisation's portfolio.

An Innovation Lab functions best when 'Innovator's DNA' behaviours are combined with Lean thinking and a process for the generation and refinement of potential ideas. Our process for ideation is illustrated in **Figure 2-12**. The model seeks to open up the idea generation process, and align with organisational goals and desired outcomes.

Figure 2-12: The Ideation Process

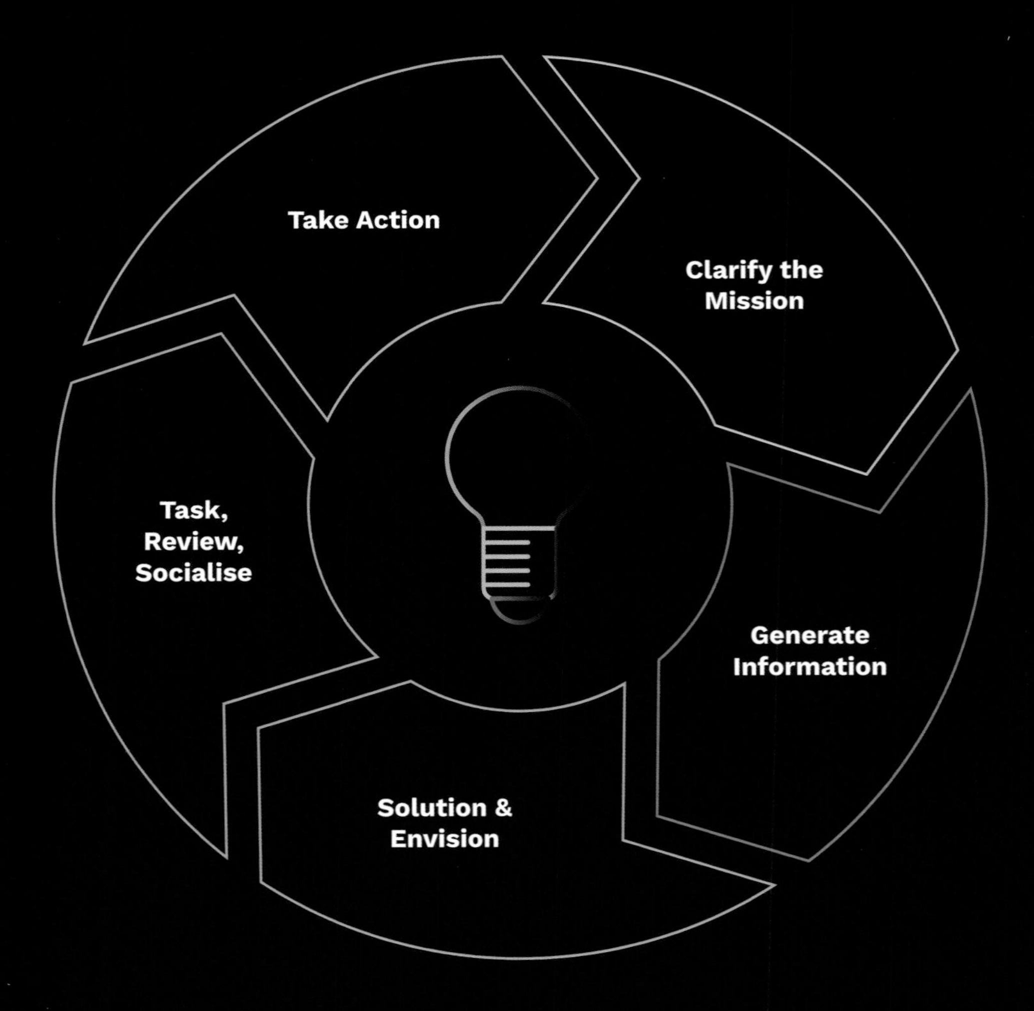

Hackathons

A Hackathon is a useful tool to enable Agility and idea generation around a specific problem. Taking place over one or two days, a Hackathon has a single objective, usually to produce a basic functioning solution to a given problem. The team, ideally formed from different disciplines, attempts to address the objective either as a competition - with multiple teams attempting to solve the same problem - or collectively as a single group.

The competitive approach allows alternative options to be explored with left-field solutions that may not normally be considered. Due to the fixed timescale, the focus is on addressing the problem and not creating a production-ready deliverable. Indeed, the emphasis is on innovation and exploration. Enterprise Agile provides the appropriate Hackathon structure, through Stand-ups and Show and Tells, which are used to share information as the event progresses. Mini-Sprints, that might only last 3 hours, can be used to explore and potentially discard ideas.

The Hackathon should ring-fence the attendees from their day-to-day tasks, with everyone being co-located - often off-site - to ensure there are no distractions. Allowing a team to focus on a problem this way can be very liberating. A Hackathon can act as an interesting introduction to concepts such as DevOps, with members from different disciplines working together, demonstrating how the removal of traditional barriers between development and operations can open up new Agility.

The advent of the Cloud allows Hackathons to be undertaken without the need for purchasing hardware or software licences and can leverage free trials provided by the various Public Cloud vendors. This allows teams to evaluate options and services very quickly.

Key Points

1. The successful modern organisation has technology at its core as an enabler, rather than a discrete supporting function.

2. Multi-speed IT provides a useful model for introducing Agility to systems that engage customers.

3. Agility can be increased by taking a product perspective of continuous change rather than discrete projects.

4. Technology delivery is guided by the organisation's culture and values system.

5. Innovation Labs are a powerful tool for creating new ideas and introducing Agility into the organisation.

Chapter 03

A Pattern for Delivering Value

Our aim with this book is to highlight good practice for using Agility to introduce and enhance technology products. In the opening chapters, we explored the challenges facing organisations and the rationale for our approach. In this chapter, we describe the patterns and practices for delivering value.

No 'one size fits all' methodology or approach is appropriate to every change initiative. Rather, one of several common approaches can be adapted to suit the needs of the organisation, framed by a supportive culture and values system.

Increasing organisational Agility is a journey and is not achieved by rigidly implementing a new operating model. Success comes from embracing Agile techniques and an Agile mindset.

Concepts

The Evolution of Agile Methods

What we now describe as 'Agile methods' began appearing in the early 1990s, before the Agile Manifesto. These early methods focused on developing individual software applications in isolation. Born out of the frustration of working in a process-heavy environment, software engineers sought a more effective way of working closely with users to develop the software they needed.

Many of these early methods eschewed all process and were often criticised for letting software projects become 'developer playgrounds' with insufficient formality for enterprise-scale change initiatives. This frustration with early attempts at Agile led us to develop the Enterprise Agile approach. We aimed to help clients enjoy the benefits of greater flexibility and efficiency, whilst retaining predictability and achieving a 'No surprises endgame' for delivery projects.

Recent developments have seen the growth of scaled Agile approaches that seek to address larger change initiatives. Whilst some of these are gaining traction, they are still largely software-focused and do not always link effectively to organisation governance and business change.

XP

Extreme Programming (XP) is an early Agile methodology dating back to the late 1990s. It identifies twelve practices and several supporting activities, values and principles. Most commonly known for pair programming, XP also promoted practices such as programmer welfare through development at a sustainable pace.

Whilst not often applied in a textbook fashion, some of the core elements of XP remain at the heart of Agile delivery, notably continuous integration and test-driven development. A criticism of XP is that it is best suited to small teams and does not scale effectively.

(R)UP

The Unified Process (UP) refers to the generic process that was popularised as the Rational Unified Process (RUP) after the commercial toolset of that name and to a lesser extent in the Open Source version, Open UP. The key elements of UP are a project lifecycle comprising four phases: Inception, Elaboration, Construction and Transition.

The previous version of Enterprise Agile extended several UP principles including a focus on risk and architecture, with iterative and incremental delivery. The strong link between UP and the RUP toolset caused many to think it was a commercial methodology requiring the toolset and was in part a factor in its declining usage.

Scrum

Also originating in the 1990s, Scrum is what many people will recognise as a common Agile approach. Scrum provides definitions of roles, events and artefacts, many of which have entered common parlance and some of which have been adopted by the Enterprise Agile approach. Scrum also defines a set of values that are fundamental to its successful adoption and some of these are also shared by the Enterprise Agile approach.

Scrum has become a very popular Agile method and has proven effective, particularly on small scale initiatives. In response to the desire to take Scrum principles and apply them to larger-scale problems, newer methods such as Large Scale Scrum (LeSS) have emerged.

LeSS

Large Scale Scrum (LeSS) is an attempt to identify how Scrum can be scaled effectively across multiple teams working on a shared product. Formalised in 2005, LeSS combines years of experience in product development with the principles of Scrum and Lean thinking. Two variants of LeSS exist - LeSS for up to eight teams and LeSS Huge for bigger groups. It provides a framework that covers principles, structure, management, technical excellence and adoption.

SAFe

The Scaled Agile Framework (SAFe) has been through five revisions since 2012 and, through its 'Big Picture', illustrates a process for Agile delivery at scale. SAFe makes a distinction between Team, Programme and Portfolio and introduces the concept of the 'Agile Release Train'.

As a method for scaled Agile delivery SAFe has been gaining in popularity. However, it has faced criticism from the Agile community for being too rigid. Some also say it lacks the strong customer focus that is central to the Agile mindset.

Devops and the Convergence in Technology

In the early days of Agile software development, it was recognised that, for effective delivery, the divide between different technology disciplines such as Developers and Testers needed to be broken down. Multi-disciplinary teams focused on the common goal of delivering software that works in a live environment rather than throwing work that is development complete 'over the wall' to the Testers or the Operations Team. More recently, DevOps practices have advocated bringing together Development and Technical Operations as a single team responsible for the traditionally separate activities of building and running a software system. We address this topic in more detail in **Chapter 8**.

Figure 3-1: Convergence Within Technology Departments

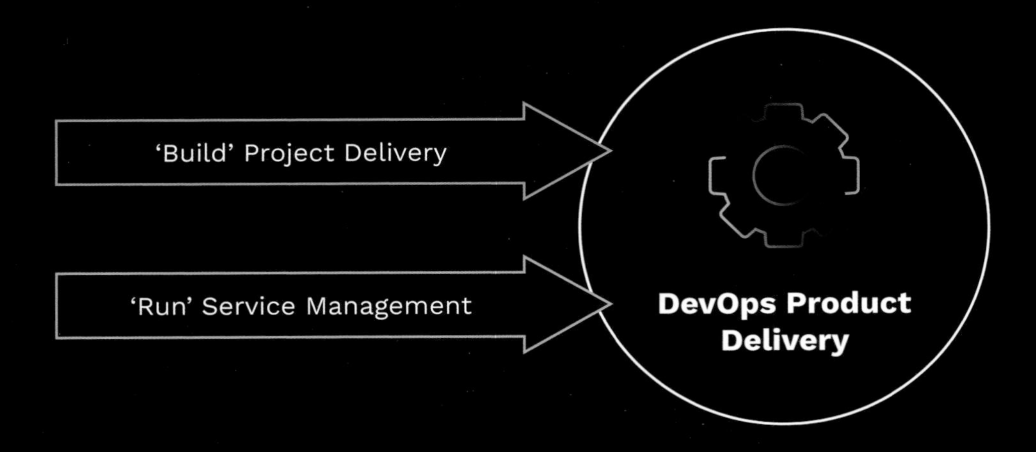

This convergence is key to achieving savings in the operational side of the organisation.

Figure 3-2: Transfer of Methods in DevOps

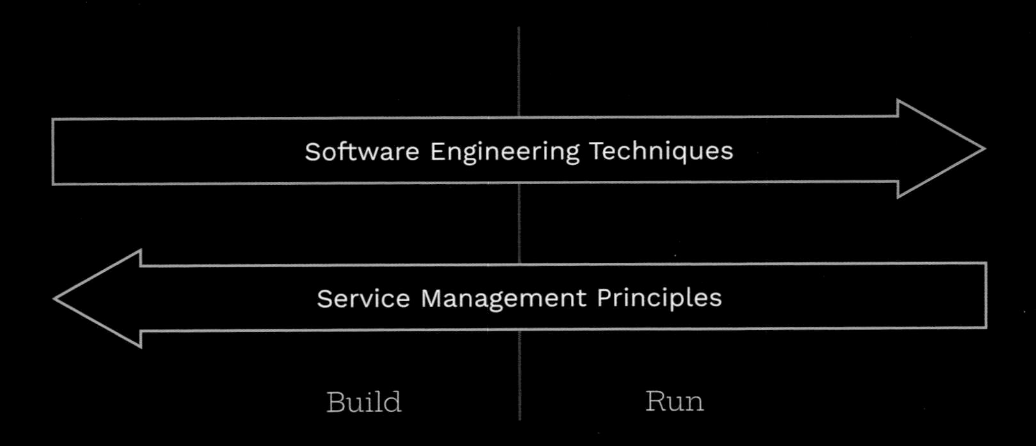

As shown in **Figure 3-1**, the adoption of DevOps techniques allows cohesive teams to efficiently build and run products for their customers.

Software engineering techniques and automation have moved over the line from project delivery into operations, while service management techniques have moved back into development. It is the automation of many error-prone manual processes that reduces the barrier to rapid change and takes much of the effort out of operating a technology product.

Continuous Delivery

Regardless of the mechanism for getting change into the hands of users, during delivery we would always want to divide change into bite-sized pieces. At the end of each piece, the team reviews where they are and solicits feedback. Typically, this means working within time-boxed periods known as 'Iterations' or 'Sprints' that focus on delivering measurable outcomes as a result of a set of changes. After one or more Sprints, the changes are released to the user. This forms the basis of incremental delivery.

It is also possible that changes are immediately released to the user independent of each other. This model offers greater flexibility and is often better suited to small scale change and relatively mature products.

Continuous delivery is a method of fully automating software production, quality assurance and deployment using a delivery pipeline through which software change can flow, enabling deployment into production at any time.

Irrespective of the overarching delivery pattern adopted, continuous delivery and the use of repeatable automated processes is powerful and forms a key part of the Enterprise Agile approach.

Cloud as an Agile Enabler

It is worth calling out Cloud as a facet of the delivery pattern and a key enabler of Agility. Agile methods have historically focused on the production of software. Treatment of infrastructure delivery is often scant or non-existent. Traditional 'tin and wires' infrastructure provisioning led to project plan dependencies and inhibited Agile ways of working.

With Cloud, or more specifically software-defined infrastructure, increments of change to products can include not only the application software but the corresponding changes to the infrastructure too, packaged and released simultaneously. This opens up a powerful new paradigm in systems delivery and enables new architectures based on lightweight microservices to be easily deployed.

Different Change Scenarios

In defining our thinking around delivering change, we have explored several common scenarios that we see regularly and have considerable experience of. Organisations must address a huge variety of change initiatives, but we feel these scenarios cover the bulk of the cases.

Frequently occurring initiatives in Business to Business (B2B), Business to Consumer (B2C) or Government to Citizen (G2C) include:

Web-Scale Platform Evolution

Large modern technology organisations often embrace Agility at scale. Where they have a single product and no significant legacy, they can apply Agile methods across the organisation and release change often. Examples include companies such as Facebook, Spotify, etc.

Change Programmes

Often requiring significant capital investment and business change, these programmes typically arise as a result of mergers and acquisition, the need for a platform refresh or the expiration of outsourcing agreements. The scale of the change, funding model and often 'big bang' nature of cutover impacts the level of Agility achieved.

Enhancement Projects

Most organisations run projects continuously to enhance the technology products within their portfolio.

It would be possible to write a whole book on the philosophical point of 'Is there such a thing as an Agile project?' Greater Agility is achieved by releasing often and making value-based decisions on delivery priorities. This can be at odds with traditional project funding processes which require an agreed business case upfront.

Greenfield Project

Creating a new, relatively standalone product should be undertaken in line with Agile ways of working. Feature priorities are addressed based on user needs and business value to create a Minimum Viable Product (MVP). Once launched, the MVP can be enhanced incrementally based on customer feedback.

Proof of Concepts

Small scale PoC work is a prime candidate for Lean and Agile working methods. With this type of work, a fast feedback loop is a powerful tool to direct the effort of the team towards the objectives.

Agility in all Scenarios

At a time of transformative new digital technologies and globally disruptive events, the challenge becomes how to use Agility throughout the entire organisation to more rapidly and reliably adapt to shifting client, consumer or citizen demands. It is easy to see why small-scale changes are good candidates for Agile delivery, particularly on mature products. The adoption of Agility in larger solutions tends to be in organisations that have adopted a product (rather than a project) perspective and have placed technology at the heart of the organisation.

Agility is often lost on large scale change programmes, where several factors impact the level of Agility:

1. **Funding** – Change programmes typically involve a large capital investment that requires a detailed upfront business case and scoping exercise
2. **Delivery Model** – It can be difficult to deliver change in small pieces, particularly on large programmes that might, for example, be replacing a legacy product
3. **Vendor Model** – Where several suppliers are engaged, it is too easy to form silos that create barriers to Agility and the end-to-end delivery of value
4. **Architecture** – Appropriate architecture is required to enable delivery to be decomposed effectively on large programmes.

Within this book and the Enterprise Agile method, we describe techniques to enable Agile ways of working in all of these scenarios.

BJSS Opinion

Releasing Change to the Users

Earlier we discussed different types of change initiative and how these might be delivered through continuous product innovation or discrete projects. Whenever possible, we want to break down large changes into smaller, manageable chunks and put them in front of real users to get feedback. Piecemeal introduction of change allows for regular course corrections. These subtle direction changes keep the product aligned with the market and optimise the value derived by the organisation.

The constructs used will depend on two key factors:

1. **How the organisation allocates funding and measures value delivered**
2. **The process by which change can be delivered to the user.**

There are situations when frequent releases are not possible, for example replacing a legacy trading system - all users need all functionality and all have to be in the same market – so a big bang transition is unavoidable.

Ideally, you would want to release change to users often and as small incremental features, because:

1. **The users benefit from new product features**
2. **The organisation gains value**
3. **The Product Team receives feedback to refine the roadmap**
4. **Change becomes a low risk 'Business as Usual' activity.**

There are, of course, many real-world constraints and differences across sectors and products. Continuously delivering change to a social media networking application is likely to be easier than to a commodities trading platform, for example.

It is worth spending some time exploring the factors that impact release cycles. Firstly, let's tackle a key challenge for many organisations – perceived risk. We purposefully use the term 'perceived risk'. It is often a very subjective assessment based on prior experience that may or may not be relevant. Many organisations unintentionally develop a risk-averse culture, perhaps based on the reaction to a previous failed release.

Attitude to risk often leads to a self-fulfilling prophecy. Change is perceived as risky; this results in additional process and a high 'release tax'. As a result, changes are made less often and releases become bigger, and riskier, as a result. The automation and DevOps techniques we talk about in this book are key to breaking out of this cycle.

A further important determinant of the change cycle is the impact on the user and other products and services. Where a change involves new ways of working, new people in new roles and so forth, then more up-front planning is required. These non-Agile real-world constraints, such as recruitment and training, get in the way of continuous change. This can be approached by breaking the work down into manageable chunks that address specific aspects of the new ways of working, including subgroups, or even individual new roles, as they are introduced.

Another category of impact concerns integration with other technology products, some of which may reside outside of the organisation. In these circumstances, changes have to be aligned with change in other upstream or downstream systems. This is why appropriate architecture is so crucial to achieving Agility. Good enterprise architecture will enable integration across systems changing at different speeds.

When Large Scale Change is Unavoidable

As discussed, releasing changes to existing products often comes down to attitude to risk and an assessment of the impact or scale of the change. One common class of problem is worth exploring further.

Launching a new product involves a large change, particularly if replacing a legacy system. This situation is often unavoidable, for example, re-writing an outsourced service that is coming to the end of the contract.

The functionality for the new product must reach critical mass for it to be useful - this is often referred to as the Minimum Marketable Feature (MMF) set. There are two transition options - big bang or incremental. With a big bang approach, all users begin to use the product at the same time rather than it being introduced to smaller groups of users in phases.

The obvious choice is to avoid big bang due to the risk. However, that is not without challenge, particularly if modifications are required to the existing system to run old and new in parallel. Sometimes big bang is the only option, for example, when users cannot be partitioned in any way, such as on a trading platform where a single market with counterparty credit relationships exists. Big bang and incremental rollout are contrasted in **Table 3-1**.

Table 3-1: Comparing Big Bang and Incremental Transition

Big Bang	Incremental
All users begin using the product at the same time	Users phased onto new product a group at a time
Potential high risk if issue found post-launch	Allows for feedback and refinement if issues found
Upfront dry run tests to mitigate transition risk	Potentially complex to plan and execute, with a lengthy cutover period
Requires long test phases to mature product	The additional expense of parallel running with the legacy system(s)
It is clear which system is in use	Needs clarity over which product is the system of record

We have successfully transitioned systems using both big bang and incremental approaches - this is only possible by using the engineering and delivery practices highlighted later in this book.

Staying out of Trouble

Having reviewed and recovered many projects, we have identified several common pitfalls experienced by organisations delivering technology-enabled products. A small subset of these are listed in **Table 3-2**.

Table 3-2: Common Delivery Challenges

Challenge	Remedy
Failure to gain sufficient momentum due to lack of clarity and direction	o Clearly understood and communicated goals at a macro (product) level and micro (feature) level o Visible and active supporting organisation culture and values to guide team decision making
Poor results in terms of quality and progress due to lack of motivated or suitably skilled team	o Recognition that process is no substitute for ability, appropriate use of specialists and generalists o Empowered teams and individuals working towards clear goals
Persistent problems due to lack of alignment of delivery and governance models	o For large scale changes use a phased delivery pattern and link this to key governance decisions o Implement lightweight assurance including regular board and design authority meetings
Inability to know the position of delivery due to poor information	o A clear set of delivery metrics and KPIs to cover progress and quality against expected objectives and trends o Use appropriate tooling to gather data at source and avoid building an industry around reporting

Continued overleaf

Table 3-2 continued: Common Delivery Challenges

Challenge	Remedy
Lack of suitable controls due to dogmatic approach to Agile working	o Build communities to share experiences and ensure action on feedback (within and outside the team) o Develop lightweight metrics and assurance and maintain focus on organisation goals and governance
Insufficient quality in delivered solution due to poor analysis and engineering	o Quality built-in upfront using Agile test techniques rather than trying to add later through quality control o Structured analysis techniques to produce quality requirements with traceability and acceptance criteria

No single approach, method or target-operating model addresses all scenarios. Delivering technology and business change is difficult. The important thing is to consider each scenario and product within the context of the organisation. For example, unless you are a technology start-up, you rarely get the opportunity to work in a legacy-free environment.

The Enterprise Agile Approach

A Lifecycle for Products

We have covered the role of the organisation in operating and changing products. Any organisation will deliver a range of products and services to its customers. Whilst there is some variation, most products follow a similar path in terms of their lifecycle. The Enterprise Agile product lifecycle is illustrated in **Figure 3-3**.

Figure 3-3: The Product Lifecycle

Technology delivery has historically been split into 'Build' and 'Run'.

Our model can, if required, support Projects and Programmes delivering change, with the operation of the resultant product undertaken by technology operations and BAU Teams. Our strong preference, however, is for combined Product Teams undertaking Build and Run activities.

Rather than immediately focusing on these structures it is worth taking a step back and looking more holistically at the product lifecycle.

All products require some upfront work to get them to a state where they are sufficiently defined to start building and then have sufficient substance to rollout to some or all users. This is the Minimum Viable Product (MVP).

Once the initial version of the product is launched it will continue to evolve to meet growing user needs. These post-launch changes may be small features delivered continuously or, if organisational constraints make it unavoidable, larger features delivered incrementally by a larger change project.

Eventually, the product will be retired. This process can be gradual where users are slowly migrated to a replacement product and all or part of the original product remains. It can also be a more abrupt transition when existing services are turned off. This can happen when an outsourced contract comes to an end.

Within the product lifecycle are several discrete phases. The early phases prepare the organisation and team for the introduction of a new product. A key focus in these early stages is to set a course and reduce risk whilst retaining Agility. The use of these phases allows the organisation to make investment decisions and informed choices about delivery options, for example, to build or buy technology components.

The three phases of Feasibility, Discovery and Delivery act as a 'ready, aim, fire' mechanism to prepare the organisation for the commitment of developing a new product. Each of these phases has several core objectives and should link to a governance process.

Feasibility

The purpose of the Feasibility phase is to assess how an idea can meet the needs of the user and generate value for the organisation. This phase takes an idea and translates it into a more concrete concept that can be further explored.

At this stage, a small team of specialists will work for a short period to determine if the idea is sufficiently substantive to warrant further effort.

Discovery

In essence, Discovery is concerned at a high level with **validating** the problem to be solved, **how** will it be solved (both solution architecture and delivery approach), and what **measures** will be put in place to ensure successful delivery, and a refined delivery **plan**. This is often referred to as the MVP.

The aim of a Discovery phase is to de-risk subsequent delivery and hone in on the options for implementation. Discovery will not answer all questions or establish all requirements in detail, but it will establish the scope for an MVP.

A core Product Team will be formed to undertake Discovery, lasting a few weeks and delivering prototypes or product mock-ups.

The Difference Between MVP and MMF

Minimum Viable Product (MVP) – the version of a product that allows a team to collect the maximum amount of validated learning with the minimum amount of work.

Minimum Marketable Feature set (MMF) – the smallest amount of functionality in a product that delivers recognisable value to customers/end-users.

Delivery

During the Delivery phase, features of the product are incrementally delivered based on a roadmap that captures the value released to the organisation. Beyond launch, the Delivery phase supports and operates the product for the users.

A cohesive Product Team is required. This team may exist for some time until the product is retired.

The key outcomes of each lifecycle phase are summarised in **Table 3-3**.

Table 3-3: Lifecycle Phase Outcomes

Phase	Purpose	Outcomes
Feasibility	o Understand broad scope of the change, models for delivery and feasibility	o Initial Business Case o Candidate technology solutions o Resource and vendor model
Discovery	o Perform sufficient upfront Discovery to build out estimation for MVP delivery o De-risk delivery with PoCs that prove the solution architecture	o Team and Organisation o Solution Architecture o Assurance approach o Indicative costs and initial plan o Functional Catalogue o Non-Functional Requirements
Delivery	o Iteratively build out the solution required to implement the change o Deliver the technical and business change to users through a regular release pattern o Run the service and support users	o Software artefacts o Business change artefacts o Business value realised o User needs met o Solutions deployed o Support incidents resolved

Achieving MMF – The ‘No Surprises Endgame’

At the enterprise level, getting to a Minimum Marketable Feature set (MMF), and therefore delivering tangible value to customers or the business, for many products involves implementing large-scale change. It is in this scenario, where large capital investments have been made, that executives get nervous and look for evidence of predictability in delivery. It is precisely for this reason that the Feasibility-Discovery-Delivery pattern is so important as a technique to de-risk delivery.

However, this should not be confused with traditional ‘predictive’ lifecycles such as Waterfall. A balance between upfront and deferred Discovery must be struck. Just as important as charting a course during the early phases is evidencing progress in the right direction during Delivery through a process of incremental acceptance.

Figure 3-4 illustrates how incremental acceptance is achieved by running through all facets of delivery at regular intervals and validating the content and quality of the product at each stage. There are two key parts to this acceptance, firstly that the user needs are being met (functional acceptance) and secondly that the product performs adequately and can be operated effectively (non-functional acceptance).

This process of incremental acceptance and the product lifecycle of Enterprise Agile are key ingredients of the ‘No surprises endgame’ - our delivery objective for any change initiative.

Figure 3-4: Delivering Business Value

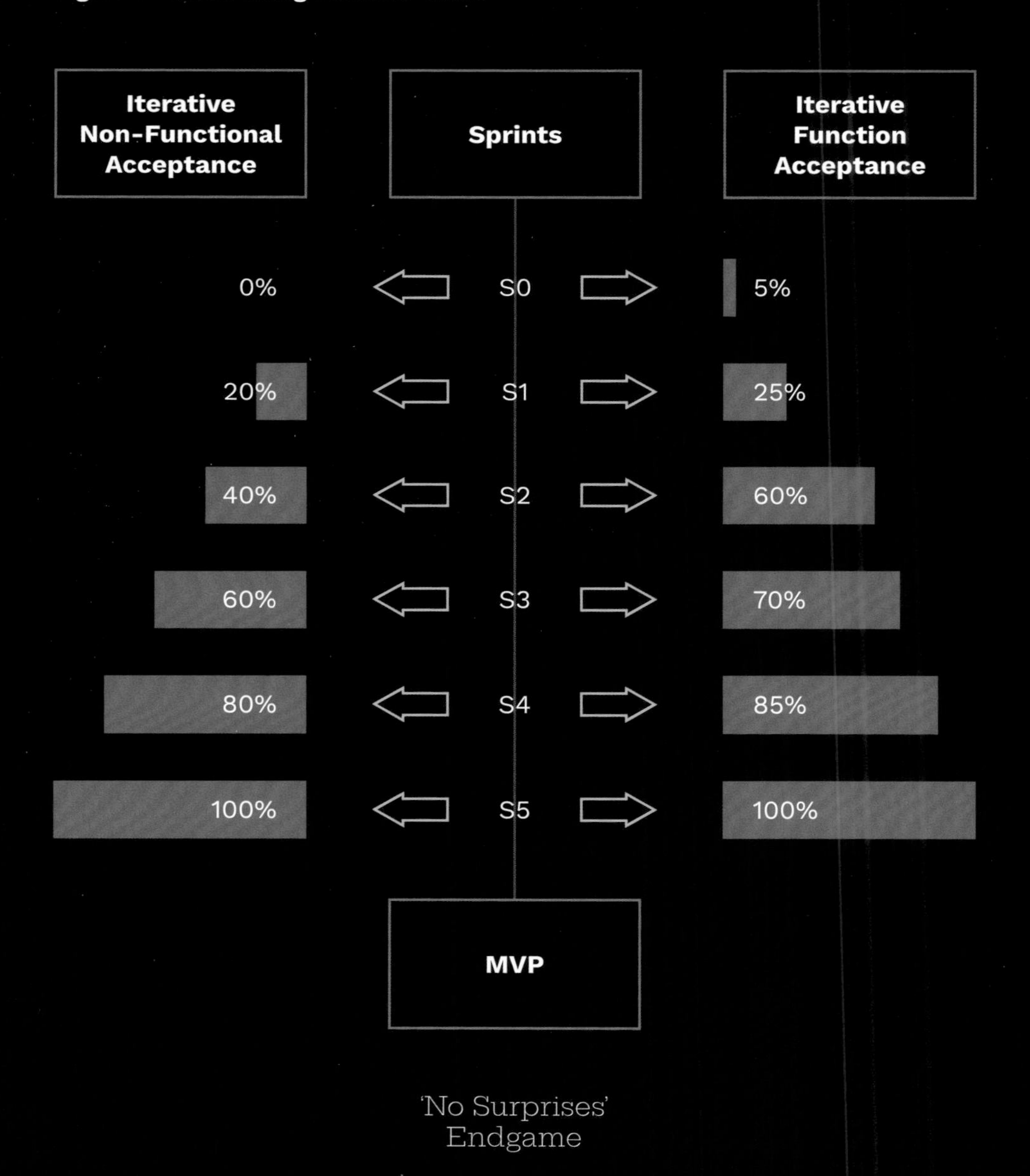

'No Surprises'
Endgame

Key Points

1. DevOps and Continuous Delivery techniques enable a unified delivery lifecycle to cover both change and service.
2. Where possible, change should be released to users regularly and in small chunks.
3. Introducing large scale change, such as replacing an existing system, requires a risk-reduction pattern to get to an MVP.
4. Enterprise Agile uses Feasibility, Discovery and Delivery phases to improve predictability in implementing new initiatives.
5. Delivery should be continuous using an automated pipeline to put change into the hands of users as required and support incremental acceptance.

Chapter 04
The Optimal Team

Effective delivery requires the correct organisation of highly capable people and the appropriate utilisation of their skills. Good teams are not made overnight, and this is a considerable drawback of delivering change in discrete projects. Continuous delivery of change by a Product Team in an Agile organisation overcomes some of these challenges.

Being effective also requires that individuals and teams be supported by the culture and values of the organisation. There is a difficult balance to strike between empowering teams to make decisions and being quasi-autonomous, and potentially losing control as people operate outside the legitimate constraints put in place by the wider organisation.

Concepts

The Return of the Full Stack Engineer

When BJSS was established in 1993, it was common for software engineers to perform the full range of tasks required to deliver a system. This often included not only cutting code but writing and executing automated tests, creating build and deployment scripts, and maintaining development and test environments.

Over the years, the software stack and the array of foundation products, frameworks and tools available to facilitate the production of a system have grown dramatically, leading many practitioners to specialise. For example, larger teams often engage specialists to maintain the build servers and develop deployment scripts.

Recently, the term 'Full Stack Engineer' has become popular. In our view, this term describes what good all-round engineers have always done - have the skill and flexibility to work on all engineering tasks required to deliver a working solution.

'Polyglot' has also recently become a fashionable term to describe a developer fluent in multiple programming languages. This too is not a new concept for us. Being skilled in several technologies can be good for the individual's career and the flexibility of the organisation but should be balanced with a desire for in-depth knowledge in a particular field. Certainly, there are cases where engineering specialism is required, for example, a DBA role. We discuss what makes a good engineer later in this chapter.

It is worth saying something about another term we often hear - 'DevOps Engineer'. This role description can cause some confusion. DevOps is a cultural and organisational concept rather than a specific engineering discipline. Often what is meant is working with scripting technologies to automate the delivery pipeline. Again, this is a task to which most Full Stack Engineers can turn their hand, although there are cases where a specialist can be useful. We avoid confusion by using the term Platform Engineer when referring to infrastructure delivery.

Self-Optimising Organisations

One of the barriers to Agility we identified at the start of this book was dealing with real-world constraints and business change. Examples of potential challenges here include staff redeployment, training and recruitment. Some thinking is emerging as to how some of these issues may be overcome and how to apply Agile principles to organisation design and business change.

One such example of this is Holacracy, a management system devised by Brian Robertson. It replaces hierarchy and large organisational change with a flat management structure and distributed authority. Whilst in its infancy, Holacracy is gaining some ground and demonstrates the desire amongst a variety of organisations to gain competitive advantage through a more flexible and rapidly changing structure and empowering people to take control of their work and challenges.

BJSS Opinion

Ability-Led versus Process-Led

Successful change initiatives are ability-led not process-led. Many organisations mistakenly rely upon process to drive a quality outcome, particularly at scale. Whilst process is important, having empowered, capable individuals in key roles is essential to enabling rapid change and innovation.

Commoditising or de-skilling technology delivery with excessive process is fraught with issues. We prefer to build teams from highly capable individuals with a mix of experience levels and a shared appetite for delivery success.

The Agile Manifesto reinforces this message by favouring People and Interactions over Processes and Tools. It should be noted that, as with all tenets of the Agile Manifesto, this is a preferred bias rather than an extreme position. Product Teams need to operate within the constraints of the organisation and maintain a regular, healthy, connected dialogue.

Countering the perception of Agile as a 'Developer playground' requires that the organisation properly aligns teams to goals and implements the 'Necessary and Sufficient' lightweight governance in preference to a return to command-and-control management.

A Supportive Culture and Values System

Product Teams must be appropriately supported by the organisation to operate effectively. The organisation's culture and values exist to guide teams in their daily work, particularly when conflict arises, or difficult decisions are required.

A healthy organisation will keep the conversation alive through regular engagement with teams and individuals. Note that, in many organisations, Product Teams comprise permanent employees, contingent labour and multiple suppliers. This presents a challenge that should not be overlooked. We strongly recommend that orientation and, where necessary, adjustments to team values are made when people are added to the team.

All individuals should contribute to, identify with, and sign up to the values of their team and the wider organisation. This simple but powerful act helps everyone move forward together. It must be clear that this is not about rigid command and control, but an evolving set of guiding principles to aid and support teams.

Figure 4-1: Aligning Individual, Team and Organisation

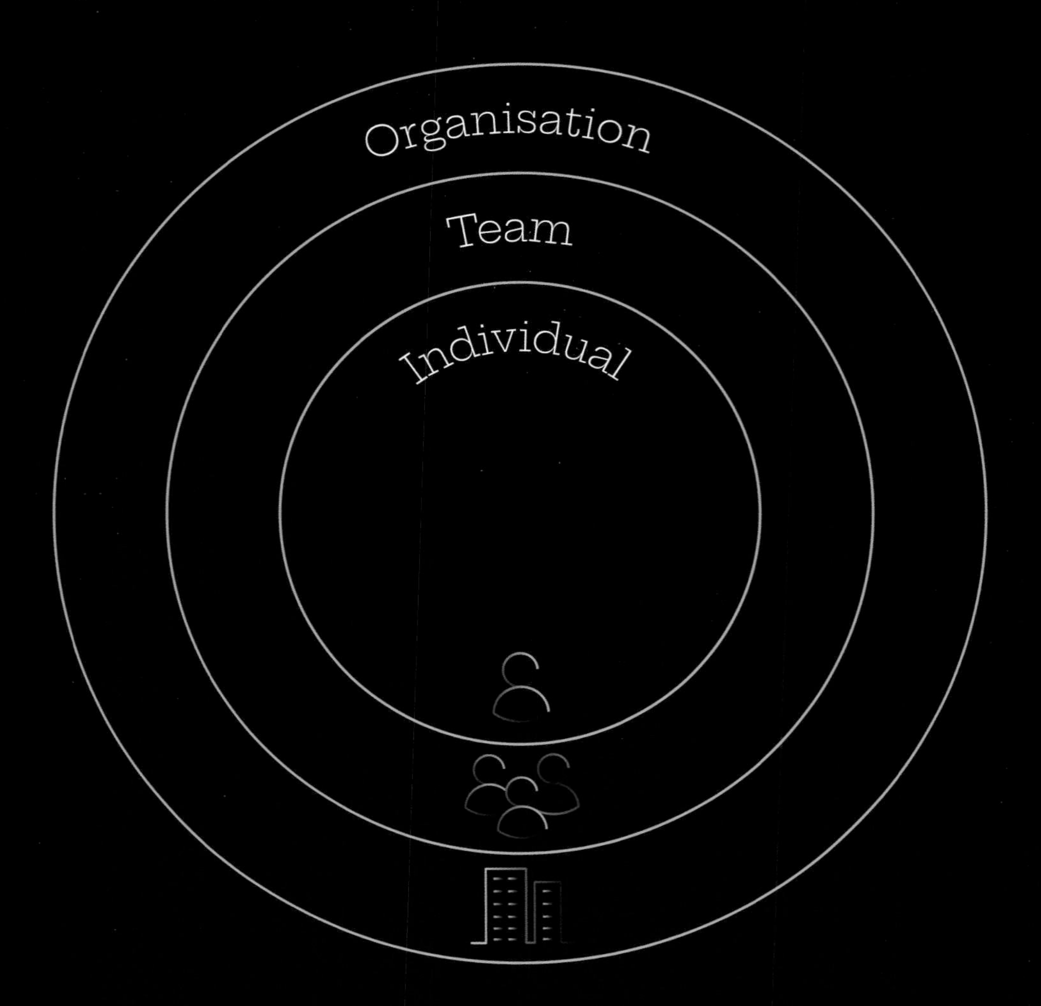

Creating Productive Teams

We are often engaged in helping organisations to initiate new projects and programmes in which teams comprise people who have never worked together. This is one of the key reasons why projects as a vehicle for delivering change can be inefficient. It is essential to consider, particularly in the Leadership Team, the characteristics of the individuals concerned. We shouldn't think of people the way we think of personal computers or desks, as interchangeable components that can be re-deployed with minimal disruption. Teams and the people within them have unique characteristics that need to be considered in the formation and ongoing operation of the team.

Various theories have been offered to describe the dynamics of a team and how a group develops. Most commonly quoted is Bruce Tuckman, who initially identified four phases of group development: Forming, Storming, Norming, Performing. This was later updated to describe a fifth phase, Adjourning.

Other similar models have been proposed, such as Tubbs' System Model (Orientation, Conflict, Consensus, Closure) and Fisher's theory of decision emergence (Orientation, Conflict, Emergence, Reinforcement).

These models can be useful to describe the evolution of a team and how they tackle problems. It is worth taking this into account when planning and considering the productivity of the team.

Figure 4-2: Tuckman's Stages of Group Development

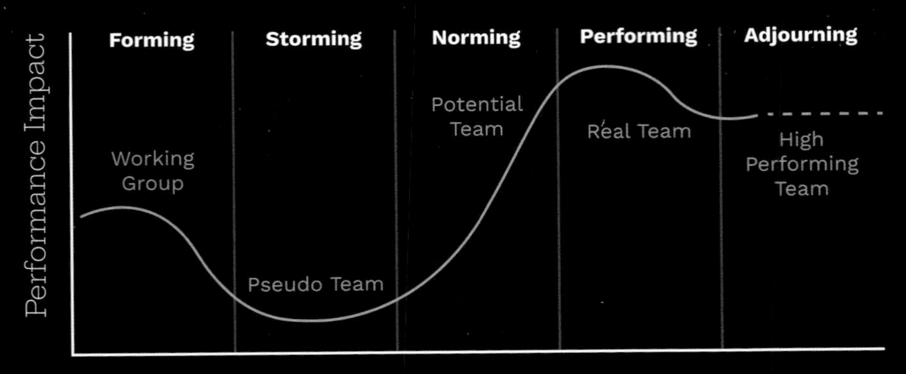

A key contributor to a productive team is clarity of goals and required outcomes. We passionately believe in keeping teams engaged and aware of the bigger picture. Team communication begins with Agile events such as the daily Stand-up, which keeps the team aligned in terms of challenges and the work of their peers.

Wider team communication should also be encouraged. This will include community gatherings for individuals interested in particular disciplines, for example, test automation or user-centred design. We also recommend that the entire Product Team is gathered together periodically for a full 'Town Hall' meeting. This should happen even if the team is large to re-assert objectives and allow Q&A.

Social functions are also a key part of getting a team to gel and operate effectively. The Leadership Team can often be buried in delivery challenges and forget this essential ingredient for productivity. The organisation of social functions is best left to someone in the team - they are often likely to have better ideas and be more enthusiastic about this aspect than the Management Team.

Considerations for a Productive Environment

The physical environment can have a considerable impact on the ability of the team to perform. Spaces are required that support the different modes that people work in. It must be possible to work quietly and concentrate on technical tasks. In addition, the environment must allow teams to collaborate and work together. This support should go beyond just traditional meeting spaces. Allowing for osmotic communication and quick informal problem solving as a team or pairing around particular problems helps keep teams productive and the work flowing.

Haworth's model for organisational space design reaffirms the relationship between environment and culture defined as **Control** (hierarchy); **Compete** (Market); **Collaborate** (Clan) and **Create** (adhocracy). The Values Framework can be a useful tool for assessing and motivating desirable behaviours through adjustments in the environment.

We are often asked about the importance of co-location to delivery, and recent events surrounding the Covid-19 pandemic have forced many of us to challenge our preconceptions regarding the effectiveness of remote teams. With the option to co-locate suddenly removed, many teams had to adapt their ways of working to comply with the restrictions imposed in the wake of the pandemic.

There have been numerous benefits to individuals of widespread remote working: regaining the time spent on commutes, the ability to spend more time with family, staying connected with people (and people) via Zoom. However, it should not be forgotten that the change has been less positive for others, with some colleagues missing in-person interactions in the office and struggling with impractical workspaces, such as those in shared accommodation.

Nonetheless, in a large proportion of cases, the overall productivity of teams and organisations as a result of the pandemic has not seen the dramatic downturn that many expected. Our experience of this dramatic change has been largely positive.

Figure 4-3: Competing Values Framework

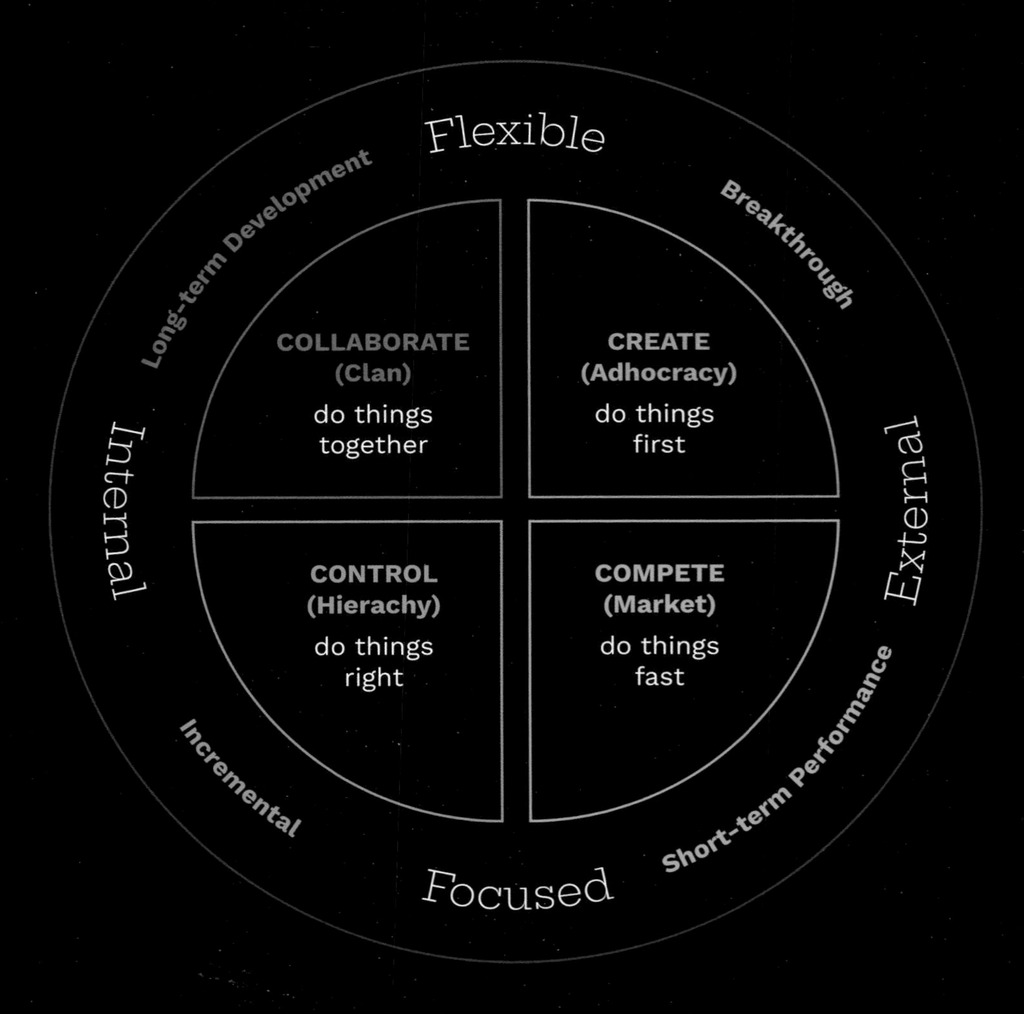

At the time of writing, the expectation for an entire organisation to congregate daily in shared office spaces is declining. The forecasts are for a 'hybrid' (or 'blended') working model, in which teams and individuals split their time between working in the office and working remotely.

Our advice is to, as much as possible, mimic the conditions where a Delivery Team is co-located. For example, the efficiency of frequent face-to-face communication is invaluable, even if it's over video conferencing instead of in person. The shift to hybrid working patterns may also offer advantages, such as increased availability of resources, accelerated ramp-up, greater opportunities to take on board diverse opinions, and sharing accountability for work across organisational boundaries.

Note that, whilst running Agile delivery engagements across multiple sites comes with those benefits, significant up-front investment is required to achieve the desired outcomes.

Even before the Covid-19 pandemic, we had a lot of experience of effectively delivering multi-site engagements across our UK and US Delivery centres. Note that success depends on more than the implementation of 'communication technology', important though these tools are. Investment in training, both for the leaders and the team members, organisational constructs around line management and end-to-end project assurance processes are also required.

The biggest challenge is that of human behaviour and the understanding for the team of what is involved in this type of engagement.

For smaller co-located engagements, project tracking formality can be more lightweight, such as the use of whiteboards and cards. In the multi-site scenario, each site can still make use of these lightweight resources. Overall cohesion requires that all data be made available via tooling allowing data sharing with people where they cannot immediately make use of the physical resources on that location. Great care must be taken to maintain this supporting technology - an area where truly digital businesses have an edge over more traditional organisations.

We make use of technology-based communication tools to maintain cross-site Agility, share key engagement data and maintain a close eye on the detail of our multiple deliveries.

The Enterprise Agile Approach

A Brief Guide to Organisation and Teams

To navigate the people and organisational aspects of Enterprise Agile, a brief overview of key concepts is provided here.

First, let us consider the building blocks of the delivery organisation:

- **Individuals performing specific tasks relating to change and service delivery - we promote the notion of 'T-shaped' individuals**
- **Delivery and Service Teams, which are highly cohesive teams of individuals working toward common goals**
- **The Product Team, which consists of one or more teams and a leadership function.**

These elements create a scalable method for organising people to build, maintain and enhance products. An effective leadership function, comprising Product Management, Delivery Management and Solution Architecture, is at the heart of the successful Product Team. We will now explore each of these concepts in more detail.

The Product Team

The Agile organisation comprises several building blocks aligned to our hierarchy of concerns. Certain roles are fulfilled at an organisation level, at a product level and within Engineering and Business Change Teams. The broad picture of the Product Team and the relationships they have is shown in **Figure 4-4**.

At the heart of any Product Team are the three key roles of Solution Architect, Delivery Manager and Product Manager. These key positions decide what changes are made to the product and how the ongoing service will be delivered.

This nucleus of the Product Team has the responsibility for managing the Delivery and Service Teams and the relationship with user groups and stakeholders. The remainder of the Product Team is responsible for delivering change and supporting the product.

The Product Team will work closely with the Design Team that may comprise Service Designers, Visual Designers, Content Producers and Analysts. The Design Team investigates and interprets pertinent information to design the optimum product or service. This process establishes a framework for the Product Manager to own.

The size and specialisms of a Design Team will depend on the complexity of the overall experience - i.e., how difficult will it be to motivate desired behaviours, and how challenging or numerous are the business processes and customer touchpoints to achieve those behaviours. For particularly complex projects demanding organisational restructure or multi-faceted orchestration and oversight, a Service Designer may form part of the core Product Team.

Figure 4-4: Product Team Structure

The basic building block is the ‘T-shaped’ technologist. These individuals are assembled into cohesive Delivery Teams, with potentially multiple teams for a particular product.

Most Engineering Teams will be multi-disciplinary and charged with delivering end-to-end features that meet user needs and add value to the organisation. General-purpose Feature Delivery Teams may be supported by specialist Engineering Teams. For example, a non-functional Test Team providing assurance of the complete integrated product against the non-functional requirements for the solution. Care should be taken to avoid these specialist teams becoming single point dependencies such that they are bottlenecks to the overall delivery of the product. In these instances, the specialisms should be integrated into the Delivery Teams so that these teams may continue to be autonomous. This may be achieved by restructuring the team, through a formal education programme, or via shadowing.

In addition to Engineering Teams, Service Teams will be required to deal with customer service enquiries and support the usage of the product by the organisation and external users.

In the Agile organisation, there are also likely to be Business Change Teams that update manual processes and execute organisational change.

The Shape of the Individual

We expect teams to include a diverse range of people. The Product Team will comprise technologists, domain specialist and managers, in a coherent unit organised for effective delivery. Most technologists have some kind of specialism - development, testing, analysis, database design, etc.

A common question is to what extent specialists should be used within technology delivery rather than generalists. Achieving the benefits of Agility requires a team of people with diverse skills working together towards a common goal. However, too much specialisation risks creating silos, inefficiencies and key person dependencies that are hard to overcome. For technology personnel, we always look for 'T-shaped' individuals, as illustrated in **Figure 4-5**.

Figure 4-5: 'T-shaped' Technologists

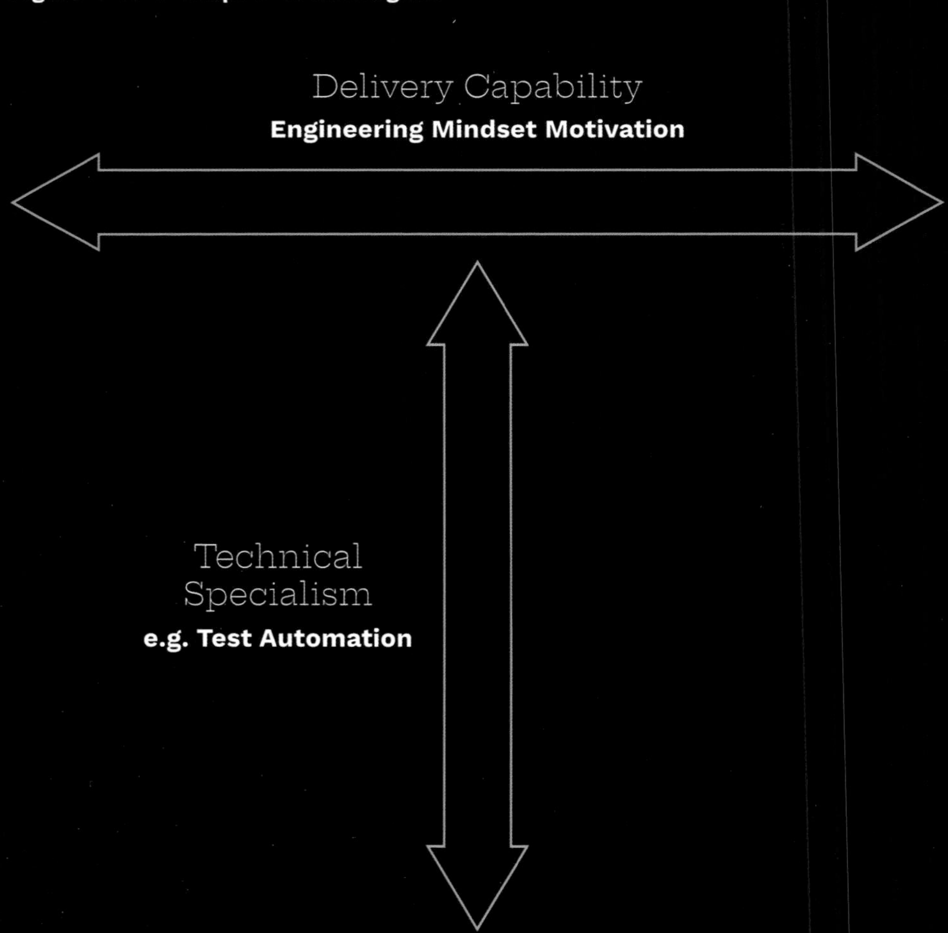

At their core, everyone on the team has a passion for delivery, a solid understanding of Agile principles, and a good engineering and problem-solving mindset. This core is supported by specialist technology skills, perhaps in test automation tools or software-defined infrastructure.

Strong technologists should always be able to learn the next test tool or programming language. When hiring into teams it is important to focus on the core attributes of the individual rather than hiring only for specific technologies.

These same specialised-generalist principles are also applied to managerial personnel. All managers are expected to have a strong knowledge of Agile and project and service management principles. In Enterprise Agile, managers are expected to support delivery, not just report on it. It is also likely that managers will have a specialism in the same way that 'T-shaped' technologists do. For managers, this may be expertise in infrastructure delivery or test management; for Service Design professionals this could be research or information design and architecture.

The Key Delivery Roles

Certain key roles must be filled for teams to successfully build and run the product. Depending on the scale of the organisation and product, not all roles will map to different individuals. Some roles are also quite broad and in larger organisations will be split across several people.

As we have already discussed, the organisation has a role to play in setting certain boundaries and constraints for Product Teams as well as providing support and guidance.

Table 4-1: Key Organisational-Level Roles

Role	Responsibilities
Product Sponsor	o Provides funding o Governance oversight
Enterprise Architect	o Guides on architectural standards and supports their adoption o Architectural governance oversight

The Product Team requires effective leadership and roles in this space are pivotal. **Table 4-2** outlines the key roles involved in leading the Product Team. The emphasis here is on leadership rather than management. The Leadership Team charts a course for the product and empowers the Delivery and Support Teams to do their daily work.

Table 4-2: Product Leadership Roles

Role	Responsibilities
Product Manager	o Understands the business domain and user insights o Owns the Product Roadmap o Leads the service design activities o Accountable for maximising the value of the product delivered by the Product Team
Delivery Manager	o Plans and coordinates business and technical change o Manages change and service o Ensuring delivery meets business objectives
Solution Architect	o Owns the big picture of the solution o Supports the adoption of architectural standards o Manages the technical governance process

The teams of technologists, domain specialists and customer support analysts deliver the real work of implementing and supporting change. The key roles within those teams are listed in **Table 4-3**.

Table 4-3: Team Roles

Role	Responsibilities
Team Lead	○ Guides the work of the team ○ Removes blockers and escalates issues
Service Designer	○ Defines the optimum approach or solution to meet business and audience goals ○ Considers interactions across all channels and touchpoints ○ Provides research skills
Technical Lead	○ Coaches and mentors technologists ○ Accountable for technical design; implements key frameworks
User Experience Lead	○ Establishes principles supporting ideal experience ○ Recommends solutions and features through testing with end users
Analyst	○ Organises user needs ○ Aligns delivery to outcomes
Digital Analyst	○ Tracks metrics relevant to Key Performance Indicators ○ Analyses and reports on key data

Continued overleaf

Table 4-3 continued: Team Roles

Role	Responsibilities
User Researcher	o Designs research using a variety of methods, from observation, interviews and usability testing, to surveys, focus groups and analytics o Identifies themes from a variety of data sets to uncover insights and make evidence-based decisions
Designer	o Defines the structure and visual style of a solution o Sets UI rules for technologists to implement
Content Producer	o Creates copy, imagery, videos or any other type of content required for the solution
Developer	o Implements technical change o Maintains the delivery pipeline
Tester	o Develops approaches to build in quality o Creates and executes test packs
Platform Engineer	o Maintains and improves infrastructure automation, CI environment and application release
Support Analyst	o Receives and triages support incidents o Works with the team on problem management

As we discussed earlier in this chapter, the concept of the 'T-shaped' Engineer is nothing new. Typically, it specifies a broad range of capabilities combined with in-depth knowledge of at least one technical discipline. This is particularly applicable for the Platform Engineer. The engineering role has evolved from the requirement for expertise in a single subject matter, such as networking, to an understanding of the entire infrastructure stack delivered as software-defined Cloud services. This has led to the breakdown of boundaries between Infrastructure Architecture, Infrastructure Design and Infrastructure Deployment, with the Platform Engineer requiring an understanding of the entire solution rather than a single subject. In addition, the introduction of Infrastructure as Code necessitates an understanding of software development techniques and automation.

Agile Software Engineering has historically been delineated alongside Development, Test, and Platform Engineering roles. With the introduction of Infrastructure as Code, these disciplines have moved closer together and share many principles. In each case, the engineering requires in-depth discipline and specific knowledge (such as Java, Selenium, Terraform/AWS), and shares many aspects:

- **A shared codebase**
- **The requirement for code quality (including code reviews)**
- **Consistent change control processes.**

There are several organisational benefits to be realised:

1. **Cross-training between roles becomes easier, providing career flexibility**
2. **Project resourcing challenges can be overcome with multi-discipline engineers**
3. **Improved quality and velocity through consistent approach across disciplines.**

Focused Delivery Teams

The building block of the organisation for delivering technology change is the Delivery Team. These teams are deliberately constructed cohesive units working collaboratively towards common goals. There isn't a universally applicable formula for the type and number of individuals in the team, but there are some reasonable guidelines. Typically, we expect to see Delivery Teams configured such that:

1. **One individual can ably support the team - this implies an optimal team size of about 6 + 3**
2. **It includes all the skills required to deliver an increment of valuable change**
3. **All are focused on a common goal – delivery of specified features.**

Irrespective of the method, all technology delivery comprises activities to analyse, develop, test, build and deploy. All of these activities need to be covered by the individuals within the team. By working together on the goal of delivering a feature to the user, these teams avoid the creation of the traditional silo mentality that has historically existed between functions such as Development and Test.

Figure 4-6: Example Delivery Team Structure

Figure 4-6 provides an example of a technology Delivery Team with all the elements required to design, construct and deliver a solution to the user.

Responsive Service Teams

As products increase in scale, it may be necessary to complement the Delivery Teams in the Product Team with Service Teams that operate the product and respond to user queries. Each team may contain a mix of resources specialising in dealing with users and resolving incidents. Where a defect or insight is found, the Service Team passes it to the Delivery Teams for resolution or enhancement. This proactive approach uncovers new opportunities for product improvement. In traditional IT support terms, Service Teams undertake first and second line support, and Delivery Teams undertake third line support. Service Teams should include service agents who deal with customers and diagnose basic issues together with more technical resources who may use tools provided by the Delivery Teams, or the underlying platform, to fix incidents.

As the Product Team scales further, Service Teams may focus on particular groups of users or parts of the system. As with Delivery Teams, all the members of Service Teams are focused on a common goal – providing a great service for users.

Effective Team Leadership

Getting the right people to lead teams is pivotal to success. There are two aspects to this which may or may not be filled by one person. Firstly, a strong lead is required to prioritise the activities of the team, track progress towards goals, raise issues and remove blockers that impede delivery.

The second side to leadership is more technically biased, taking a lead on design, mentoring the team and upholding the constraints and standards set by the broader organisation. Often the best technologist in the team is not the right person to perform the former of these roles but may be suited to the latter.

Organising Change Across Delivery Teams

When multiple Delivery Teams are engaged in delivering a product, a decision is required as to how to divide work between them. There are two schools of thought:

1. **The teams could have an affinity with components or parts of the system**

or

2. **The teams could be organised around cohesive end-to-end features that cut across potential technology or component boundaries.**

There isn't a definitive answer, although we have a strong preference for feature teams rather than component teams. We often change from one type of team to the other during a project, starting with component teams then moving to feature teams later when the basic structure is in place. There are advantages and disadvantages to each approach, as outlined in **Table 4-4**.

Table 4-4: Team Affinity

Feature Teams	Component Teams
Focused on end-to-end delivery and the common goal of creating business value	Easier to allocate work across feature dependencies
Clear responsibility for fixing issues, avoids defects being thrown 'over the wall'	Allows specialist teams to work on specialist technologies
Ensures continuous and regular integration across components	Enables multi-speed delivery across different systems
Creates greater awareness of the full technology stack across the team	May more efficiently facilitate sharing of components across multiple Product Teams

A key thing to remember is that success requires alignment of delivery model, team organisation, architecture and vendor management. If you engage multiple suppliers and they are providing expertise for specific elements of the technology stack, feature teams may not be the answer.

Real-world constraints often mean a hybrid model is used in many organisations. For example, the software vendor may maintain the back-office operational fulfilment package, while cohesive feature teams maintain multi-channel customer engagement systems. It is also possible for the position to move with time as the early stages of delivering a new product require focused work on frameworks.

In our experience, wherever there are hand-offs required between teams to secure end-to-end delivery, a level of coordination is required of each of the teams involved. Whilst this coordination may be achievable, it will inevitably create an overhead for each team and may require additional time and people for the delivery.

Scaling the Model

When the overall Product Team becomes larger than around five Delivery and Service Teams, it is probably time to think about how to adapt the structure. Traditional thinking would suggest creating a hierarchy and an additional layer of management. To an extent, there is no avoiding some form of organisational structure to coordinate across the growing team, but any structure should be lightweight and pass the Enterprise Agile 'Necessary and Sufficient' test.

Several models have been offered by organisations employing large-scale Agile delivery techniques. Some organisations employ terminology such as 'Clans' and 'Tribes' to describe groupings of teams. In Enterprise Agile, we adopt the more straightforward nomenclature of Streams, Capabilities, Communities and Teams to describe bigger team structures and organisational containers.

A key driver in our thinking about larger teams is the balance between empowering people to take ownership of their work and quality of delivery, and the organisation's need for some consistency of approach and easily digestible information on status and progress. A key to success in larger teams is effective communication. Structured and formal channels should be supported by informal ad-hoc communications, enabled by the working environment and suitable technical and collaboration tools.

In Enterprise Agile, several key constructs help support the growing team:

- **Stream** - A group of teams working on related functionality or components of the system
- **Capability** - A logical grouping of team members undertaking the same job function
- **Community** - A group of people with similar interests looking to promote improvements in a particular area.

Focused Streams of Activity

As the number of individual teams grows, they may require some logical grouping and additional coordination. For this purpose, we use the term 'Stream' to describe a collection of related teams. Teams may be grouped by function such as Delivery, Service and Business Change, by functional area or by technical component. There are clear advantages to each, but our preference is for functional area first and technical component second. We are keen to avoid silos and promote the concept of tightly bound teams working toward common goals based on delivering customer value. To be successful, the organisation of Streams should align with the technical architecture and any supplier model and incentives.

When there are several Streams each with many teams, it may be necessary to replicate the Product Leadership function across each Stream. This ensures that there is sufficient delivery management, solution architecture and product management bandwidth to coordinate and lead the work of the team as illustrated in **Figure 4-7**.

Figure 4-7: Multiple Streams

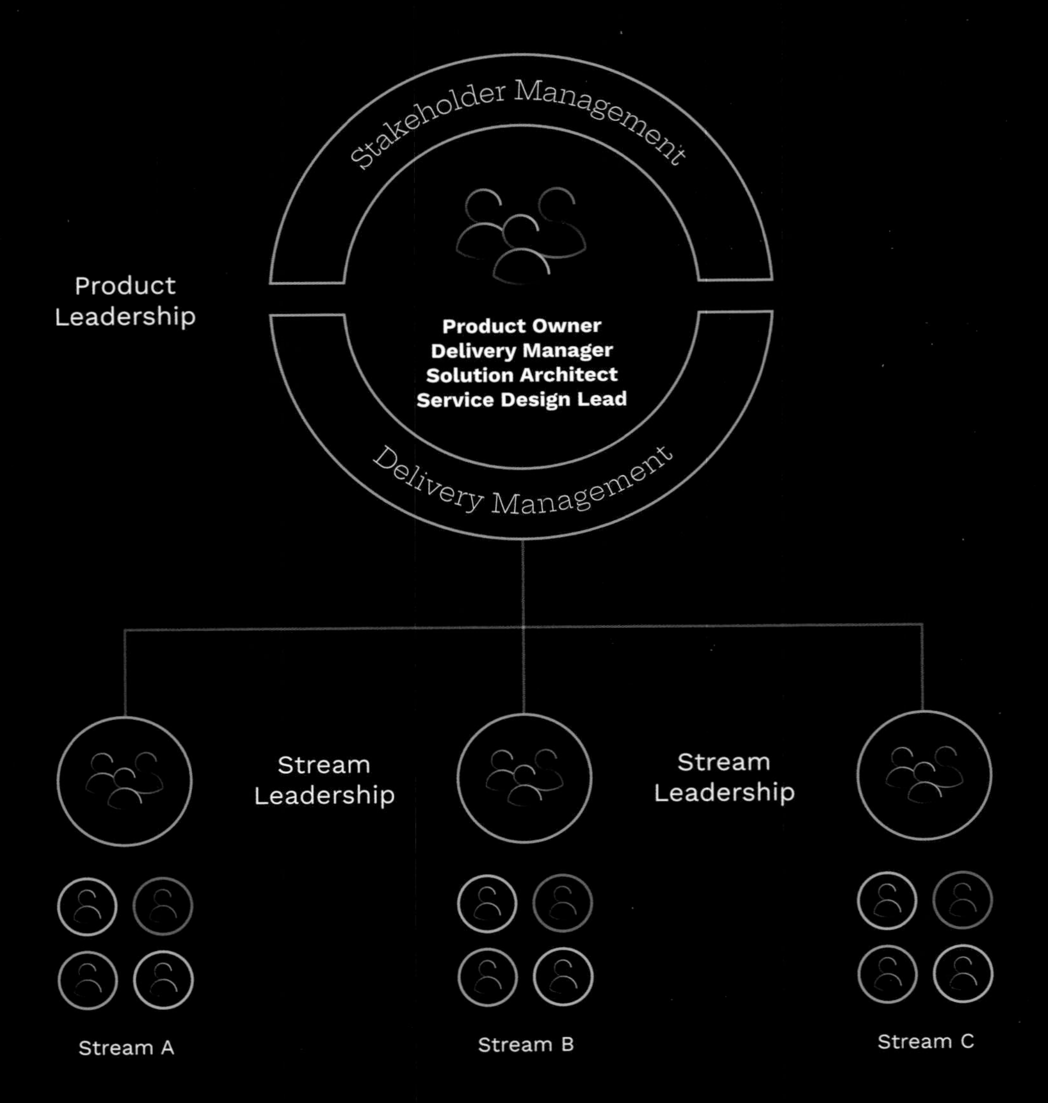

Leading Consistency Through Capabilities

When multiple teams exist, it is useful to lead the work of the same job function across these teams. For example, a test capability may exist to group together the Testers across several teams and share best practice, ways of working and tools. A Test Lead may span the teams and provide guidance, support, best practice on working methods, and a lightweight governance function.

This secondary alignment of the individual to a Capability, in addition to the primary role of delivering as part of the team, provides a useful structure to support people in their daily work. The use of Capabilities is illustrated in **Figure 4-8**.

Figure 4-8: Capability Leadership

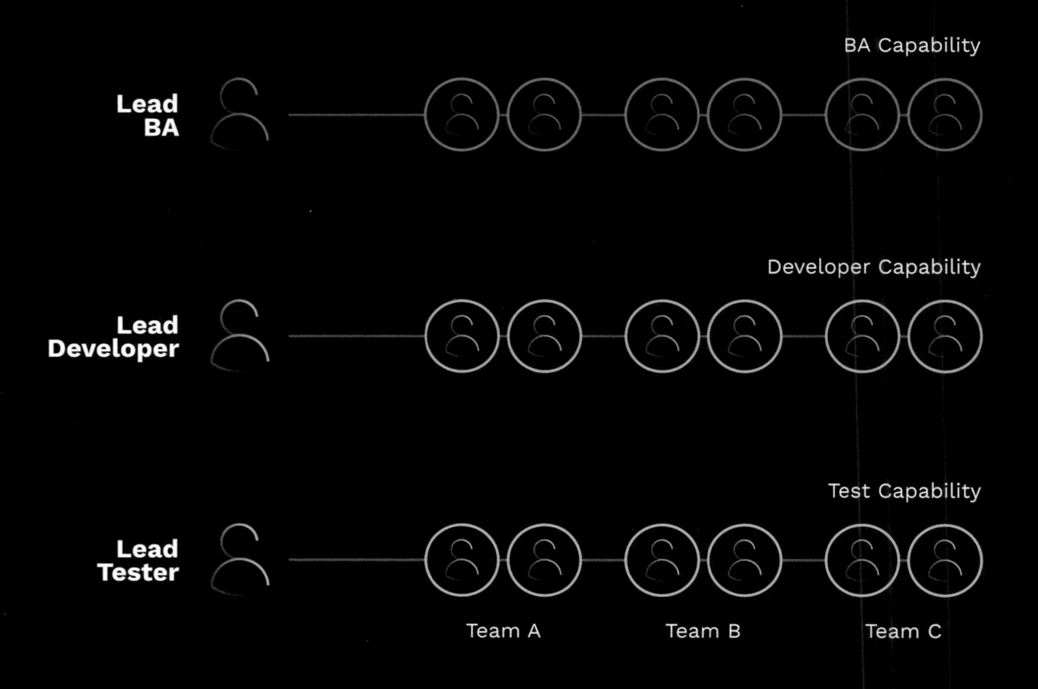

Building Communities for Continuous Improvement

If, as we suggest, technologists are located within Delivery Teams tied to products, then we hope that their primary affinity is to the product. Whilst this achieves focus on product delivery, it is important for both the organisation and the individual that there is a broader fabric of community within the technology domain.

Figure 4-9: Communities Spanning Multiple Teams and Products

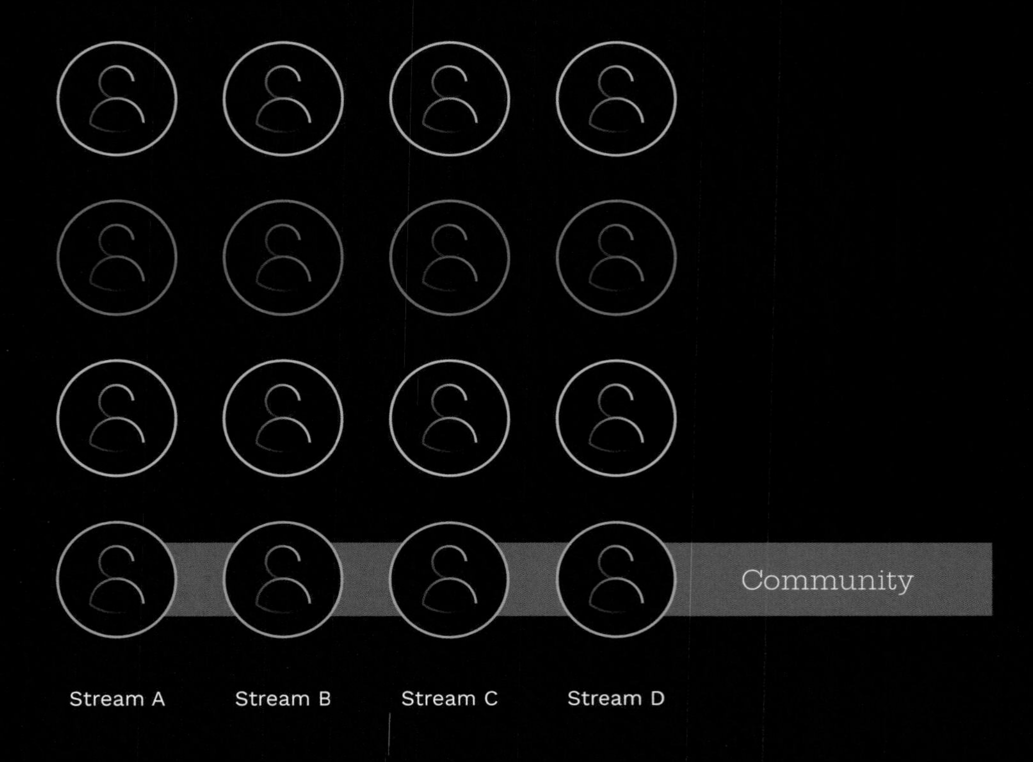

Creating Communities for particular groups of individuals or specific skill areas helps develop people and the organisation through improved sharing of ideas and knowledge. It allows the organisation to experiment and innovate from the ground up, supported by lightweight governance.

A typical way to build a Community is to encourage knowledge sharing through appropriate tools and to bring together interested individuals from across different Product Teams regularly. Ideas and improvements to working methods or tools identified by these groups are likely to contribute to the appropriate governance process, such as a Technical Design Authority.

Key Points

1. Team decisions and priorities should be guided and supported by the culture and values system of the organisation.
2. Delivery is ability-led and effective teams are made from 'T-shaped' individuals who all have broad experience of Agile delivery coupled with a specialism.
3. Change and service should be delivered by cohesive teams with everyone working toward a common goal.
4. A strong leadership function, comprising Product Management, Delivery Management and Solution Architecture is required to drive delivery.
5. Build self-sustaining communities from the bottom up to share ideas and promote good practice within specific technical areas.

Chapter 05
Effective Leadership

At the heart of a strong Product Team is a leadership function that can guide and direct the delivery of features that meet user needs and add value to the organisation. The number and type of individual roles may vary according to the scale of the service provided and the structure of the delivery and operations functions.

Leaders need a full 360-degree view of any initiative to manage effectively, both outwardly to stakeholders and also within the Delivery Team. They need to be capable of working with the broader organisation on strategy and to enable good governance. Effective leadership of empowered teams is where the most leverage is gained for organisations looking to thrive in the modern economy.

Concepts

Project & Service Management Leadership Convergence

Several recent innovations in technology are combining in a new model for building and running the products and services that organisations rely upon.

The rise of Cloud computing and the era of 'software-defined everything' means that software engineering practices are taking over the full technology stack and heavily influencing not just the build, but also the running of services - the DevOps model.

However, DevOps is not just about the technology of continuous delivery. It is a cultural and organisational shift that requires a new way of thinking about how to change and support products.

In addition to the expansion of software engineering practices into technical operations, service management thinking is moving back up the line into delivery. The lifecycle of a product does not begin when software is delivered to Operations, but when an organisation conceives and initiates the production of the idea.

Traditionally the 'Build' of a product was separate from the operations required to 'Run' it. This led to two separate disciplines of Project Management and service management. Increasingly, these areas overlap.

BJSS Opinion

Four Key Leadership Components

A good Product Team requires three elements of leadership, often provided by three or more individuals:

1. **Delivery (project and service) management**
2. **Product domain expertise**
3. **Solution architecture.**

Each has a role to play in working upward with the wider organisation and stakeholders, and downward into the team delivering change and running the service.

Figure 5-1: 360 Degree Product Leadership

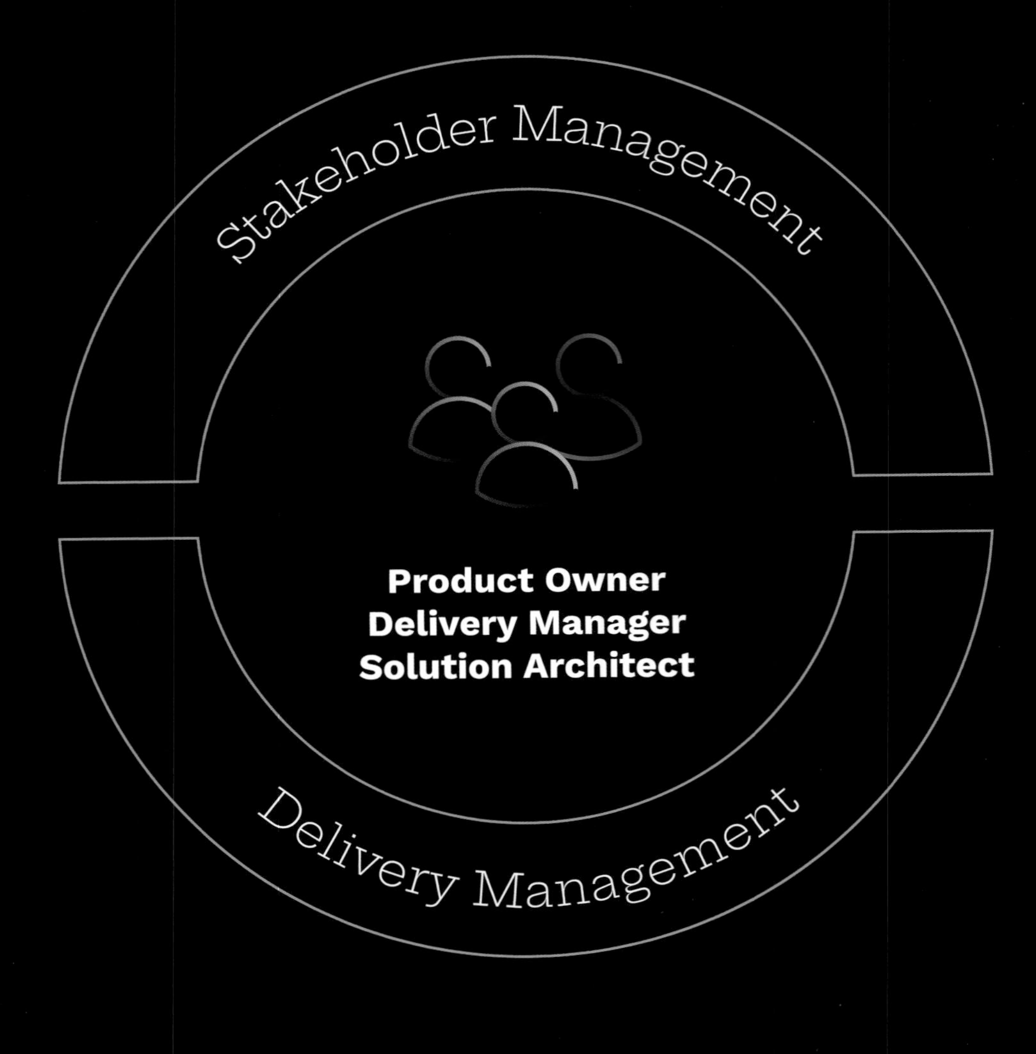

The common responsibilities of each of the key leadership roles are explored in **Table 5-1**. Whilst the three leadership roles work together to change and support the product, the responsibilities we outline do imply some structure. Ultimately, as the plan and budget holder, the Delivery Manager is accountable for the delivery of changes and the service for the product.

This does not necessarily mean there is a strict reporting line from the Solution Architect and the Product Manager into the Delivery Manager. Sometimes, this relationship can be a complex dynamic; for example, the Product Manager is provided by the organisation, and the Delivery Manager and Solution Architect are from a third-party supplier.

Table 5-1: Responsibilities of Key Roles

	Delivery Manager	Product Manager	Solution Architect
Outward Responsibilities	o Manage allocated resource and budget o Reporting including service KPIs and delivery metrics o Escalate risk and issues to the organisation o Ensure delivery against business goals	o Understand and prioritise user needs o Help define the roadmap and contribute to organisational strategy o Communicate with the customer	o Actively manage technical risk o Product alignment with enterprise architecture o Contribute to the technology community
Inward Responsibilities	o Remove delivery blockers from the team o Manage and motivate the team o Own the plan	o Ensure a common understanding of user needs o Make priority calls on delivery o Support test and assurance activities	o Coach and support teams in understanding the overall solution architecture o Promote good practice and awareness of enterprise architecture o Review and contribute to detailed design work

The most important point is that all three areas must work together to deliver a product focused on user needs that adds value to the consumer as well as to the organisation.

‘Necessary and Sufficient’ Governance

Governance often has a bad reputation amongst Delivery Teams. It conjures up thoughts of bureaucracy, red tape, and reasons not to do things. We have already established that the modern organisation needs to change at a faster pace and continually evolve its products to meet user needs. To do so, the role of governance must be to guide and support with judicious management of risk.

Infrequent, onerous approval gates are replaced by lightweight, regular guidance. This requires a mindset change for sponsors and executives. Teams must be trusted to deliver and provided with regular support to do their jobs. Executives have a responsibility to the organisation to manage risk and ensure that people and resources are deployed effectively. Discharging this responsibility requires engagement and strong leadership.

Teams have a part to play in building this trusted relationship through demonstrating value-add to the organisation, and by being open and transparent about challenges that exist. The judgement required here is a key skill of the Leadership Team. Too often, change initiatives spiral out of control due to a loss of confidence by stakeholders. This can become a bigger problem than any underlying delivery issue. Teams need to demonstrate they are in control whilst not hiding problems.

Defining the Business Challenge

A well-defined business challenge is critical to project success. Strategy should be the foundation of any Discovery phase – providing the direction and boundaries for future decision making. When an organisation is clear on the problem to solve and objectives to meet, an investigation to surface internal and external insight can begin. It is this insight, particularly that of the audience, that enables the selection of promising ideas that reduce the risk of releasing unwanted products.

Tools like a Value Proposition Canvas ask teams to consider product benefits, features, and experience through the lens of audience needs, wants, and fears. The aim is to surface a differentiating idea that will satisfy customers' needs.

Figure 5-2: Value Proposition Canvas

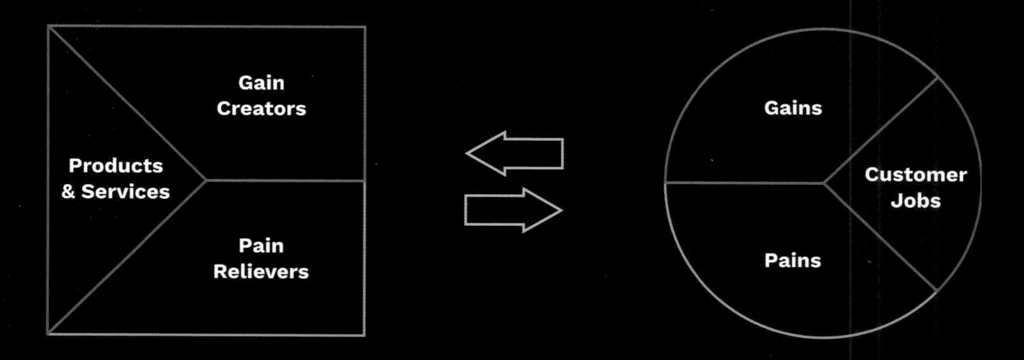

Developing a subsequent Business Value canvas can help to consolidate disparate business, audience, and market insight to identify the attributes needed to support a successful business or service. This approach asks you to consider:

- **Who are the potential partners in your network, and what resources or activities are available to you?**
- **What activities and resources are needed to support the value proposition?**
- **What are the characteristics of your value proposition, and what form will it take?**
- **Who is your audience, what factors differentiate them, and what do they need from the experience?**
- **Which channels will you use to bring the product or service to market, and how will you use them to reach your audience segment?**
- **How will you charge for the product/service and what costs do you need to cover to remain viable?**

Estimating Work

One of our aims for this book is to help organisations build predictability into their delivery process. The techniques we describe can help with this, and a key point is to break change down into smaller pieces and release often. Another essential factor is the process by which work is estimated and sized, particularly when this is being undertaken to advise funding for a Minimum Marketable Feature set (MMF).

Traditional project planning relies on decomposing the perceived work and then estimating based on the effort (in person-days) required to complete it. The drawback with such work breakdown structures is that they require significant upfront Discovery work and assume that functionality is relatively fixed. Both of these factors do not lend themselves to Agility.

Alternative Agile methods of estimation take a more holistic approach, sizing pieces of work based on relative size, risk, and complexity to get an overall view of the effort required. A common method is to use story points to mark the relative estimate of valuable items of work (sometimes captured as user stories). Typically, the numbers used are something like a Fibonacci sequence (1, 2, 3, 5, 8, 13, 21, 34) to demonstrate increasing uncertainty in larger, more complex stories.

The strength of story points as an abstract concept can also become a significant weakness during Delivery. We have seen many projects go awry due to the intangible nature of the metrics being used. For small-scale change and the work of a small team, simple use of story points and a velocity (the rate at which story points are currently being delivered) may work. The drawbacks of story points on larger programmes and MMF delivery can be significant and do not aid predictability, notably:

1. **Many business sponsors do not understand the abstract concept of story points and want (need) to work in clear effort and monetary terms**
2. **Story points can lead to a lack of transparency over progress, particularly when they are diluted through re-estimation. Delivery of story points gives the illusion of progress even though the backlog is not reducing.**

We would urge some caution when using story points, particularly in conjunction with third party suppliers and contracts. Delivery of story points does not always equate to progress towards the end goal and is certainly not a measure of supplier productivity.

On the other hand, when used well, story points and relative estimation can prove to be a far more reliable forecast for delivery than traditional estimation and planning techniques.

The Enterprise Agile Approach

Taking a Risk-First Approach

We are strong advocates of active risk management and a risk-first approach to delivery. Risk takes many forms. Some risks are under the control of the Product Team, some they can influence, and others are external to the organisation that they are unable to affect.

When considering implementing change to a product, it is essential to take time to consider risk, its source, and what can be done to influence or manage it. Taking a risk-first approach means tackling unknowns early, providing the opportunity to fail fast, or adjust plans while there is still time to do so.

In practical terms, the risk-first approach provides confidence in the solution being delivered. This is affirmed through robust and ongoing consultation with the audience(s), and the active participation of the entire team in applying their skill and judgment to recognise potential risks, and considering innovative approaches to address them. It is in this area where the Delivery Manager and Analyst are expected to make a significant contribution. We believe that managers should be actively driving towards no surprises in delivering change, not simply reporting on it. The manager is expected to fly ahead of the team to look for potential obstacles.

The Enterprise Agile approach includes the following elements to help realise the risk-first principle:

The Product Lifecycle

Use of Feasibility and Discovery phases ahead of Delivery to manage risk to delivery, and ensure the solution meets audience needs.

The Delivery Pipeline

Fully automated software build and deployment using repeatable processes rather than manual, error-prone alternatives.

Quality Built-In

Well thought through test approaches and important considerations such as security, privacy, and accessibility to ensure a high-quality product is delivered and assured.

Architecture Centric

Proving architecture early in the product lifecycle through the delivery of valuable features, and ensuring that architecture evolves in a controlled manner.

Sprint Planning

Making sure the high-risk areas of technical or functional delivery are addressed in the early Sprints of the release.

Implementing Good Governance

It has been our experience that clients expect something specific delivered against a plan, for a particular date and a specified budget – all agreed in advance. To achieve this over an extended period in an Agile engagement requires appropriate governance.

Most clients have existing frameworks with which we must conform. At first sight, these often appear to be heavyweight processes with significant documentation overhead. However, they usually include the essential gates designed to inform senior management decision making and minimise corporate risk. It's perfectly possible to make an Agile delivery approach work in this type of environment, and a 'Necessary and Sufficient' documentation set can provide the level of documentation and information required to support such decisions.

A good governance process should fulfil three key aims:

- **Inform** – Provide suitable performance indicators
- **Escalate** – Offer a route up in the organisation to raise critical issues
- **Assure** – Keep the product aligned to organisation goals.

This process will involve regular meetings to discuss progress, status, key risks, and issues. We believe that these should be focused and aligned to the Sprint and Release cadence. This ensures they support the delivery of Sprint plans, as well as report on the end of Sprint deliverables and the achievement of Release commitments. This is discussed in more depth in **Chapter 7**, where we consider the value of Sprint backlogs, earned value, and a commitment to deliver.

We think that appropriate project governance is a vital element in the success of all projects, especially Agile ones, and that it can be achieved without a burdensome level of overhead.

Bridging to the Organisation

The key governance review meeting between the Product Team and organisation executives is the Programme/Project Board or, perhaps more appropriate in an Agile organisation, the Product Governance Board. This provides the Product Team with the opportunity to request additional support from the sponsor and to raise issues. The board performs the function of steering product development to maintain strategic alignment and levels of service received by the end-users. Conflicting priorities may be escalated to this group for guidance.

Figure 5-3: Flow Between Governance Board and Product Team

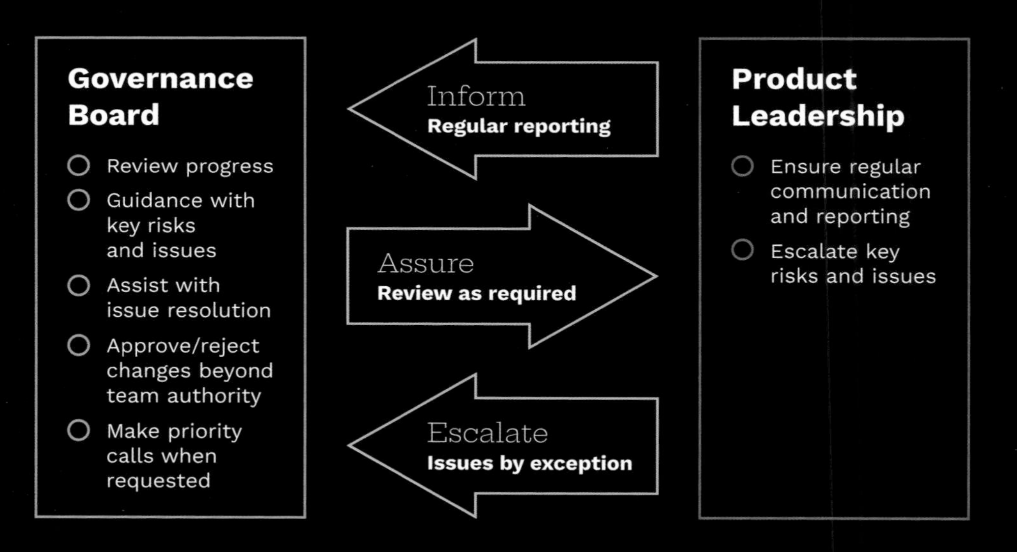

Diligence Within the Product Team

Good governance is also important within the Product Team itself, particularly as it grows. As far as possible, the Product Owner should be trusted by the organisation to make decisions about the product independently. That said, there are occasions where decisions that are impacted by strategy, or that may impact the product within the wider organisation or portfolio, may require some additional oversight and ceremony. One area we believe that some ceremony is required is design decision making. Using a Design Authority to record key design decisions is a powerful tool to help plot and record the course the product takes over time.

There are two facets to the Design Authority: functional design decisions and technical design decisions. We recommend both are discussed at the same forum. Taking decisions in isolation of a discussion about delivery impact should be avoided. This group should be diverse and include those managing the delivery of change, not just the service design, technical, and analyst communities.

The frequency of the product design authority meetings may vary. The more intense the phase of delivery and volume of change, the more frequent the meetings are likely to be. This keeps change flowing and minimises the number of decisions at any one time. Always bear in mind that any delay resulting from a team waiting for an authority's decision will impede the team's, as well as the wider organisation's, ability to be responsive and Agile.

The workings of the Design Authority are likely to be tied to the Sprint delivery pattern. This ensures that areas of design related to work for the following Sprint can be guided as necessary as requirements are further elaborated. The Design Authority will operate within organisational constraints, such as enterprise architecture.

Figure 5-4: Product Design Authority

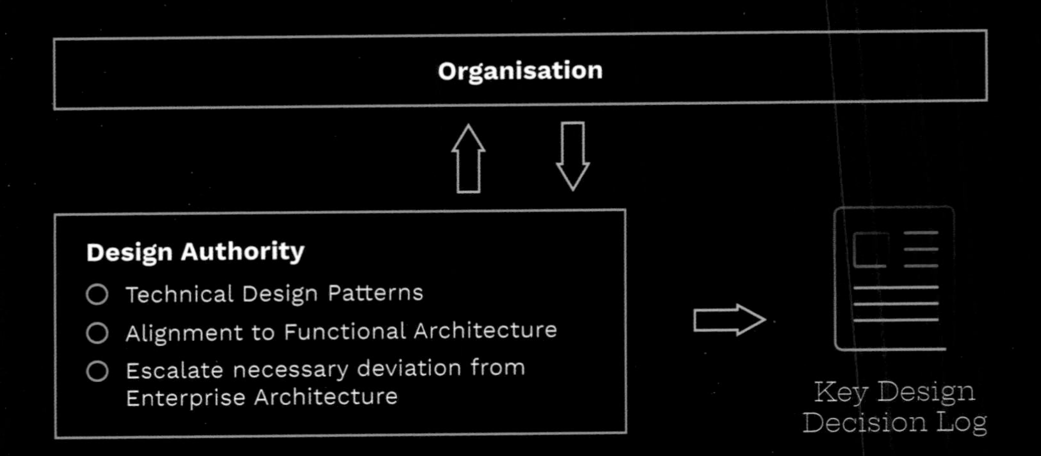

The Ongoing Importance of Planning

Agility does not mean foregoing a plan. Managing change requires planning, but the real measure of success is demonstrable progress towards the required outcomes. No team should slavishly follow a plan without reference to defined goals. The level of planning depends on the scale of the change and the level of Agility across the organisation.

Roadmaps typically exist at the organisation and product level. A roadmap is a statement of intent, and suggests a phasing and rough timing for initiatives. A plan is more detailed, but still subject to change. The Sprint backlog describes a commitment by a team to deliver a specific goal. Whilst there may still be some flexibility in how the goal is delivered, the planned backlog items and tasks required to deliver them should be understood.

Products that are relatively standalone and mature can evolve through continuous product innovation and require little planning. The replacement of a legacy system with a 'big bang' cutover and many dependencies on third parties requires much more work. Planning is usually most important during the inception of a product and getting to MMF and launch.

We recommend that plans are layered with successive levels of refinement. For the majority of small initiatives, a single-level Sprint plan is often sufficient. For large-scale changes, there are commonly three layers of planning that roll up into each other.

High-Level Plan

Planning at a high level will capture the major milestones and interactions with other products and services across the organisation and any external dependencies.

This high-level plan is generally outside the remit of the Product Team and manages portfolio-level dependencies. This plan is key for larger-scale change programmes and is often expressed as a flight plan to bring together multiple, related workstreams and products.

Mid-Level Plan

The mid-tier of planning focuses on the work of the entire Product Team, their interactions with each other and the bringing together of business and technical change.

This artefact is the key guide for the Product Team and is owned by the Delivery Manager with input from all the team leaders. It is this plan that the governance process tracks against.

Low-Level Plan

A low-level plan looks at the day-to-day work of individual teams delivering change and supporting the product. This layer is the most fluid and often exists within the delivery pipeline tooling. This equates to the individual Sprint Plan used to deliver change and release valuable increments of the product.

Planning Across Lifecycle Phases

The role and level of planning evolves across the lifecycle.

Feasibility

At the Feasibility stage, the key activities are understanding the objectives of the initiative. It is critical to define the value that the initiative will provide for the customer (internal or external) as well as the benefit the initiative will deliver for the organisation.

Feasibility can often be brief, perhaps even only a few days and involving a handful of people. Planning activities at this stage involve ensuring that key stakeholders are engaged, the candidate delivery options are validated and understood, and a suitable proposal, including an initial draft plan for delivery, is prepared.

Much of the effort in Feasibility should focus on building a robust plan for Discovery that allows for that phase to conclude successfully.

Discovery

Several essential objectives must be achieved during Discovery - an intensive phase designed to reduce risk and increase predictability during delivery.

Where Discovery is more than a couple of weeks duration, a Discovery phase plan should begin the operation of a Sprint pattern. This allows for Agile principles of a regular heartbeat to facilitate course corrections and demonstrable progress.

In contrast to many traditional initiatives, the Discovery phase may result in the initiative being cancelled if it reveals that the customer demand cannot be validated or the solution cannot be provided whilst still delivering the benefits defined for the organisation in the Feasibility stage.

Delivery

The Delivery plan is a Sprint-based plan that, whilst allowing for refinement and change, is aimed at providing some degree of predictability – particularly up to the point of MMF. An initial Sprint plan for the MMF is built during Discovery.

Generating a Sprint Plan

It is useful to have a view of a few Sprints ahead to link Agile product delivery with other fixed, real-world dependencies. One scenario where a Sprint plan is most useful for a longer duration is in the delivery of a Minimum Marketable Feature set. This is generally because the initial product delivery has some challenging real-world constraints and deadlines, and the organisation is seeking more predictability.

Creating a Sprint plan requires that suitable structured analysis has been undertaken to create a set of estimates against the required scope. Developing the plan is then a matter of allocating work to Sprints based on a set of priorities and the estimated capacity of the Delivery Team.

Estimating for MMF

The bulk of the effort to create an initial Sprint plan for the Minimum Marketable Feature set is identifying the features required and estimating the work involved. The process of generating the scope for the Minimum Marketable Feature set and structuring requirements is covered in more detail in **Chapter 6**.

If the research and analysis work has produced a backlog of epic features (any large, complex, or risky piece of work that cannot be delivered within a Sprint) to deliver, a good way to generate the estimates for the plan is to take a top-down approach and 'shirt size' the requirements. The Discovery phase of the product lifecycle should yield a functional scope against which to estimate. There are three distinct stages of creating the estimate.

Build the Model

The build of the model is a case of listing out all of the feature epics and applying a shirt size to them. We normally use five shirt sizes: XS, S, M, L, XL. It is often useful at this stage to adopt a blind estimating technique where members of the team do not compare results until the exercise is completed, so as not to bias each other.

After this stage, we have identified the relative complexity of the epics and flushed out any unknowns. It is also possible to see the potential variance based on different estimators' understanding of the problem. The conversations that this process generates can be a useful way of ensuring there is a common understanding of the requirements across the team.

Calibrate the Model

It can then be useful to assign numbers to the model. To do this, we will take a representative sample, perhaps up to 20% of the epics, and decompose them into stories. These stories are then sized in ideal days. It is essential at this stage to take a representative set of epics across the product and of different shirt sizes.

From this stage of the process, we can determine the average effort required for the delivery of each size and get an overall effort for the MMF in ideal days. Factoring in an efficient ratio and capacity for defects allows a total required capacity to be attained and a Sprint plan to be built.

Test the Model

There is no substitute for doing actual work to determine the accuracy of the estimation model. For a large product build, certain elements of the solution will likely be prototyped during Discovery. These pieces of work could be used to recalibrate the model.

Generally, we recommend that the same teams that conducted Discovery should carry on into Delivery to ensure that the learnings are not lost. If this is not possible, it will be necessary to adjust the 'actuals' from the Discovery phase if they are applied to the overall model. Certainly, delivery metrics from the first few Sprints should be fed back. It is also worth bearing in mind that the productivity of new teams, whilst initially low, will increase during the early stages of delivery.

Managing Changes to the Plan

The purpose of greater Agility in the organisation is to allow for flexibility and responsiveness to adapt to evolving user needs. In this environment, change is inevitable and should be encouraged.

There does, however, need to be some direction and stability as provided by the roadmaps and plans created for individual products. Whilst Product Teams should be empowered to do the things that users need and release value for the organisation, change should not be unconstrained.

Where a baseline scope has been created for a Product Increment or Minimum Marketable Feature set, it may, in exceptional circumstances, it may be necessary to use Change Control to govern this. The use of a Change Control process ensures that any revised scope remains true to the organisation's goals and that any outside dependencies can be adjusted. It also allows for expectations to be managed if particularly large features come in or out of scope, adjusting delivery dates or the need for (interim) manual processes.

Minor changes as a result of regular story elaboration and items moving between Sprints would not normally require Change Control. Major scope changes at the epic level require visibility, and this may include formal decision making.

Active Raid Management for Improved Predictability

Even if you can embrace continuous product innovation and exploit Agile techniques across the organisation, you will still face changes presented by the outside world. Active RAID (Risks, Assumptions, Issues, and Dependencies) management is still as important as ever to avoid unpleasant surprises.

We often find that these terms are misused, so it's worth a quick recap of the definitions.

Table 5-2: RAID Definitions

Term	Definition	Example
Risk	An identified threat to delivery	The supplier may not be able to provide suitably skilled staff at the right time
Assumption	A documented expectation based on the facts available at the time. A change to the assumption could jeopardise delivery	There will be no regulatory or compliance changes during the delivery project
Issue	An actual problem that impedes delivery	An issue has been identified in a core foundation technology product that inhibits the non-functional requirements being met
Dependency	Required input from elsewhere within or outside the organisation. Should have a due date	The procurement agreement with the Cloud service provider will be signed by 1st Jan 2022

Materialised risks, false assumptions, and missed dependencies all result in issues. Teams also identify blockers through their daily Stand-up meetings. Blockers that cannot be dealt with through team interaction also need to be raised and recorded as issues.

Reporting

A key element of a Product Team leadership role is providing timely, accurate reporting to enable fact-based decision making and interventions. When too little or too much information is provided, time-poor stakeholders cannot rapidly understand the current position, and become frustrated. The Leadership Team must clearly articulate the current position, supported by several relevant KPIs and metrics.

Table 5-3: Suggested Reporting Contents

Definition	Example
Summary	Narrative to briefly describe current status
RAG status	Red/Amber/Green to reflect current product status often split into sub-categories: o Value o Progress o Quality o Service o Team o Suppliers
Outcomes planned/delivered	Outline of the outcomes planned for the reporting period and the outcomes delivered
Key RAID changes	Any significant movement in RAID

Continued overleaf

Table 5-3 continued: Suggested Reporting Contents

Definition	Example
Metrics	Example key metrics supporting the current position: **Progress** o Sprint Burn-down o Release Burn-up **Quality** o Defect find/fix rate o System availability **Service** o Volume of incidents o Performance against SLAs

Concerns arise when information is reported that does not represent the complete picture. This can quickly become a distraction and result in demands for further information. Before long, the Product Team is spending a disproportionate amount of time servicing questions rather than delivering. In the absence of the right information, stakeholders make judgements based on perceptions. If this point is reached, it is time to stop, take stock, and agree on a recovery plan to remedy the key issues and return to fact-based conversations.

Metrics and data collection for reporting should be built into the delivery tooling and, as far as possible, be automated. Minimal effort is required from the team to record the tasks being worked on if the tools are set up correctly from the outset.

It should be clear that delivery metrics are best used to understand the rate of progress and product quality to aid planning and continuous improvement, rather than a stick with which to beat team members. Reporting should echo the message coming out of the Sprint ceremonies, such as estimation and planning meetings and Show and Tells.

A good report may include the key elements described in **Table 5-3**.

Keep the Information Flowing

Whilst regular reporting is required to keep stakeholders informed, this should not be the sole source of information. Delivery, service, and quality metrics should always be visible to the team and stakeholders.

There should be no surprises for anyone in terms of the status of delivery and progress towards agreed goals. The use of whiteboards and, preferably, screens in the team environment is to be encouraged. It is straightforward to get most modern tooling to display a dashboard to highlight progress, quality, and service metrics.

The current delivery position should always be very visible to teams and stakeholders. Everyone is signed up to working towards a set of common goals, and progress towards these should be of interest to everyone.

Key Points

1. A strong leadership function should cover three components: Delivery Management, Product Ownership and Solution Architecture.

2. 'Necessary and Sufficient' governance should be put in place with clearly defined paths for Information, Escalation, and Assurance.

3. Estimation for Minimum Marketable Feature set involves building, calibrating, and testing a model based on the Discovery phase feature backlog.

4. An initial Sprint plan for delivering a Minimum Marketable Feature set is required and this is built during the Discovery Phase, but subject to change based on feedback from the first few Sprints.

5. Active Risk, Issue, Assumption, and Dependency (RAID) management is still required in Agile delivery, particularly in the bridge to the non-Agile world.

Chapter 06

Understanding Human-Centred Design

The last decade has seen a radical shift in the way organisations solve problems and design products or services. Human-centred design is a mindset and a method. It is a practice of understanding human behaviours and identifying insights that inform the design and delivery of better user experiences.

A mature User Experience (UX) approach seeks to meet both internal and external audiences' expectations by deliberately designing their experience to create the greatest value for both the user and the organisation.

Human-centred design extends to planning and organising internal teams, systems, infrastructure, and communication to deepen the connection between the organisation and the user.

There is a multitude of terms and models used to describe all elements of Human-centred design. While this can be confusing, the most important point to remember is that the user need should be paramount at the outset of strategic product and service proposition development, and throughout the delivery process.

Concepts

Understanding User Needs

Inaccurate assumptions, bias, departmental silos, and many other challenges reinforce the importance of a Human-centred design approach for successful delivery. When user needs are identified, they can set the shared strategic vision for all contributing teams and stakeholders.

Empathy is one of the first steps in Human-centred design. Methods and tools that help Agile Teams build empathy with users embed a better understanding of user needs within the team and, subsequently, with the wider stakeholder group. This first step generates the crucial insight required to create solutions that are fit for purpose.

User research is a way to embed empathy within the team. The insight generated reduces the risk of development, providing the team with the confidence and understanding to build the right product or service at pace. There are many different research techniques, from qualitative in-depth observational field studies, guerrilla testing and face-to-face interviews to quantitative analysis of user data.

Primary research, i.e., research that you conduct yourself, can be supplemented with other sources. This is often referred to as triangulation. Using more than one method to collect insight on the same topic can assure the validity of research. For example, call centre records or digital analytics provide good insight. Many online reports and resources are also available, for example, Google Trends and Google Correlate. 'Review' sources like app and retail stores can also be useful.

Empathising with users through research is often followed by 'affinity mapping', which means grouping the insight into commonalities and patterns which enable categorisation. Personas are an example of research-based fictional characters that represent groups of users. Personas provide a visual tool to help embed a common language and user focus across a team. High-priority persona types and corresponding user needs, often written as 'stories', will inform design, and strategic and tactical prioritisation of 'features'.

Figure 6-1: Research Triangulation

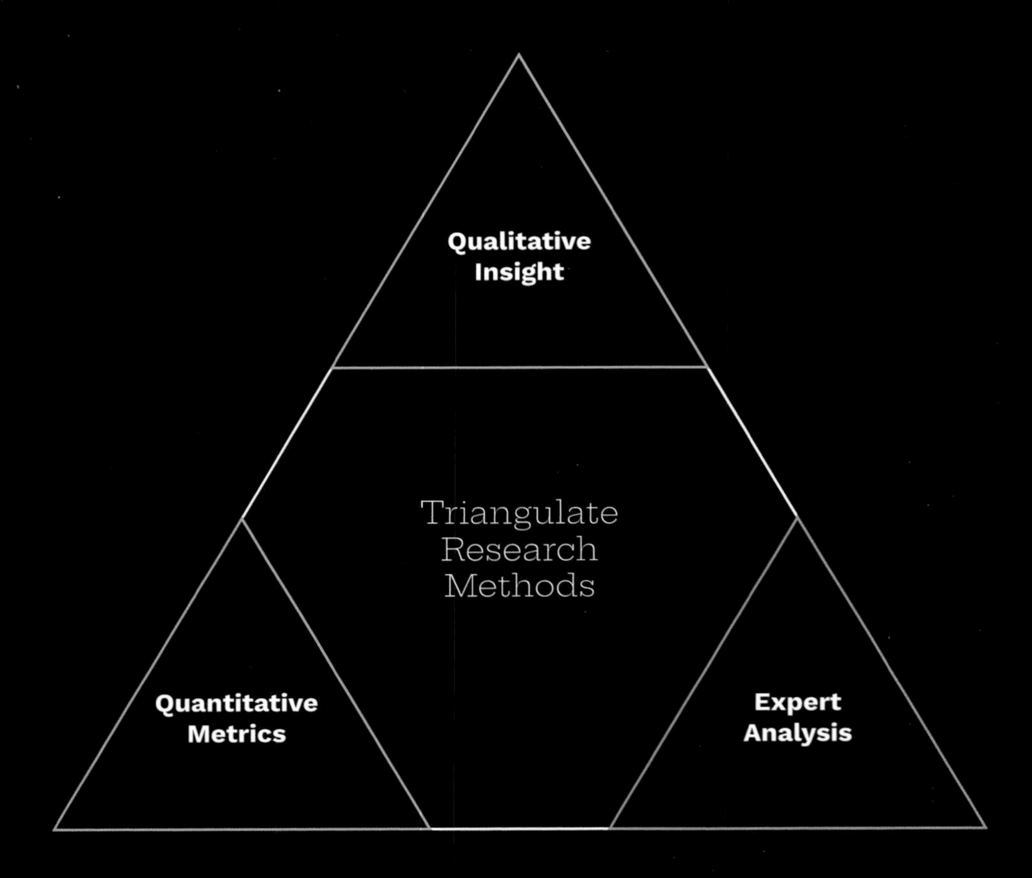

Evaluating the User Journey

Empathising with user groups is key to designing great experiences. A user journey map is a visualisation of the process a user goes through to accomplish a goal. It identifies tangible and emotional stages along the process, as well as gaps and inefficiencies. It visually represents how and why users make decisions. A journey map identifies user needs, pain points, and journey barriers, as well as 'loops' or other nuances.

Creating a journey map is a collaborative activity that aligns stakeholders around a problem to be solved. Creating the user journey map is essential to engage users of the product or service and proxy internal stakeholders. Engage stakeholders from across the organisation, and identify those likely to know where the opportunities to develop and improve are.

Identifying the right altitude for the journey map will depend on the problem to solve. Getting the altitude right is important. Too focused and you will miss opportunities or fail to understand context, whilst a high-level view may prevent you from identifying the gaps and inefficiencies that require digital intervention and solution design.

Figure 6-2: User Journey Map

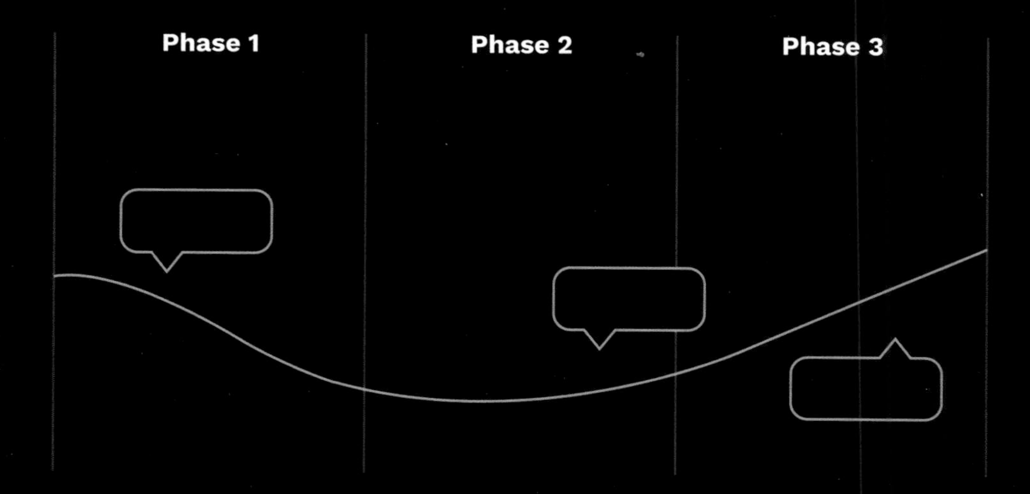

Changing Human Behaviours

Designing an experience that motivates positive action determines whether a solution is successful or not, and requires an understanding of human behaviours. Principles from behavioural economics - 'the study of psychology into the analysis of the decision making' are often used in Human-centred design to encourage or deter behaviours. A typical example is the habit-forming social network notification icon which frequently persuades you to return.

This field of thinking underlines that human decision making is often emotional and not rational (even when we fail to see it ourselves). Recent digital technology has attracted attention to this knowledge through 'dark patterns', stimulating counter-movements like 'circular' and 'ethical' design.

Shaping a Human-Centred Organisation

Once seen as a nice-to-have, Human-centred design has now proven its commercial value – Wharton University concluded that the return on investment of good user experience ranges from $2 to $100 for every $1 invested. This can be a powerful persuader for sceptical or resistant stakeholders.

Organisations that become more human-centred advance through four stages of maturity:

1. **No design** - Design plays little to no role in the organisation; the user perspective is barely considered, and if it is, it relates to isolated initiatives
2. **Design as styling** - Design is only relevant in terms of form or aesthetic considerations. External suppliers usually drive any specific user experience considerations

3. **Design as process** - Design is a process in the development of products and services; the organisation implements specific and holistic processes to improve user experience

4. **Design as strategy** - Design drives innovation and the continual improvement process. The organisation views and acts on user insight strategically. Design is an integral component throughout the value chain.

Figure 6-3: Adapted from the Danish Design Ladder

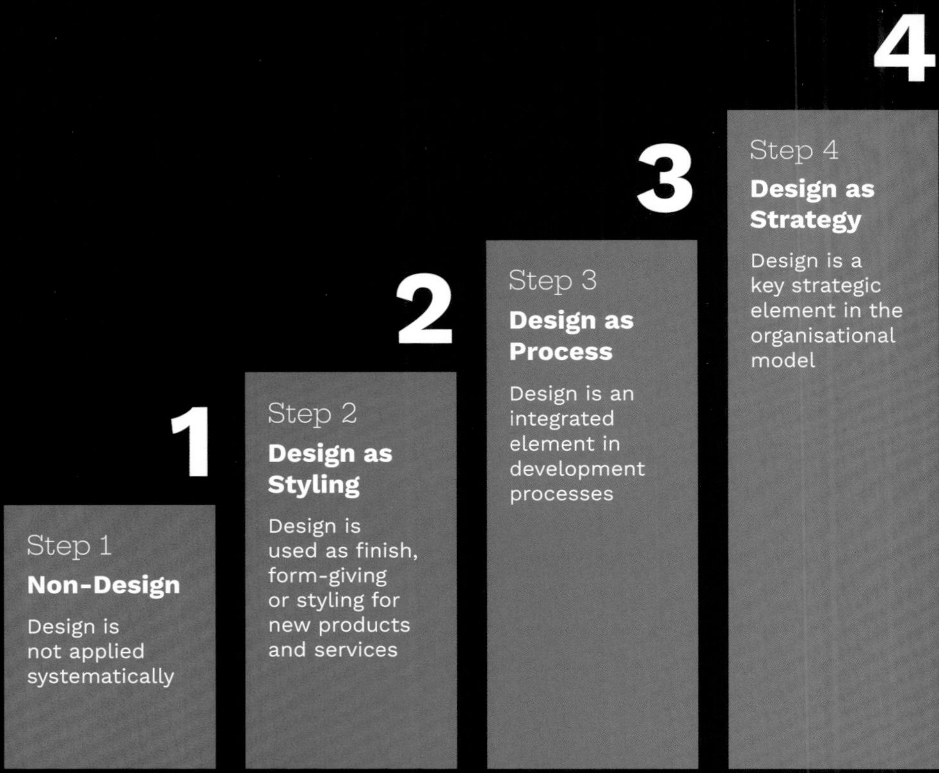

1

Step 1

Non-Design

Design is not applied systematically

2

Step 2

Design as Styling

Design is used as finish, form-giving or styling for new products and services

3

Step 3

Design as Process

Design is an integrated element in development processes

4

Step 4

Design as Strategy

Design is a key strategic element in the organisational model

The drive to create better experiences for all users - this includes colleagues as well as consumers - should be a continuous goal for everyone within an organisation. A human-centred mindset should not be relegated to marketing or digital departments, or considered to be visual improvements alone. The greatest benefit is realised when a human-centred mindset is adopted throughout an organisation.

BJSS Opinion

Embrace a Human-Centred Design Approach

Human-centred design is often synonymous with an interface or interpreted as interaction, navigation, and interface design. This view places the ownership of a 'good user experience' solely with a User Experience Designer. Human-centred design is all-encompassing, including the above and ranging through (but not limited to) organisational strategy, systems integration, process modelling, content design, accessibility, and performance. A complete understanding shows that no single person is responsible for the user experience – instead, it's a collaborative team effort across all departments and partnerships. This includes involving those who support the product in delivering change – a key reason we advocate adopting a DevOps culture and associated practices.

It is not sufficient to introduce Human-centred design towards the end of a project, or expect visual enhancements to improve function. A more organisationally-mature approach introduces exploratory and strategic user research to validate, quantify, and set the direction of an initial idea or purpose from the outset. This establishes a clear vision - enabling the Product Owner and the Agile Team to make decisions confidently and deliver a solution based on user insight.

Figure 6-4: Adapted from the Research Funnel, Emma Boulton

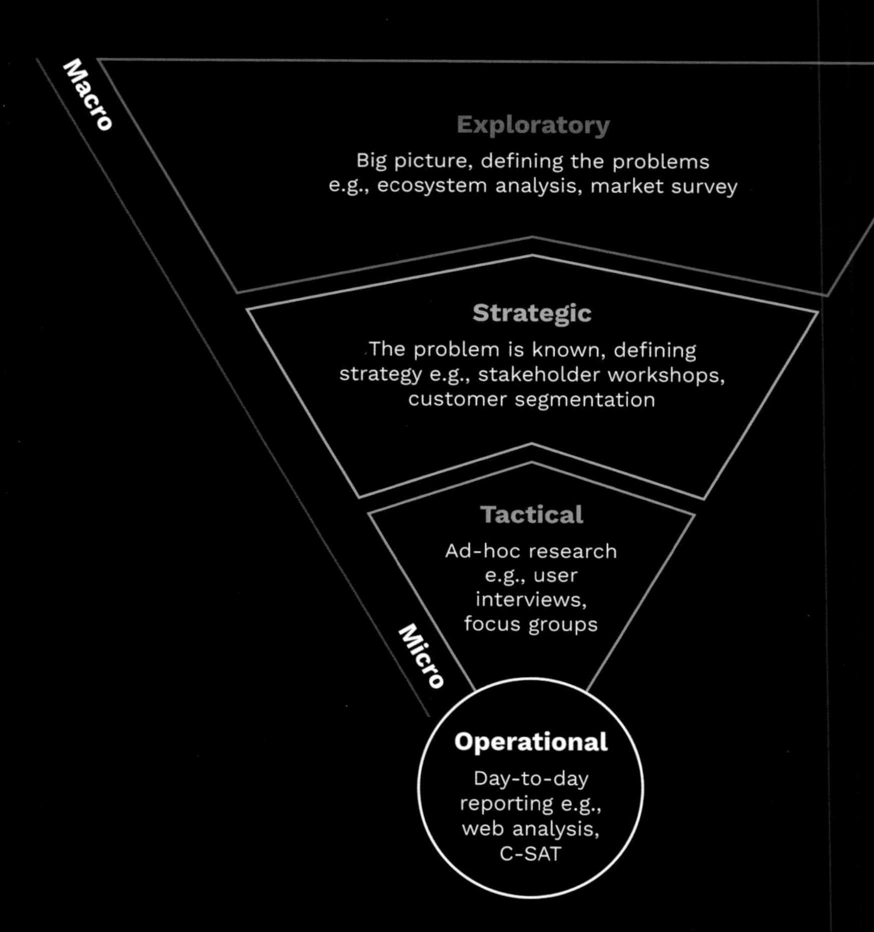

Agile Teams should continue to involve users using tactical user research to test and iterate products and services during Sprints. The most effective processes build regular user testing into Sprint planning - optimising the solution through development and into live environments. Frequent testing and optimisation can encourage stakeholders to embrace a release early and often approach generating value more quickly.

Generate Value Through Service Design

Service design is the design of services from the perspective of its users (both the consumers of the service and the deliverers of the service). Service design can help develop an entirely new service or improve an existing service.

A service helps people do something - like being treated for cancer, buying a house, or doing your annual tax return. Service design looks at the whole start-to-end process, including waits, channel changes, escalations, and anything that can go wrong in delivering the service. It also designs from front to back - from what users need to do, through the supporting technology and processes, down to the underlying infrastructure, integrations, and legal constraints required to make it all work.

Successful services will create value for both the user and the organisation. This is often achieved by identifying the opportunities at the intersection of human desirability, technical feasibility, and commercial viability.

Figure 6-5: Human-Centred Design

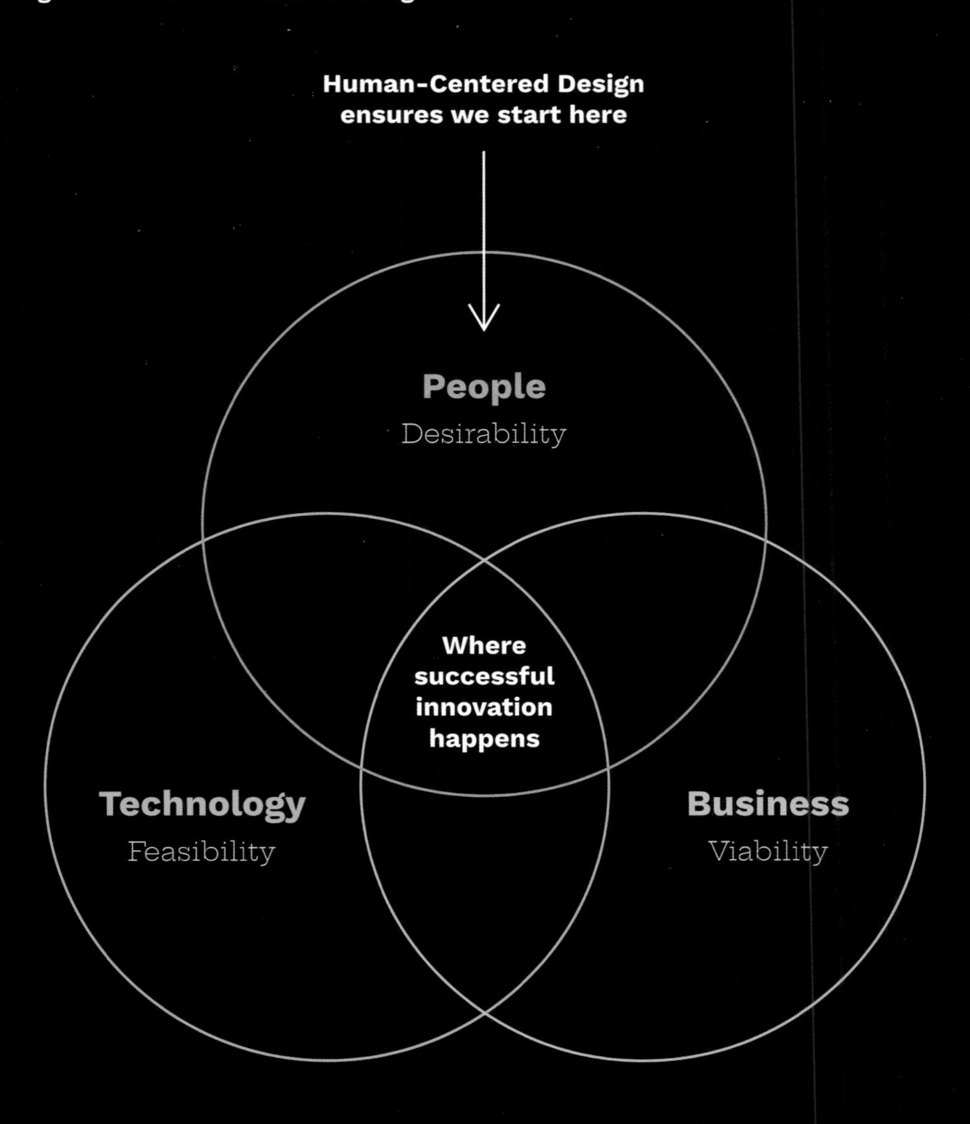

When an organisation embraces service design, multidisciplinary teams are created, bringing together Designers and other professionals, such as marketing, sales, technical systems, product, and legal specialists.

The multidisciplinary team collaborates to analyse, empathise, ideate, and design each interaction between customers and the organisation.

We recommend including service design as a critical component of any project involving users, and adhering to the following principles:

- **Human-centred** – The experience of all the people affected by the service is considered
- **Collaborative** – Stakeholders from various backgrounds and functions and representative users are actively engaged
- **Sequential** – The service is visualised and orchestrated as a sequence of interrelated actions
- **Iterative** – An exploratory, adaptive, and experimental approach is taken, iterating toward implementation
- **Real** – Needs are researched with users; ideas are prototyped and tested with users
- **Holistic** – Services are designed to sustainably address the needs of all stakeholders throughout the experience and across the business.

In most cases, users want a quick and easy-to-use product or service that is right first time. Organisations are likely to achieve this by taking a holistic view to identify and improve gaps and inefficiencies in the product or service. A service design blueprint is a key tool used to help organisations achieve this goal.

Introduce a Service Design Blueprint

A service blueprint is a visual operational tool that presents the components of a service in enough detail for stakeholders to analyse, implement, and improve it.

Creating the blueprint is a valuable collaborative task that brings together multidisciplinary stakeholders to share insight. The multidisciplinary team produces the blueprint together. A service design blueprint includes user actions, internal team actions, touchpoints, processes, workarounds, and technology interactions. The line of interaction through the middle divides the front stage (what consumers see) and the backstage (what's happening behind the scenes). A service blueprint may also recognise other relevant in-progress programmes or opportunities that have already been identified.

Figure 6-6: Service Design Blueprint

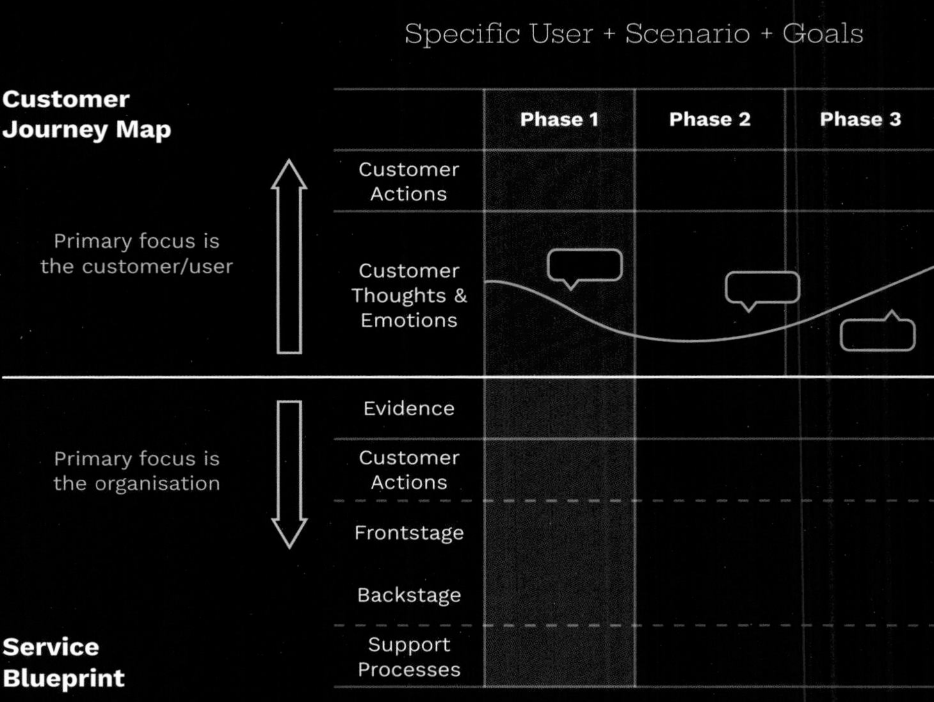

An ‘as is’ blueprint is usually created first to understand the existing state of a service. This will identify the gaps and inefficiencies that should be improved to create more value. It will also identify areas that are performing well that can be celebrated and benchmarked. Creating a ‘future-state’ blueprint can then follow.

A service blueprint focuses stakeholders on the real problems to solve. The blueprint will prompt and enable prioritisation activities with key stakeholders, informing a shared roadmap to realise the change required.

Set Strategy with Evidence-Based Design

Evidence-based design is the deliberate intention to base strategic and tactical decisions on the best available research evidence to improve outcomes for users. Within a rapidly changing environment, user expectations and behaviours are evolving at pace, making evidence-based design important for organisations to stay relevant and reduce the cost and risk of change.

There can be a view within organisations that there is not enough time or budget to gather evidence within the timeframes available. Yet, there are many ways to achieve evidence-based design with minimal budget and time. Guerrilla research, in particular, is a quick, low-cost way of understanding user behaviours and experiences. It is usually done in public spaces and does not require a rigorous recruitment process. Evidence can also be achieved quickly by running user tests with just five users. This provides valuable insight to inform the focused iteration of a product or service. Further tests can then be helpful in subsequent Agile Sprints.

It is essential through assurance and governance that insight gained through research is shared with stakeholders to inform commercial and technical strategy. Everyone within an organisation should be encouraged to understand the real needs and expectations of both external and internal users. This will lead to a greater level of human-centred organisational maturity.

Structuring the evidence clearly, for example, using visual tools such as blueprints, journey maps, personas, and roadmaps, will support teams across the organisation to collaborate towards a strategic vision by:

- **Delivering a framework by which human, technical, and commercial change can be aligned and implemented effectively**
- **Enabling the organisation to prioritise based on the features that deliver the most value**
- **Allowing inter-dependencies between features to be identified, informing allocation of work to Delivery Teams**
- **Providing a basis for estimating the size and scope of changes and capacity planning in the Delivery Teams**
- **Allowing a link back to technical and functional architecture to inform the risk associated with the change**
- **Providing traceability and a mechanism to track the progress of the change through delivery within the context of the problem domain**
- **Adding rigour to the analysis process making it more effective**
- **Providing assurance that the right questions have been asked and the appropriate sources consulted**
- **Documenting in a lightweight manner the decisions that have been taken and the route to arriving at a particular functional solution.**

Time and budget allocated to evidence the real user need will inform an authentic focus on building the right thing, which will increase value for users and the organisation, and the likelihood of innovation.

Remove Barriers to Human-Centred Design

Human-centred design performs best when it is a shared mindset across an entire organisation. This will often require a culture shift.

Embedding enterprise-wide Human-centred design concepts can be challenging, and the process takes time. Traditionally, commercial and business interests have taken a higher priority. This approach can lead to costly mistakes that can be avoided by aligning human, commercial, and technical requirements concurrently. Significant benefits and innovation will be realised when these once siloed groups collaborate to identify opportunities to create value.

While organisational culture is developing, there can be a conflict between user needs and the technical feasibility and commercial viability of addressing those needs. Taking the opportunity to reframe any potential conflict into a positive drive for collaboration and transparency around strategy and prioritisation is a step in the right direction.

Focusing on outcomes is a great way to elevate the language and conversation towards the value provided by Human-centred design - 'who' and 'why', and the velocity provided by Agile delivery - the 'what' and 'how'.

Developing enterprise-wide Human-centred design maturity requires focus on these integrated factors:

- **Strategy** - Strong leadership and commitment at executive level, a healthy budget, roadmap planning, and resource prioritisation
- **Culture** - Active organisational-wide communication and engagement about the benefits, building wide working knowledge, cultivating UX careers and practitioners' growth
- **Process** - Embedding the systematic use of UX research and design methods into all areas of product development and service design

- **Outcomes** - Intentionally defining and measuring the results produced by user-centred design initiatives. Sharing insights and successes widely across an organisation.

Many organisations promote themselves as 'user first' without having a direct dialogue with users. It is essential to educate leaders and decision-makers about the financial and cultural benefits that authentic evidence-based Human-centred design brings.

Human-Centred Design Evolution

Human-centred design continues to be an essential ingredient of organisational strategy. With continuing advances in technology and human behaviour, leaders and decision-makers have never been more important to building a deep empathy for the people they want to engage. It also helps organisations to become more innovative, flexible, and faster in delivery.

The basic expectation an organisation must meet is a functional, usable, reliable solution. Organisations that gain a deeper understanding of users can then develop differentiators around emotion to attract and retain engagement. Human-centred design can elevate an offering above the competition.

Evolving examples of elements that require a Human-centred design mindset and approach are AI, Voice and Virtual/Augmented Reality, all of which are in their infancy and have huge potential to continue to disrupt how organisations and society operates. Users will drive best practices in conversational design, context-driven content, audio cues, and virtual gesturing.

To remain relevant, leaders and decision-makers must tap into the mindset of users to find the key to innovation. We encourage organisations to create an ongoing dialogue with internal and external users, and experiment with technology to secure their relevance in the future.

An important area of development in Human-centred design is sustainability. It has long been recognised that design plays a crucial role in ethics. It is now recognised that design also plays a key role in supporting the world to harness a commitment to sustainability, helping organisations to create behavioural change to improve the wellbeing of all people and the environment.

The principles of Human-centred design correlate strongly with the behavioural economics concept discussed earlier.

The Enterprise Agile Approach

To compete in a constantly evolving environment, organisations need to operate with focus, flexibility, and speed to bring high quality, differentiated products and services to market. The risk of a laser focus on velocity is that the overarching need to 'get something delivered' can lead to experiences that don't meet real customer needs and fail to deliver value. By integrating Human-centred design and Agile methods within multidisciplinary teams, it is possible to release efficiently with the confidence that the user will have a seamless experience with the new or evolved product or service.

'Design is not just what it looks and feels like. Design is how it works.'

Steve Jobs, Entrepreneur and Inventor, 1955-2011

The Who & Why of Delivery

Enterprise Agile focuses on the 'what' and the 'how' of delivery, and aims to increase delivery velocity by breaking up the planning and scope into smaller units. Human-centred design looks at the 'who' and the 'why' of a problem. New ideas are generated through a series of user-focused exercises that culminate in identifying a solution. Human-centred design aims to create value for the user and the organisation by focusing on users' needs and asking questions about the specific problem to solve.

Enterprise Agile and Human-centred design are complementary mindsets and methods that ensure user stories have strong acceptance criteria. The 'so that' (the 'why') part of the story is as well understood by Agile Teams as the 'how'.

Successful Agile Teams will include Human-centred design disciplines. Human-centred Designers (including user experience, user interface, content design) will challenge the team to identify what they know rather than what they think they know. Questions might include:

- **Did you begin Discovery by interacting with your users and understanding their problem?**
- **If yes, how many users did you interview? Is this number enough, or should you speak with more users?**
- **Is your problem well defined into an actionable problem statement?**
- **Is it possible to further break down your problem into sub-problems?**
- **When was the last time you revisited your problem statement?**

This attention to detail can mean backlog refinement takes longer, but the benefits include better stories, greater user understanding, and more value delivered faster. Human-centred design can be challenging to integrate seamlessly into established delivery cultures, but the benefits shouldn't be underestimated. Human-centred design will influence epics, features, and stories. It will inform prioritisation and feedback at a strategic and tactical level.

The Right Problem to Solve

Human-centred design is a mindset and method relevant during all phases of the Agile delivery cycle, including Planning, Discovery, and Development. It promotes a continual focus on:

- **Understanding the problem from the users' point of view**
- **Designing the right solution, with significant influence from technical feasibility**
- **Ensuring the solution is commercially viable and sustainable.**

Traditionally, there has been a focus on implementing a solution that meets technical or organisational requirements instead of the user need. This can result in products and services with unusable or ignored features that frustrate users.

Human-centred design uses divergent and convergent techniques to understand a problem from the users' perspective, design a solution, and deliver that solution to the market. The double diamond model has been used to guide this process since the British Design Council popularised it in 2005. There are now many models that support teams with the Human-centred design method and mindset.

Figure 6-7: Double Diamond, adapted from the Design Council

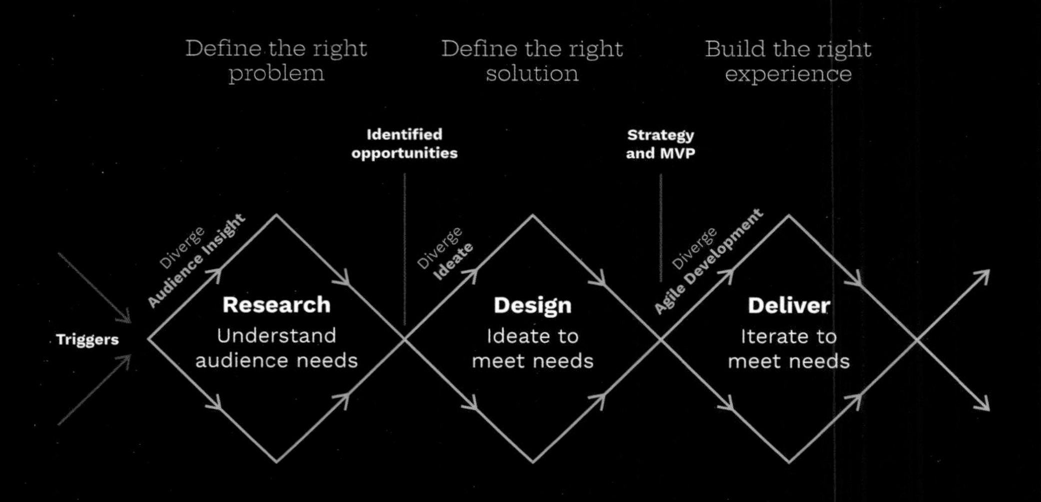

An iteration of the Design Council's double diamond model in 2021 recognises that the process is circular and that regular connection and communication outside the Agile Team are essential to maintaining success. It also recognises the importance of sustainability.

The first diamond focuses on exploring and framing the problem space, identifying the right problem to solve through divergent and convergent thinking. The second diamond is focused on creating and delivering the right solution in the right way. While real user problems are being identified and solutions developed during the process, the steps may jump forwards and backwards. Reverting is often a result of further user insight uncovered, making refinement or skipping forward necessary due to relevant insight being already available and interpreted.

Human-Centred Design Artefacts

Artefacts should be transparent, accessible by all teams and evolve as new insight is identified. The Agile Manifesto states a preference for working software over comprehensive documentation. The Human-centred design mindset leans towards a preference for visual documentation. Four Agile principles aid in producing only artefacts that record or disseminate information:

1. **Document what the user needs**
2. **Produce the artefacts that support teams during the delivery of the change**
3. **Document what work was done to support the change**
4. **Create perpetual 'working' versions that evolve with change.**

Human-centred design and Agile are collaborative methods. The Agile Team and stakeholders will use the visual artefacts and tools produced during research and collaborative workshops to set the vision, identify problems, and prioritise and test solutions. There are many artefacts and tools that can be produced. Here are a few of our favourites:

Personas/Archetypes

Personas and archetypes are research-based fictional characters representing user groups and act as visual tools for easier comprehension. High-priority persona types and corresponding user needs, often written as 'stories', will inform design and can be used to support strategic and tactical prioritisation.

Journey Mapping and Service Blueprinting (Current State)

'As is' or current state user journey maps and service blueprints visualise the users' physical and emotional interaction with an organisation across touchpoints. Identifying the current state enables the clear identification of gaps and inefficiencies in the current offering. Further information on journey mapping and service blueprinting is provided above.

Wireframe

A wireframe is a static, low-fidelity visual representation of different layouts that form a product. Wireframes are used to communicate structure, content, and functionality, helping Delivery Design Teams create a shared understanding of a future vision. Wireframes are often used as a precursor to prototypes.

Prototype

There are many kinds of prototypes to suit all timeframes and budgets. There are low-fidelity paper prototypes which are typically hand-drawn sketches of the intended solution.

Mid-fidelity prototypes are visually complete representations of solutions but usually not functional. High-fidelity prototypes are visually complete and interactive models which users can explore.

Integrating Human-Centred Design

Both Human-centred design and Agile are fluid methods providing guidance rather than instruction. It is important to remember that 'one size does not fit all' in terms of organisational transformation, user need, or products and services to deliver. With this in mind, it is helpful to take a Lean approach, and use the best elements of both methods to deliver the right solution properly within the specific landscape. In general, we recommend that organisations or departments integrate Human-centred design within Enterprise Agile. This can be achieved by following this process:

- **Engagement** - Start small, integrating one or two teams. Focus on the quick wins, the high-value, low-risk opportunities to gain experience using Human-centred design and Agile together. As the capability matures, expand to more challenging initiatives
- **Adoption** - Create more cross-functional/multidisciplinary teams to design and develop solutions. The teams should promote frequent collaboration across disciplines and frequent collaboration with users
- **Sustainability** - Collaboration and co-creation are essential to achieve successful and sustainable integration. Teams in supporting functions, such as legal and finance, will also need to adapt to new collaborative ways of working. If an established Technical Development Team integrates withHuman-centred design, provide training in the value of empathy, definition, and ideation to achieve the right balance of design and development. Embed the understanding that Human-centred design is relevant during all phases of the delivery cycle
- **Success** - Full integration will result in a clear understanding across all Agile Teams of the 'who' and the 'why' of what they are delivering as well as the 'what' and the 'how'.

Just like Agile, there is no endpoint with Human-centred design. The mindset to promote is to continually gather user insight to identify changing requirements and evolve products incrementally. Users and their insight are integral to the product and service development process, and critical to the successful convergence of Human-centred design and Agile methodologies.

Key Points

1. Human-centred design is a mindset and a method. When it is disconnected from product design and engineering, or applied retrospectively, its impact is severely compromised.

2. Human-centred design without the user is a surprisingly common mistake. If you genuinely want to understand the problem, there is no avoiding talking directly to users.

3. Well-structured visual information beats duplicated and daunting volumes of data. Human-centred design artefacts that are minimal, memorable, and shareable will significantly impact teams and stakeholders.

4. Too often, organisations fail to apply what they learn. Don't disregard user insight due to uninvestigated technical barriers, resource constraints, or personal opinion. The users should set the vision; without this approach, the final result will be compromised.

5. Design experiences that are grounded in psychology and with regular testing. Prototypes have the added benefit of helping stakeholders to imagine the end goal.

Chapter 07
Crafting the Product Increment

New increments of functionality are periodically released to users by the Product Team. This increment may consist of technological enhancements or new features. Irrespective of delivery method, the new features help evolve the product in ways that improve the experience for the user, address an unmet need, and add value for the customer and to the organisation.

Historically, releasing increments of change carried significant overhead. This typically builds up in an organisation over time. Change carries a perceived or actual risk, and processes are introduced to counter this. This 'release tax' means releases occur less frequently, become bigger and are inherently riskier. As a result, the problem is perpetuated. Continuous Delivery and DevOps techniques help organisations break free from this trap.

Concepts

The Product Increment

The unit of change is the Product Increment. This is the delta that gets released to users following implementation by the Product Team. A Product Increment may be small and consist of a single simple change or be much larger and contain many changes.

When making a change to a product, it is important to consider the full stack of elements required and to release this as a cohesive unit. Implementing the change should involve releasing the technology and supporting processes simultaneously.

Figure 7-1: Full Stack Product Increments

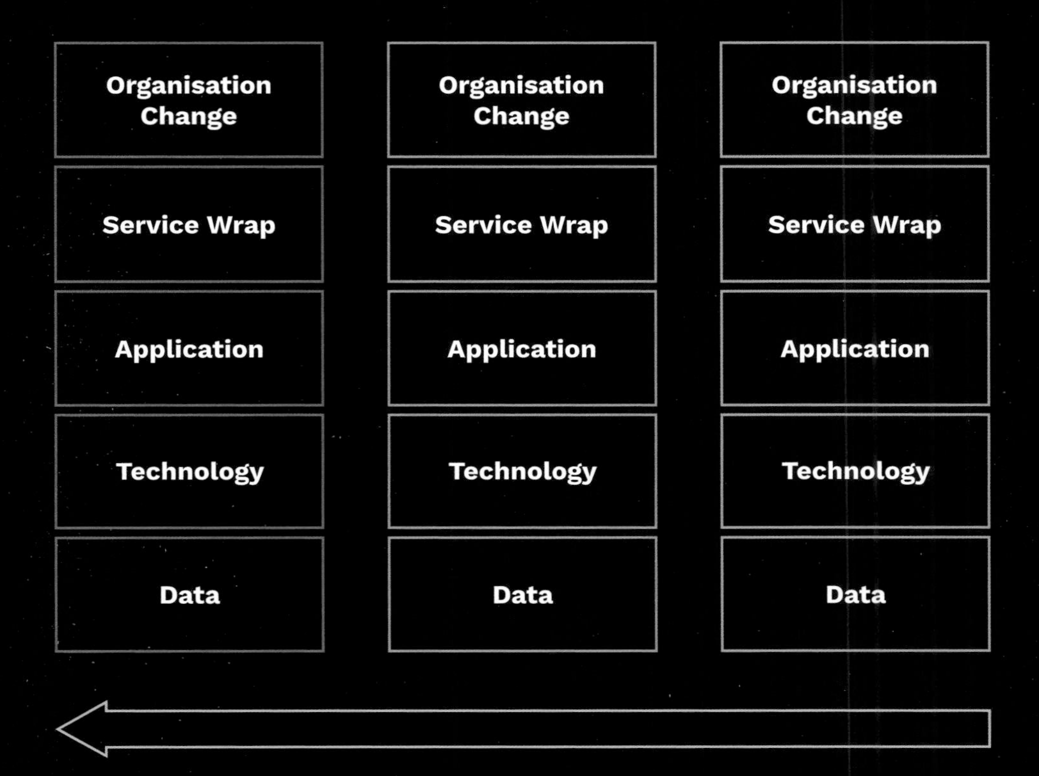

A cohesive Product Team will work to ensure that an increment of change to the product is inclusive of all components required to provide value for users and the organisation.

This full stack of change incorporates data, technology (application and infrastructure), Service Wrap, and organisation change. This can be a challenge when the Agile technology delivery meets the non-Agile world of people change, recruitment, training, etc. This is where the real breakthrough in organisational Agility can occur.

Success here is easier to obtain for digital products and systems of engagement than for systems of record. Well-structured analysis around user needs and a compelling user experience will minimise the need for areas such as user training. The layers of the full stack are explored further below.

Organisation Change Layer

Deals with the business impact created through updates to the technology components of the product and/or changes to manual, non-technology-driven product features such as fulfilment and logistics.

Where a new user feature is realised in both technology and organisational change, these activities should be aligned in the Product Increment.

Service Wrap Layer

Defines the supporting people, processes, and technology to 'run' the technology product in line with user expectations and agreed service levels.

Changes to the underlying technology infrastructure and application should result in corresponding and fully aligned changes to the supporting processes.

Application Layer

The software required to realise the features of the product that are delivered through technology. Changes here are taken from the prioritised backlog of features identified through structured analysis.

Infrastructure Layer

The underlying platform on which the application software resides. Rapid Agile change is easier to obtain here when using software-defined infrastructure in some form of Cloud solution.

The underlying configuration management database (CMDB) should evolve incrementally in sync with the application software.

Data Layer

Data is a frequently overlooked component of change. This must be considered. Changes to the data model, reference, data, test data, and production data must be factored into the change.

Failure to test a change with production data is a common cause of difficulties in getting a technology change to function properly.

Alternative Modes of Operation

There are two common ways of delivering a Product Increment. Firstly, each change can be considered in isolation and released as required. Secondly, several Features, perhaps related under a theme, can be delivered together using a Sprint pattern.

The mode used typically depends on the volume of change, size of the team, or, more significantly, the maturity of the product. Where Feature change is low in a mature product and changes are typically defect related, these are more likely to be fixed and released without a Sprint pattern.

During the development of a Minimum Marketable Feature set, or making significant or several feature changes, a Sprint pattern is more useful.

For the bulk of the work we do, we find a Sprint pattern and the associated events very useful and, in the case of any significant new product development, essential.

Table 7-1: Pattern Alternatives

Mode	Characteristic	Usage
Sprint Container	o Work for each Sprint is planned and estimated upfront o Activities around each Sprint to wrap up and feedback on team performance o Typically aligned to the Scrum framework	o Delivery of several Feature changes or an MVP
No Container	o Work taken as required into Delivery Teams o Low ceremony based around moving tasks through a small number of discrete phases o Typically aligned to the Kanban method	o Delivery of small, discrete feature changes or defects

BJSS Opinion

Always Use the Process

A key part of the power of Agile is the feedback loop - an ability to fail fast, learn, and make many minor course corrections rather than storing up and having to deal with a big problem. The Sprint events we describe in this chapter embody this thinking. The use of the Sprint enables the adoption of Lean thinking and a learning loop as illustrated in **Figure 7-2**.

To get the benefit of the activities required to plan, monitor, and control a Sprint, they must be undertaken systematically. All too often when we are engaged in project or programme recovery, we see that these basics have slipped in some way, such as:

- **Retrospectives are cancelled because the team is too busy**
- **Incorrect participation in planning sessions**
- **Show and Tell meetings moved out**
- **Sprints extended.**

Get into the rhythm of Sprint delivery and stick to it!

Figure 7-2: Lean Thinking Learning Loop

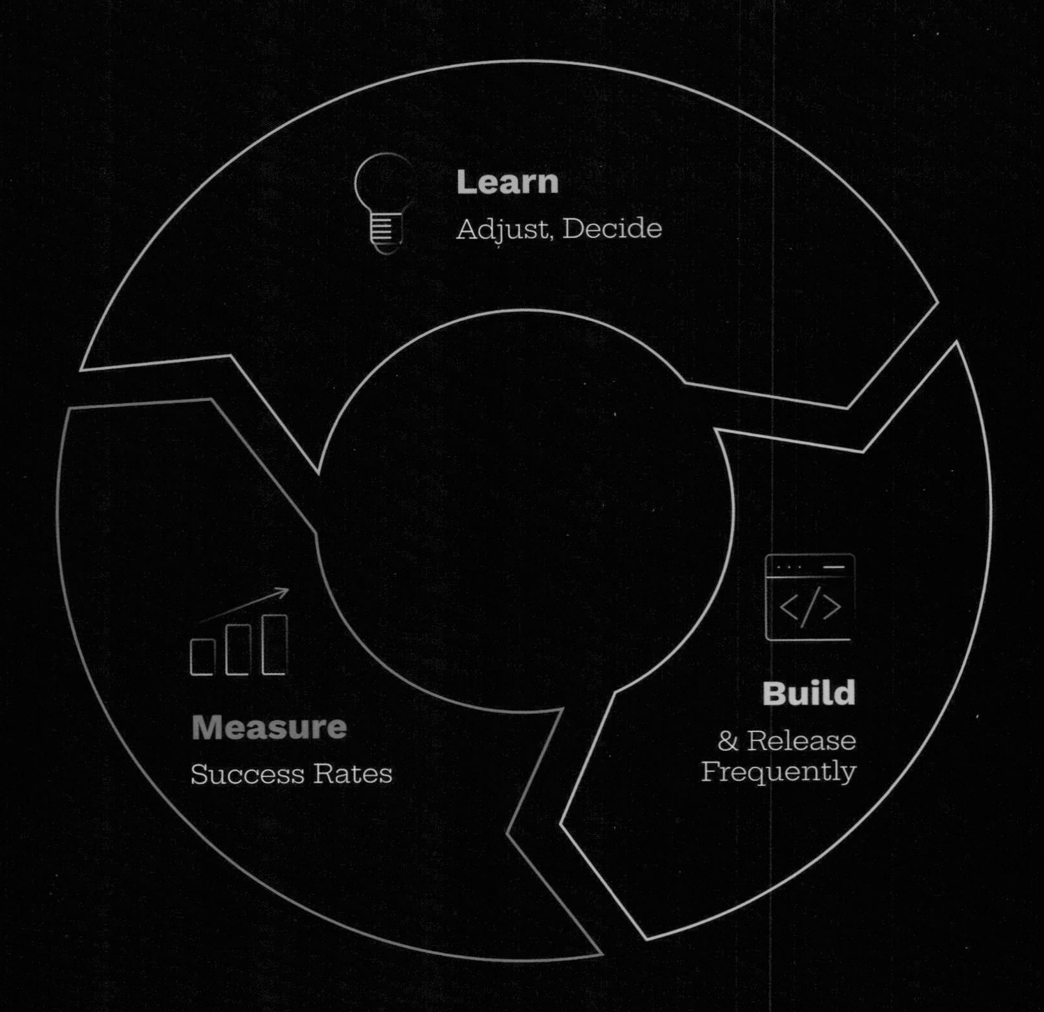

The Enterprise Agile Approach

Starting and Finishing a Story

We want to be confident that, in developing a Product Increment, it is complete on delivery and meets quality expectations. To achieve this and run a productive delivery pipeline relies upon understanding what 'good' looks like, both before and after implementing the change.

Commonly used techniques for achieving this include the use of a **Definition of Ready** and a **Definition of Done**. These terms should be defined and communicated in such a way that the whole team recognises them and can call out any deviations they observe.

Failure to be strong around the implementation of these criteria can easily result in the wrong change being delivered or delivered to a poor level of quality. Never, ever, no matter how tempting, fudge the Definition of Done. Change is not done until it is done! Significant issues will result from watering down the Definition of Done. Transparency over delivery progress will be lost and, in our experience, the team rarely catches up.

Using a Definition of Ready ensures that requirements, usually expressed as user stories, are completed to a high standard and provide a strong basis for estimating and tracking against. Teams often use the acronym **INVEST** to provide an effective and easy to remember Definition of Ready. This definition may be modified where required, provided that all the team sign up to it.

Table 7-2: INVEST acronym for Definition of Ready

Letter	Definition	Description
I	Independent	Isolated from other stories
N	Negotiable	Will be refined during delivery
V	Valuable	Adds value to the product and organisation
E	Estimable	Can be estimated
S	Small	Will fit into a Sprint
T	Testable	Has acceptance criteria

Similarly, a Definition of Done is produced in agreement with the team and clearly communicated. Implementing a good Definition of Done can be problematic. This should be an auditable checklist that is sufficiently exhaustive to safeguard delivery and quality without being too unwieldy.

'Done' is often an emotive point. Ultimately, a change is not done until it is in the hands of users. This is where some teams find it useful to have multiple layers of Definition of Done that map to the relevant endpoints for particular activities. It is essential to be clear on expectations around the Definition of Done with stakeholders. Nobody likes an unpleasant surprise and to be told something is finished when it isn't.

We find it useful to link the Definition of Done back to the V-model. To avoid complexity and ensure proper Agility, we believe that there can be no more than three levels of Definition of Done. This is mapped to a simplified V-model in **Figure 7-3**.

Figure 7-3: Layering of the 'Definition of Done'

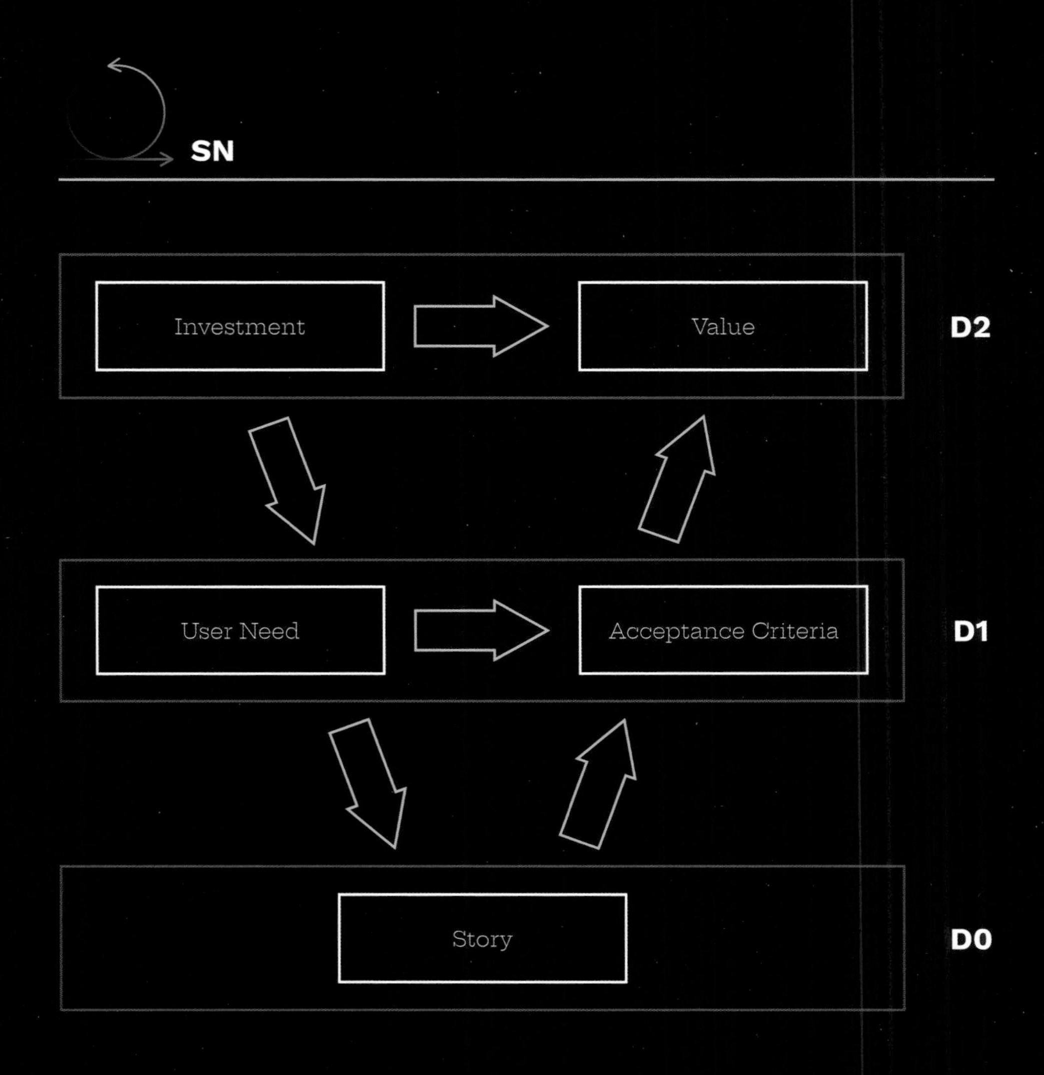

The Definition of Done at each layer corresponds to satisfactorily meeting the criteria a particular group has of the change.

D0 is likely to be more technical and include things the team wishes to achieve to ensure product quality and maintainability. An outline of the layered definitions is provided in **Table 7-3**.

Table 7-3: Layered 'Definition of Done'

Layer	Done	Typical Definition
D0	To the satisfaction of the Product Team	The team has completed the delivery of the story, tested it to satisfaction and updated associated documentation
D1	To the satisfaction of the specifying user	The story has been tested and accepted by the broader organisation, and is deemed to meet the acceptance criteria
D2	Released to the user community	The story has been released and is in use across the user community. Value can be generated for the organisation

Sprint Delivery Patterns

The use of Sprints sets the delivery cadence, with Sprint events taking place at the start, during, and at the end of a Sprint. We are often asked about the optimum Sprint length. The team needs time to deliver stories that are meaningful to the user, but Sprints cannot be too long otherwise the benefits of the process are lost. In our experience, anything longer than four weeks is too long, and anything less than a week is too short. Our default position is for two-week Sprints.

The objective of any Sprint is to complete the planned user stories consistent with the Definition of Done. For small-scale changes, this will often mean that the solution is ready to go into production.

Our experience has shown that, for larger initiatives and in larger organisations, it is often not practical to achieve this in the short term. As a result, for larger-scale change initiatives, there are likely to be further activities to be concluded to wrap up the release and get it into production. In these cases, it should be the ambition of the team to 'extend' their Definition of Done to include more of the activities that enable a Product Increment to be released.

As far as possible, the activities to make the stories delivered in a Sprint ready for live should be undertaken in the Sprint to avoid a Waterfall-style endgame. A release will only take place when there is a meaningful Product Increment that adds value, and this may take more than one Sprint to achieve. It can take many Sprints to get to the point of an initial Minimum Marketable Feature set release. In this situation, we recommend that the path to live is still automated and rehearsed to avoid back-loaded risk.

Figure 7-4: Sprint Delivery Pattern

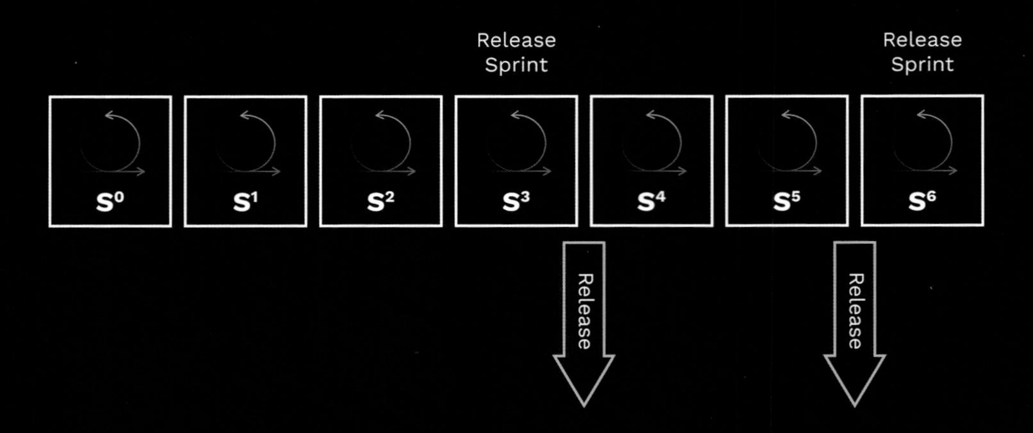

In the example in **Figure 7-4**, we have identified a theoretical Sprint delivery pattern in which a Product Increment is released every three Sprints. This pattern identifies the use of two special-purpose Sprints - Sprint 0 and the Release Sprint are used to achieve particular aims aside from Feature delivery. Where a release does not occur every Sprint, it may be necessary for a Release Sprint to be used to bring together non-Agile workstreams and activities, such as organisation change, and less Agile technology delivery of back-office systems in a multi-modal technology landscape.

Use of Special Sprints

Sprint 0

The first Sprint of technology delivery is a special purpose Sprint to prepare the ground for effective delivery in subsequent Sprints. In essence, Sprint 0 bootstraps and primes the delivery pipeline. On large-scale change initiatives, earlier phases of risk reduction, such as Discovery, may have already built the delivery pipeline to produce architectural PoCs. In this case, Sprint 0 will focus on making the delivery pipeline production quality and able to scale for use by the full team.

It is useful to build a set of technical stories with acceptance criteria to define the activities of Sprint 0, just as you would for any other feature Sprint. Whilst the specific technical tasks of a Sprint 0 will vary by product and technology stack, we have identified some key goals of a Sprint 0 below. In each case, as with any user story, it is worth identifying and recording the customer value that each technical story will bring, be it security, performance, quality, or anything else relevant to the product in question.

1. **Agile lifecycle tooling and workflow established**
2. **Code quality dashboard and static analysis tools installed and configured**
3. **Unit test framework established**
4. **Continuous Integration (software build) tooling installed and configured**
5. **Engineer code (desktop) environment established**
6. **Basic test platform available**
7. **Automated deployment script started**
8. **Team onboarding guidance developed (technical and product orientation)**

9. **Delivery metrics, collation and reporting established**
10. **Technical governance process in place.**

Release Sprints

A Release Sprint is a special vehicle for wrapping up change and getting it into the hands of users. The aim should always be to deliver production-ready software after each Sprint. There are some occasions where additional activities are required, such as final compliance steps like mobile app store verification, integration with non-Agile work streams, or alignment with certain organisational change activities.

In these situations, such work can be done in parallel to feature Sprints. Or, where the effort required may be considerable, the team can be given time away from feature delivery to focus on release activity. The use of Release Sprints cannot be mandated by any particular rules; it is a useful tool to consider when delivering complex products and change across the organisation.

The Practices of Effective Sprints

Day one and day ten of a Sprint will not necessarily be the same. There is a pattern to a Sprint that is required to ensure successful high-quality delivery of change. Specific activities are required to plan, execute, control, and wrap up a Sprint.

A small number of key activities make a Sprint successful. In our view, all are essential to ensure productive, high-quality delivery, manage expectations, and avoid surprises.

Figure 7-5: Anatomy of a Sprint

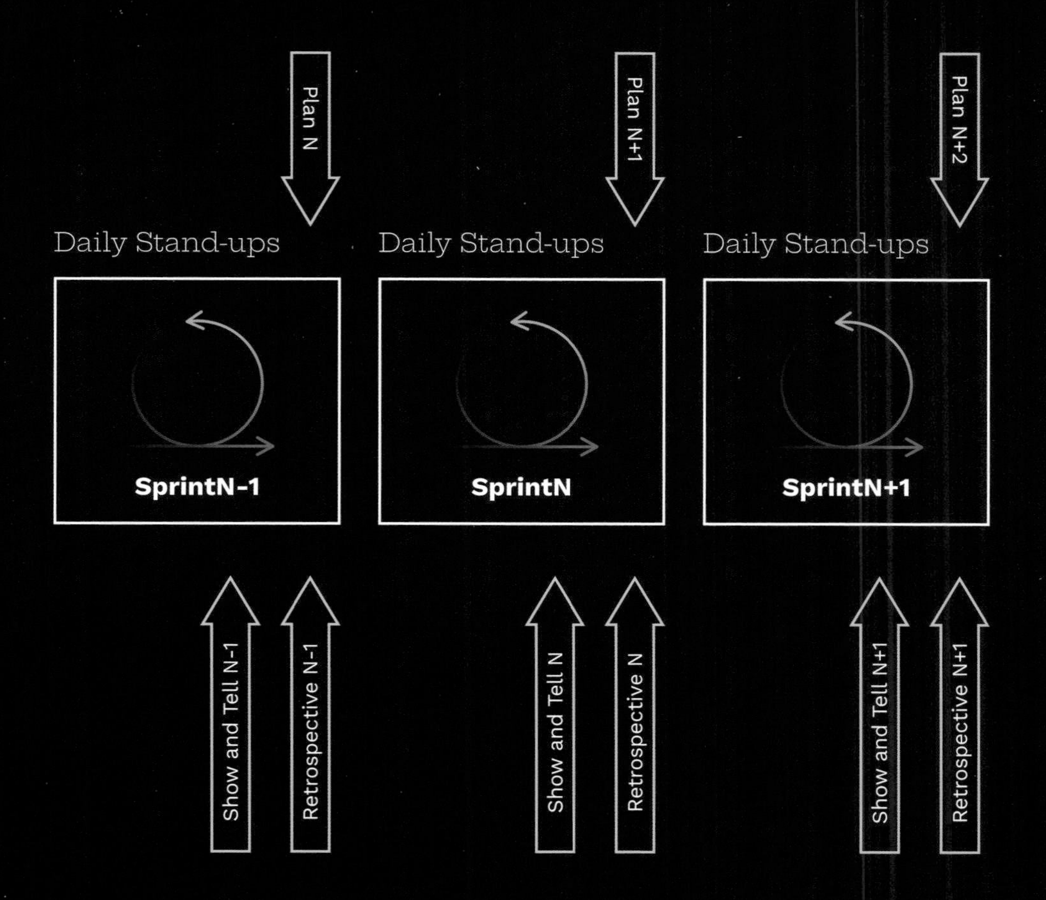

Planning

The purpose of the Sprint planning session is to agree on the work that will be delivered by the team in the upcoming Sprint. This is usually achieved by taking a set of stories that meet the Definition of Ready into the next Sprint. These meetings usually include the whole Delivery Team and the Product Owner. The team works through the prioritised product backlog and receives any clarifications on user needs from the Product Owner and Analysts.

A key part of the planning process is estimating the stories taken into the Sprint and decomposing them into the relevant tasks. In **Chapter 5**, we discussed the estimation process used during Discovery. At that stage, blind estimation techniques can be useful, however, at Sprint planning, we recommend consensus-based estimation. Teams may use a form of Agile planning poker to arrive at estimates. Using this method, the story is discussed, and each member of the team offers their estimate. Sometimes, this is done by showing a card from a set with the Fibonacci sequence numbers on them.

The advantage of this estimation technique is that it flushes out unknowns and information that not all team members might have. Not only does it support knowledge transfer across the team, but it is also likely to result in better estimates.

For this session to be effective, some work will have to be done in advance by Analysts with the team to ensure that the candidate stories are suitably elaborated to be developed and meet the Definition of Ready. In addition, Analysts and Team Leads will be working ahead by one or two Sprints to manage any dependencies with the leadership functions to ensure the story is independent of others.

Working ahead of the Sprint planning process may also throw up some design work and decisions. Where necessary, these should be taken to the design authority before Sprint planning. When filling a Sprint with stories, in some cases it may be prudent to include capacity for defects and support incidents.

The output of the Sprint planning meeting should include:

1. **The Goal of the Sprint** - The goal defines why the Sprint is valuable to customers or stakeholders with an interest in the product
2. **The Sprint Backlog** - The set of estimated prioritised stories for delivery in the Sprint, as well as a plan for delivering them as part of the next product increment
3. **Quantifiable Spare Capacity (when required)** - To handle defects and support incidents coming through that need to be addressed by the Sprint
4. **A Commitment to Deliver** - All parties involved offer their support for the delivery of the Sprint backlog; this includes external dependencies that may need to be secured by the Leadership Team.

Daily Stand-up

The daily Stand-up is the heartbeat of the Product Team. We believe it applies equally well to Delivery and Service Teams. Each team will run its own Stand-up. In a Product Team of multiple teams, each Team Lead will get together and run a Team Lead Stand-up.

The objectives of the daily Stand-up are to ensure that:

1. **Progress to the Sprint goal is reviewed and the Sprint backlog is adjusted as necessary**
2. **Any blockers are identified and quickly addressed or escalated**
3. **A plan for the next day of work is agreed upon by the team.**

To meet these simple objectives, the format is kept clear and focused. The team can use any structure or techniques they want to conduct the daily Stand-up so long as they emphasise the team's progress towards the Sprint goal. This encourages focus and supports self-management.

It is the job of the Team Lead to control the Stand-up and make sure that any debate is taken away and continued outside the meeting. Typically, the Stand-up will not take any longer than 10 minutes, and is usually best conducted first thing in the morning when the team arrive – after they have made a cup of coffee. They are called Stand-ups for a reason - these sessions should never be conducted seated in a meeting room!

Show and Tell

The Show and Tell is the end-of-Sprint ceremony for wrapping up the delivery with the key stakeholders. During Sprint planning at the start of the Sprint, all parties will have agreed to what stories are going to be delivered. The Show and Tell demonstrates those stories as either working software or other change artefacts.

We believe in establishing clear traceability, so the demonstration of work delivered is usually accompanied by a brief presentation or dashboard showing what was committed to during Sprint planning, and what has now been delivered along with a summary of any known issues. A simple example of this is illustrated in **Figure 7-6**.

Figure 7-6: Simple Traceability Report for Show and Tell

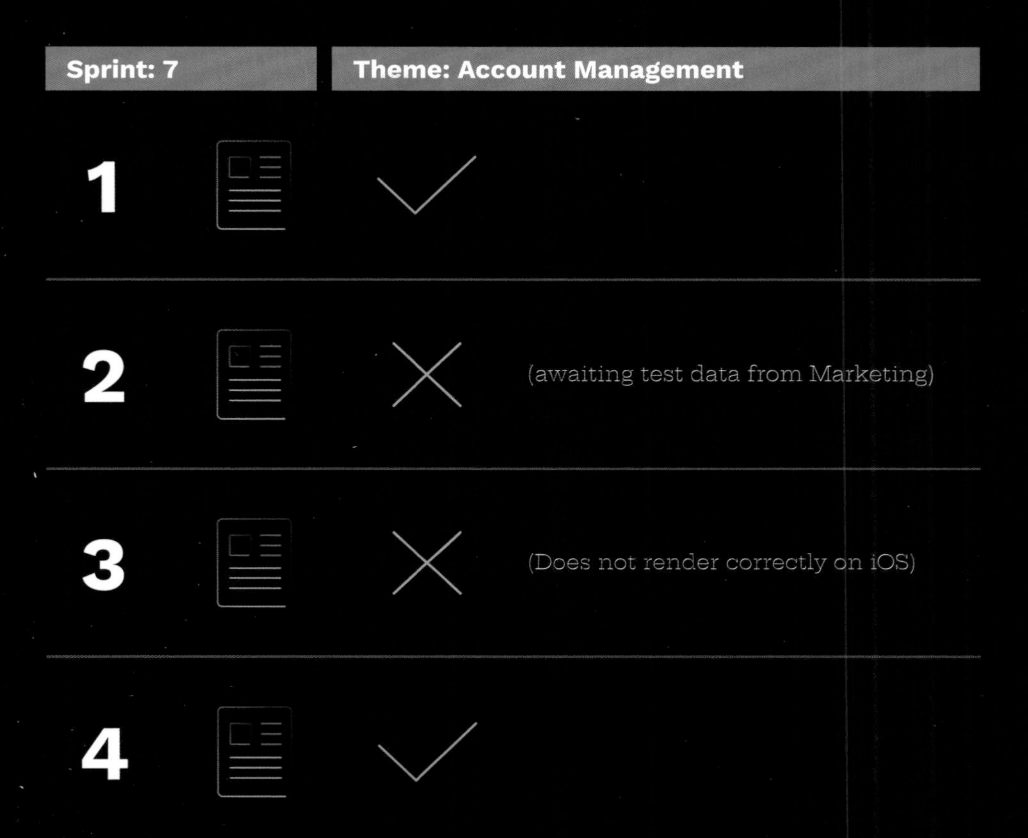

Show and Tell meetings are usually held at the end of the Sprint. The team should be ready to hold this session by the end of the Sprint.

This meeting is also an opportunity for the Product Owner to review the product backlog and adjust it in the light of changes in the environment or in response to new information. The Show and Tell is a working session and the team should avoid limiting it to a presentation.

Retrospective

The Retrospective meeting is another Agile feedback loop and is an essential part of the process. It is held within the Product Team and is used to mature the process and iron out wrinkles. The retrospective allows the team to identify what went well and what they would like to change. It also allows persistent issues and challenges to be escalated.

The format of the retrospective is straightforward:

1. **The team assembles and the Lead sets the context and reminds the team of the format**
2. **Everyone records their Good, Bad and Puzzling observations either on physical notes or in electronic format**
3. **The observations are grouped into related themes**
4. **The team agrees which theme is most likely to help them increase their effectiveness**
5. **The team agrees on at least one action that it will implement as soon as possible (ideally in the next Sprint) to improve its effectiveness. Frequently, these actions are added to the Sprint backlog for the forthcoming Sprint.**

There are many ways of categorising the feedback, however, we prefer to use three groups, as identified in **Figure 7-7**.

Figure 7-7: Retrospective Feedback Categories

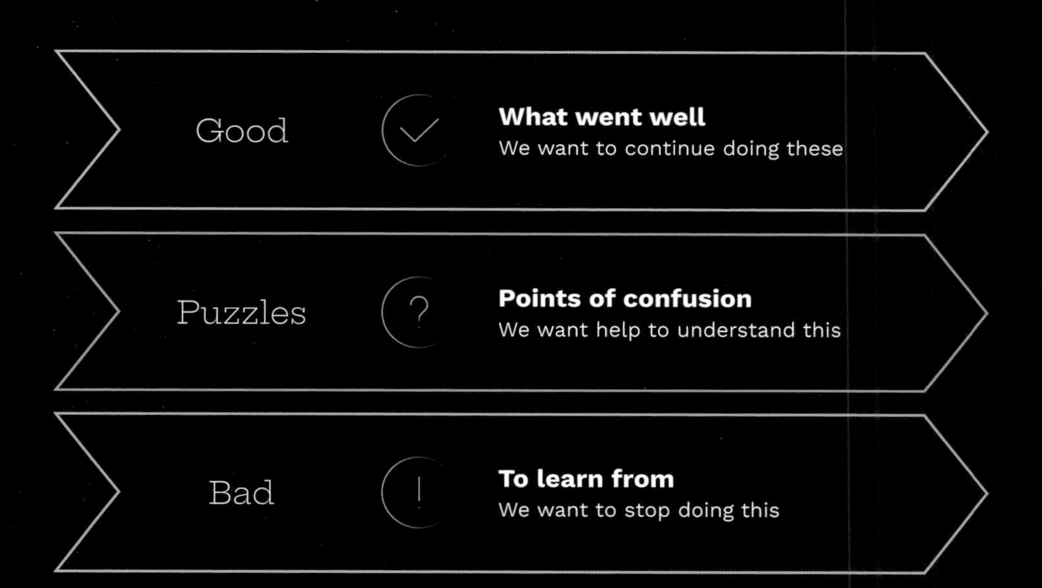

Updating the Service Wrap

As highlighted at the beginning of this chapter, the broader Product Team working together to deliver a complete Product Increment is essential to achieving organisation Agility. The change released is not just a technology update, but also a corresponding update to the supporting processes.

In **Chapter 9**, we explore how the delivery pipeline can now automate many of the traditional service functions. That said, it is still necessary to ensure that Support Teams are familiar with the new functionality and can effectively handle incidents raised by users. This work should be quite lightweight. We expect Support Teams to be working alongside Delivery Teams as part of the broader Product Team.

Service Teams will have full visibility of change flowing through the delivery pipeline and be included in broader team activities and Sprint ceremonies. The key here is not to treat service as distinct from change, but to include Service Teams in the wider Product Team.

Combining Organisation and Technology Change

The Sprint pattern is not just applicable to delivering technology change, it is also suitable for delivering the full Product Increment. Often, some non-technological change carries real-world constraints, particularly those around operational logistics and personnel that require legal and contractual input - alignment is required.

Figure 7-8: Concurrent Technical and Manual Process Delivery

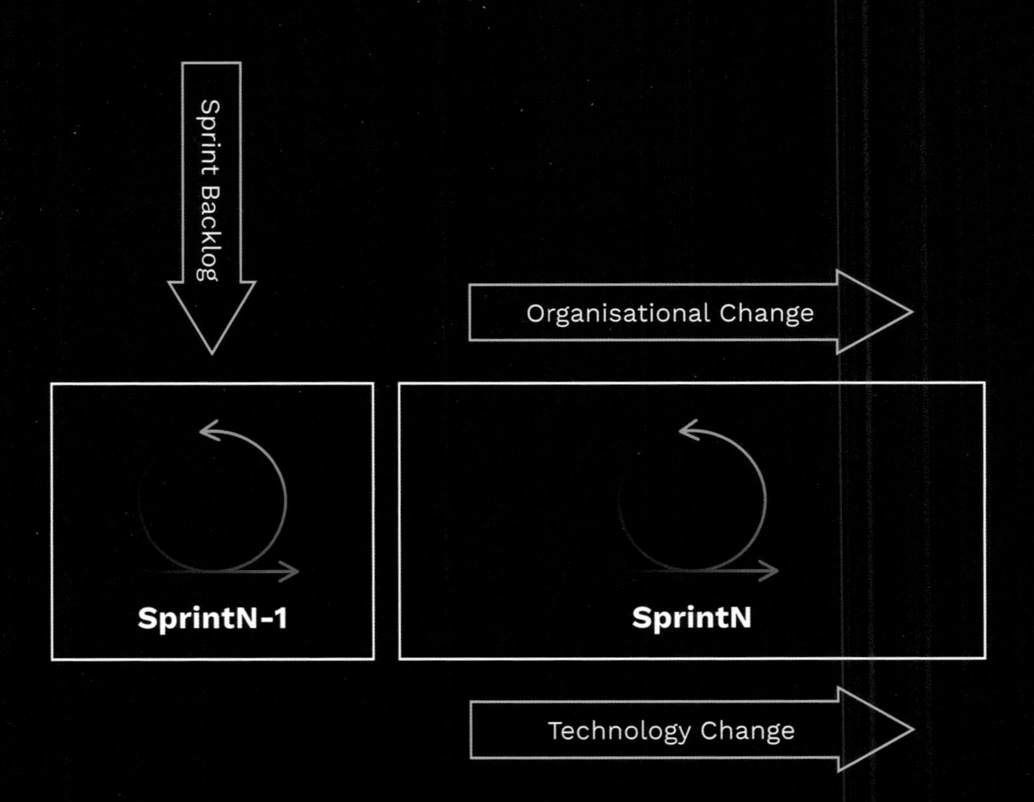

Aligning organisation and technical change starts with a clear strategy and objectives. This is essential and feeds the structured analysis work that provides the links between technology and manual processes. The User Journeys produced to describe the required changes will identify what is achieved using technology ('in-system') and what is delivered via manual processes ('out-of-system'). The Agile nature of the delivery means that scope will change, and decisions based on the value derived by the organisation will refine the in-system versus out-of-system boundary.

We recommend that the organisation change activities required to support new product features be delivered as part of the same Sprint pattern to minimise a potentially risky rollout of the change. The definition of manual processes and supporting artefacts should be produced at the same time as the related technological change and is often undertaken by a specialist team of Analysts.

Key Points

1. Make sure a deliverable Product Increment includes the changes to all aspects of the product stack - business change, Service Wrap, and technology (application, data, and infrastructure).

2. Only take stories into Sprint that meet the Definition of Ready and only earn value from stories that meet the Definition of Done.

3. Use a Sprint 0 at the start of the Delivery phase to initiate the delivery pipeline and get all the necessary tooling and automation in place.

4. Ensure every Sprint includes sessions for planning and estimating, daily Stand-ups, Show and Tells, and Retrospectives, and that these are never cancelled.

5. Align organisation change and manual process updates to the same Sprint delivery and release cadence.

Chapter 08

Engineering Quality Outcomes

Technology delivery is a fascinating discipline that combines engineering precision with a creative flair. We believe that the best quality outcomes in terms of technology delivery arise from a structured approach to engineering built around automated, repeatable processes that are flexible enough to evolve as business goals grow or change.

The field of software engineering is constantly evolving and recent innovations such as software-defined infrastructure have brought new opportunities and challenges for delivering Agile change. We have long advocated the need to remove back-loaded risk from technology delivery through continuous integration, automated test and deployment.

Concepts

Key Components of Engineering Delivery

The modern engineering landscape as popularised by the term DevOps comprises the three key components illustrated in **Figure 8-1.**

Figure 8-1: Engineering Components in DevOps

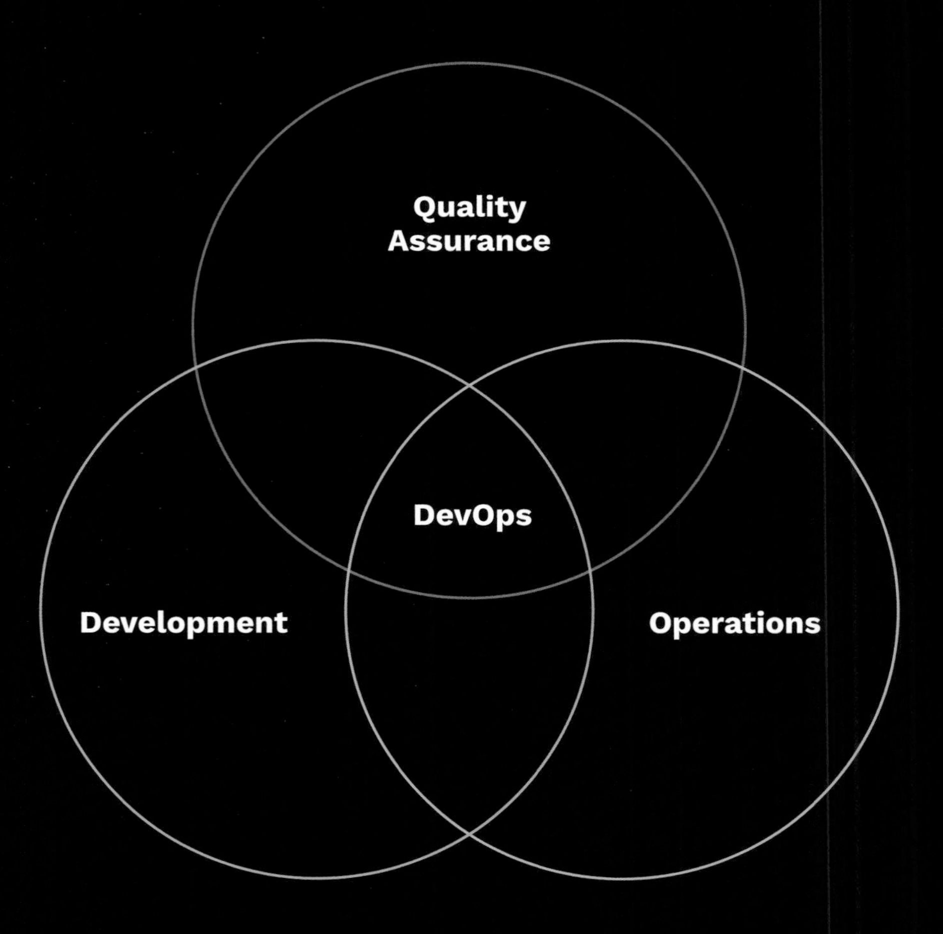

It is important to note that the key enabler to DevOps is good quality assurance through test automation (which itself needs a sound test architecture behind it to ensure appropriate coverage and relevance). Bringing together Development and Operations is considered too risky for many organisations but is essential to release change to users often and deliver the wider organisation benefits of greater Agility. Effective QA is the means of managing that risk and making DevOps a reality.

BJSS Opinion

Start With Strong Architecture

Good engineering starts with strong architecture. For a time during the early days of Agile delivery, the term 'emergent architecture' became fashionable. Coding without architecture isn't Agile delivery, it's hacking – nothing more than a code and fix approach. Whilst this might work for small-scale pieces of work, it is no way to conduct product development in a professional organisation.

Being more Agile doesn't mean allowing the engineering function to become a developer playground with no rules. The consequences of an emergent architecture are a total lack of predictability in delivery. Discovering that you must support 10,000 users after six months of development work, requiring a complete change of the technology stack, isn't the kind of problem most organisations can swallow.

In general terms, when developing a new product, the architecture for the MVP is defined upfront and tested against the core business goals using PoCs and prototypes during Discovery. This provides a level of predictability and reduced delivery risk during the implementation of the initial product version. Solution architecture is largely impacted by the non-functional requirements of the product, so early emphasis on getting these agreed is important.

Figure 8-2: Architecture Definition

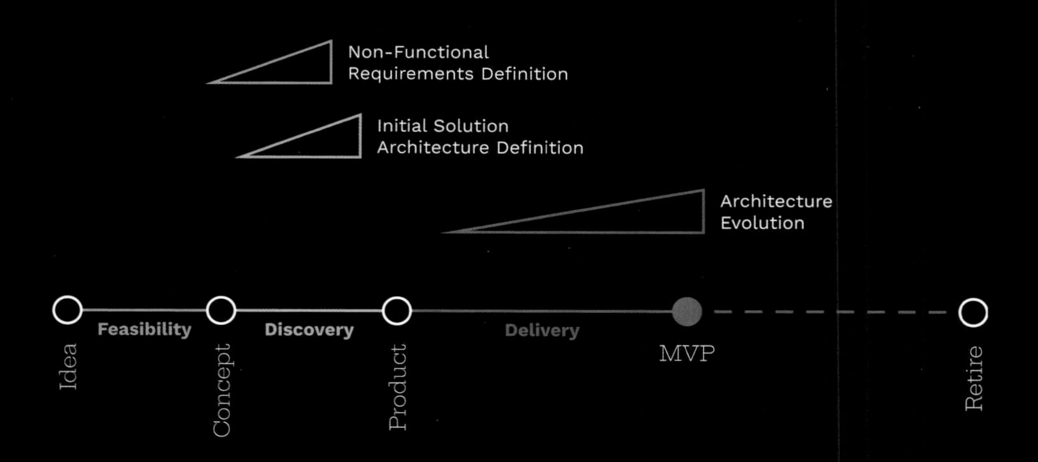

It would be naïve to assume that architecture is defined 100% upfront without subsequent modification. The architecture of the product will continue to change as the product changes, particularly post-launch.

Updates to the product architecture occur through controlled evolution and not emergence. Significant architectural changes can cause widespread disruption to the delivery pipeline if not managed correctly. In extreme cases, we have seen this completely halt delivery of functional change.

Figure 8-3: Introducing Architectural Change

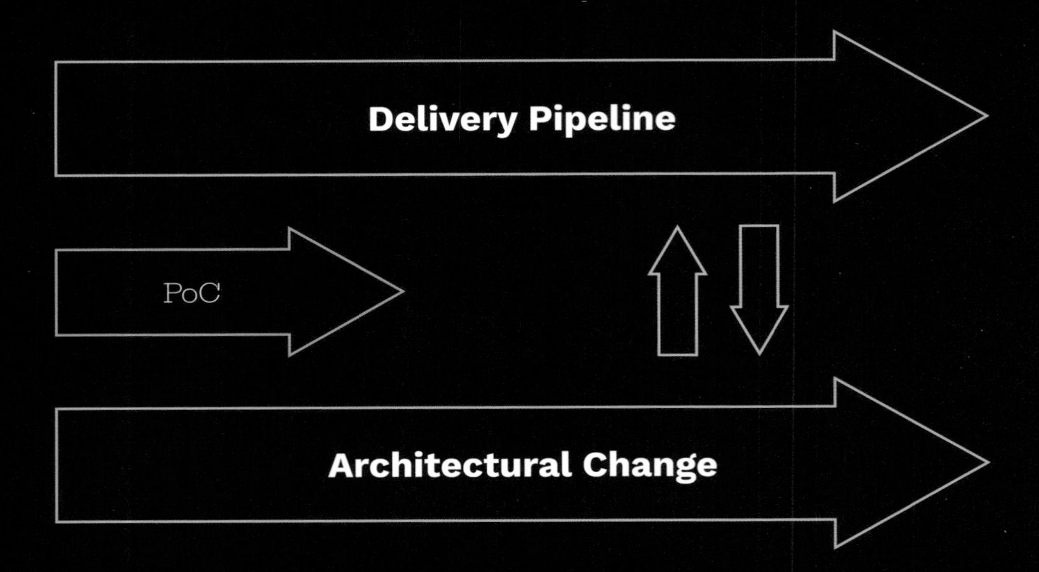

The process of making architectural change is a surgical procedure and is largely the same irrespective of where in the architecture the change is - business, application, data or technology. The change will likely comprise a large-scale code change, service integration, potential technology change, and a modification to the delivery pipeline.

Strong engineering principles executed through good configuration management, source code control and branch and merge policies are essential. The key steps are:

1. **Identification of requirement for architectural change leads to a PoC to confirm the approach**
2. **Architectural change is undertaken in a separate code branch to avoid impacting normal functional delivery**
3. **The change is merged back into the pipeline when complete or ideally periodically where this is feasible.**

The most important point is that architectural change is only committed to the delivery pipeline and shippable product when all assurance and tests have been completed. Technical changes should never break the pipeline or impact product quality.

Given the serious problems that technical changes can bring, we recommend always following these rules:

1. **There are written requirements and acceptance criteria in the same way as for functional change**
2. **Change is only made when it adds value to the organisation (this may be indirect, e.g., improving the efficiency of the team)**
3. **Implementation is undertaken within the Product Team, not by architects in isolation.**

The last point may seem counter-intuitive, but there will be long term consequences for knowledge and morale if the perceived 'hard' technical work is the preserve of an elite. The Product Team need to be able to know how to continue to change and run the product.

Measure for Success

To aid predictable delivery and continuously improve, it is essential to put in place the right measures around delivering change and service. We believe that metrics collection and reporting should largely be automated by the lifecycle tooling. It is also important that there is complete transparency over the metrics from the team all the way up to the sponsor.

There is considerable debate amongst the Agile community as to how, and if, teams should be measured. In many ways, excessive measurement is counter to the spirit of Agile development, but in scenarios where large-scale change is being delivered, measurement is essential. It is vital to gain the trust of the team by being transparent about what metrics are being collected and what they are used for.

Engineering Good Customer Service

A key component of delivering complete Product Increments is the Service Wrap - the processes and procedures that support the user when experiencing difficulty using the product.

Traditionally, the service component of product delivery has been separated from the development efforts to change the product. To be effective at rapid low-risk change we believe that 'Build' and 'Run' should be combined. **Chapter 9** provides a description of this approach and how Agile and ITIL can co-exist in a single DevOps delivery unit.

The Enterprise Agile Approach

Building the Delivery Pipeline

The delivery pipeline - the technology and tooling through which new Product Increments flow - is core to delivering technology change. Establishing the basic delivery pipeline during Sprint 0 is an essential investment. Without it, the process of delivering change relies on manual processes, poor testing coverage and a collection of error-prone and time-consuming scripts.

At the heart of the delivery pipeline is an integrated toolchain. These engineering tools should support all aspects of building and running the product. Getting these products up and running from the start of product delivery is strongly recommended. However, it is possible to add to existing product delivery where this hasn't been used in the past. On larger scale Product Teams it is sometimes the case that a specialist team (or individual) looks after tooling. This is a judgment call - we suggest that all engineers should have a good working knowledge of the tooling and how it fits together.

Figure 8-4: Typical DevOps Tool Chain

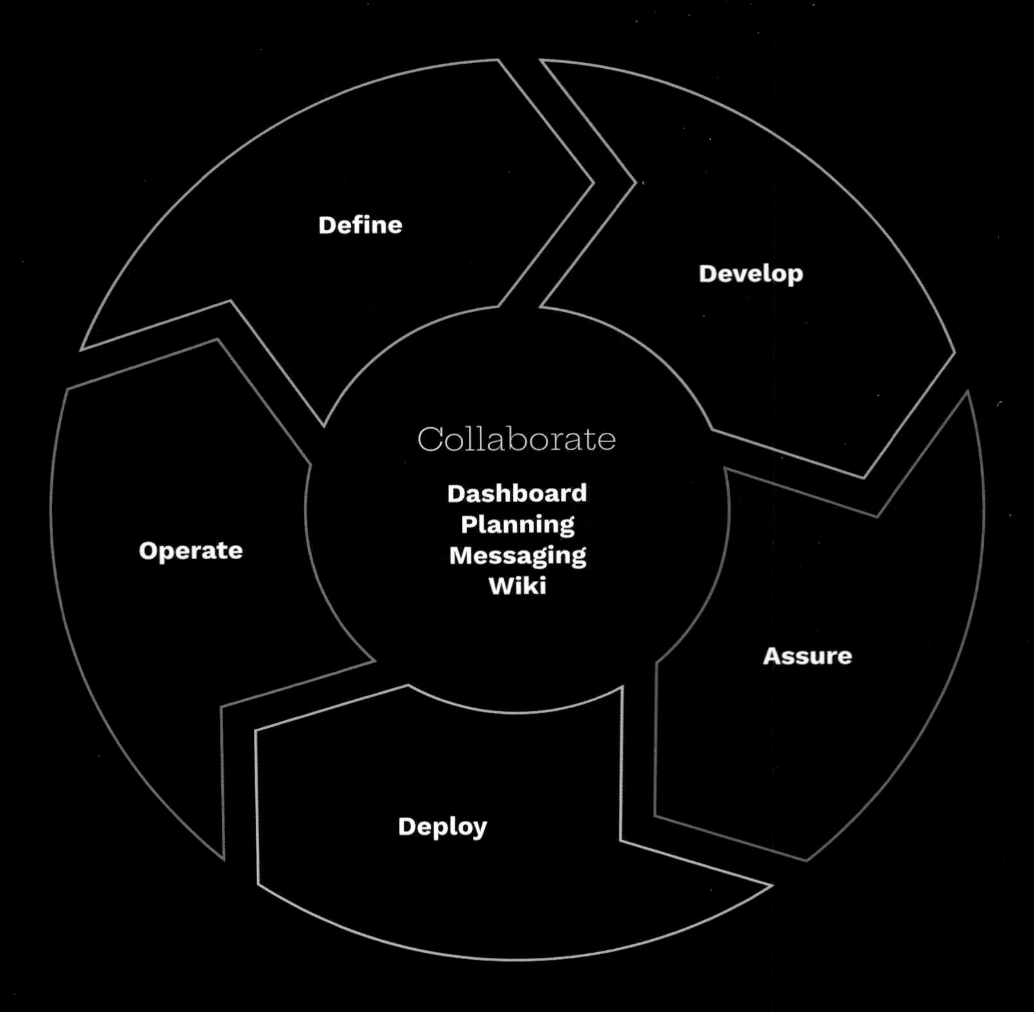

Figure 8-4 shows an example of the categories of tools in the end-to-end toolchain to support the delivery pipeline.

Operating and Improving the Delivery Pipeline

Time should be allowed both pre- and post-product launch to maintain and improve the delivery pipeline. This is also a good time to catalogue tech debt and prioritise it against new functionality or support issues. Doing so preserves the efficiency of the team and reduces the risk of failures. Required changes to the pipeline are most likely to originate from the team themselves during their normal Stand-ups and Retrospectives. These changes should be recorded as defects or new stories and added to the backlog. They are then prioritised and fed into the normal Sprint planning process against reserved maintenance capacity.

If the pipeline becomes faulty then delivery should stop. A big mistake we see teams make in this situation is carrying on. If the continuous integration process or automated tests are not working, the team must halt all feature delivery and concentrate on fixing the problem. Without the correct controls in place, there is no knowing what the product quality is. Furthermore, if tests are failing, continuing to change and add new areas of untested functionality to the product will compound the problem. If the build breaks, the pipeline is faulty and normal delivery stops – no excuses. Ever!

We expect instrumentation to be applied in production and to the delivery pipeline. Sudden increases in build times, test execution times, etc. may point to a problem that will soon impact productivity. Such issues should be recorded and dealt with as potential defects in the same way as product defects. Remember, the delivery pipeline is the vehicle for implementing technology change - it needs maintaining and repairing to continue to be successful.

Building in Product Quality

Product quality is 'engineered in' throughout the delivery process. It cannot be easily 'tested in' afterwards. This requires a clear approach to testing that ensures potential issues are identified early. It is only through these (largely automated) test activities that a DevOps approach can succeed.

Pushing frequent change through the delivery pipeline and into the hands of the users requires assurance that things aren't going to break. Test activities evolve across the product lifecycle as shown in **Figure 8-5.**

It is important to recognise that everyone is engaged in quality and test activities and that this is integral to the work of each team. The focus on testing begins at the outset and helps shape the realisation of the initial idea. Early consideration of test activities is essential to the delivery of a quality product. The first areas to consider are how the delivery of the product can be assured and the role that testing plays in this. The initial approach will consider the required test activities, levels of automation, framework, roles, environments and data.

Figure 8-5: Test Evolution Across the Product Lifecycle

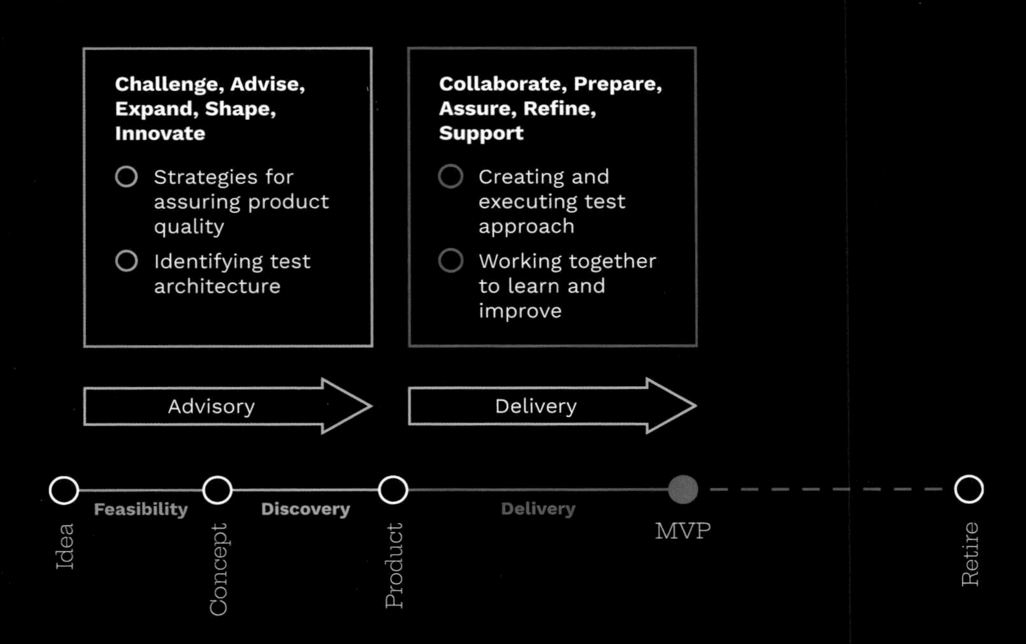

The role of testing is to ensure that a high-quality product can be delivered continuously and consistently. This requires attention to four functions:

1. **Test Leadership** - Advising and guiding the Product Owner and informing the governance process on approaches to quality and potential issues
2. **Test Architecture** - Aligning a suitable set of tools and frameworks to the product, assuring quality without creating a cottage industry to maintain bespoke artefacts
3. **Functional Testing** - Adding value through knowledge of the product, users and market to ensure needs are met and a quality user experience

4. **Technical Testing** - Making sure that the product will cope with the rigours of real-world use and meets the required non-functional requirements.

Testing has a role to play in all aspects of the product stack. Don't confine your thinking and test strategy to the application software. Data quality, infrastructure and service all impact the experience of the user.

Developing a Strategy for Testing

Using a test strategy is a powerful way to capture and focus energy on test activities. Exhaustively testing (manual or automated) all aspects of the product following a change is not feasible. An effective test strategy understands what test coverage is sufficient and directs efforts to test objectives where they are most needed based on risk and effectiveness.

Ultimately, testing aims to ensure the product can be released to users with a reasonable level of predictability and quality. A good test strategy will include the following key elements:

1. **Test Objectives** - Shaping the balance of testing methods employed and the focus of the team is derived from clear test objectives. This is likely to reflect the acceptable risk profile and external constraints such as compliance
2. **Contribution to Governance** - Product quality is one of the key measures of interest to stakeholders. The output of test activities must be articulated crisply and concisely, such that it can inform any required support or interventions

3. **Information Sharing** - The entire Product Team relies on data relating to testing to help focus its efforts, so clarity here is important. Issues arising during testing may point to the need to address skills and capability within the team or resolve design problems

4. **Test Architecture** - This may sound a rather grand term, but it is important to consider how test activities interact and overlap. Test architecture will capture the structure of the testing landscape and identify the supporting frameworks and tools required

5. **Test Method** - Consideration must be given to how the testing will take place and the execution process, the level of automation and the underpinning data and environments that will be used. This will help the team plan test tasks and interactions across the organisation.

Determining Where to Focus Test Effort

Creating automated tests is a significant investment. Not only does creating the tests require engineering skill and labour, but every product change will require further tests and updates to existing tests. When creating a test strategy and considering where to invest in automation, we find the Agile test automation pyramid in **Figure 8-6** useful. This identifies that the bulk of automation effort should be focused on unit tests ahead of service (API) tests and UI automation.

Figure 8-6: Agile Test Automation Pyramid

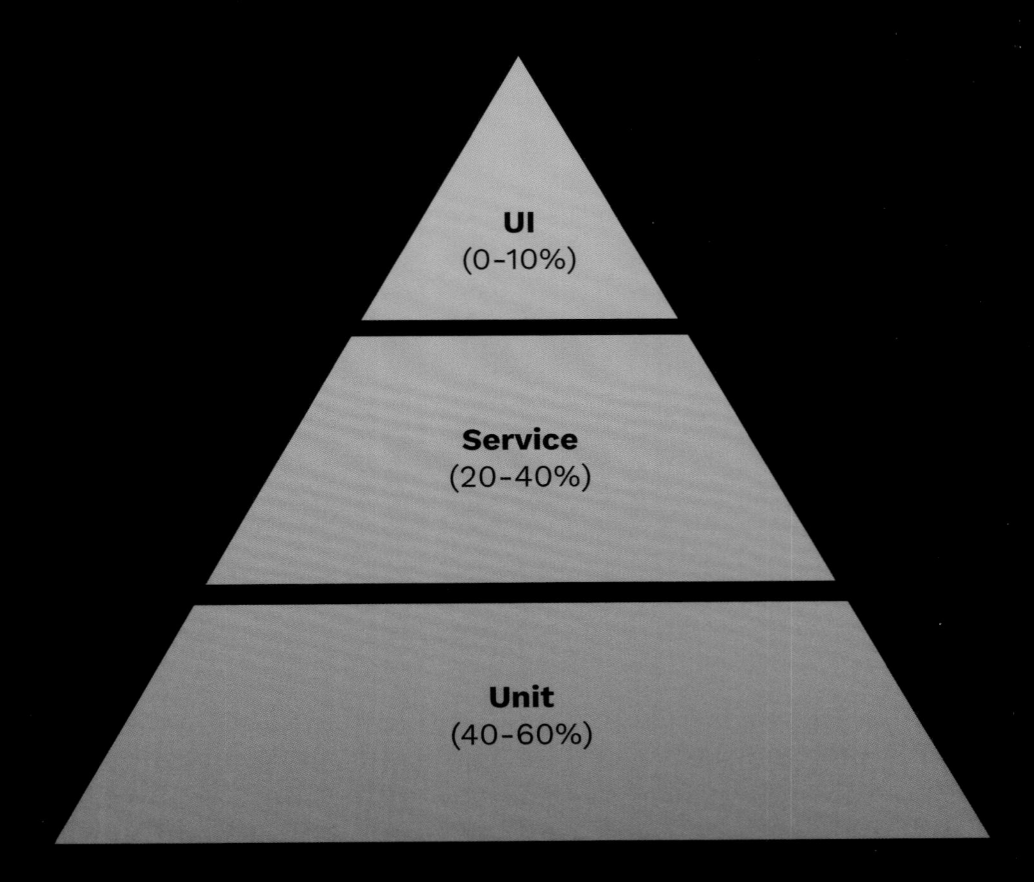

This approach offers several clear advantages. Firstly, it builds quality into the product from within. Traditional test approaches might have a team of people or large automation packs created by testers focused on the interface and not the implementation. Secondly, relying on big UI automation packs is inefficient - they quickly become brittle and are costly to maintain.

Thirdly, the bias towards unit and service tests pushes the bulk of test automation back into the development space, forcing developers to own product quality which has a general overall positive effect. It also broadens the responsibility to Business Analysts, who must ensure edge conditions are well understood and covered.

It is common to see the pyramid model extended to cover additional test phases and also suggest the level of effort to be expended on manual testing. An example of an enhanced test pyramid is shown in **Figure 8-7**.

Figure 8-7: Expanded Agile Test Pyramid

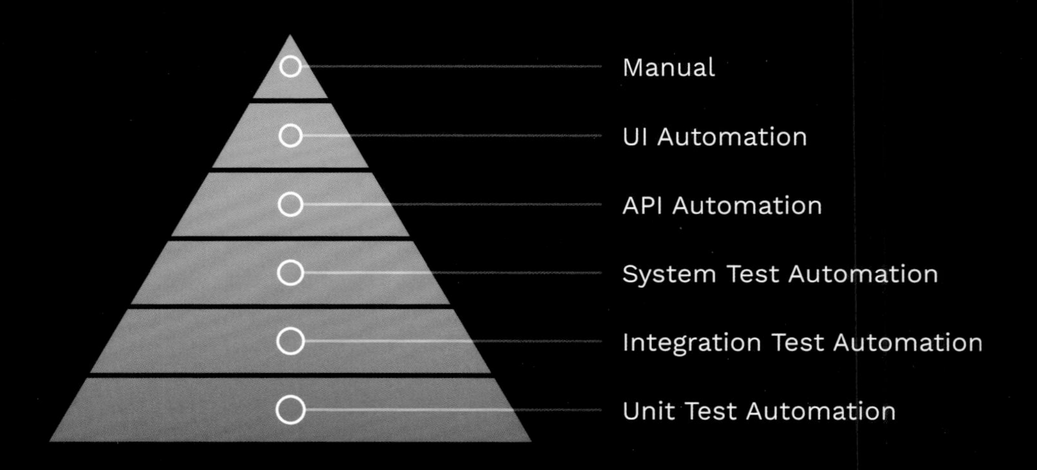

A Structured Approach to Testing

In **Chapter 6** we discussed the importance of a structured approach to Analysis. For obvious reasons, validating that layered requirements have been met necessitates a layered approach to testing. This yields consideration for the established V-model. The concept of the V-model was originally coupled to more traditional Waterfall projects. However, the principle can still apply to an Agile delivery with the 'V' repeated every Sprint (or set of Sprints forming a release). We refer to this as the W-model.

Figure 8-8: W-Model

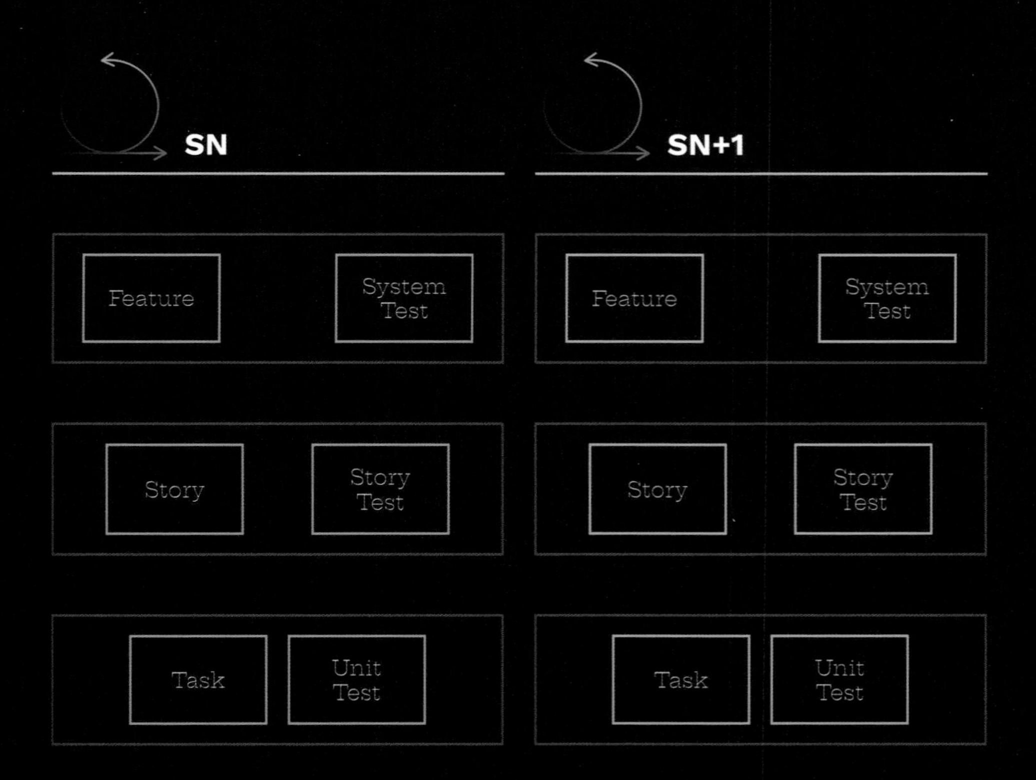

In devising the approach to testing, the team must consider the balance of requirements-based testing and risk-based testing. Both have a part to play in ensuring product quality. All stories will be written with acceptance criteria that need to be tested against; this should be a joint activity by Developers and Business Analysts to ensure the right coverage and that both business and technical criteria are included. Further testing beyond that and into obscure edge cases should be driven by risk.

It is useful (not just from a testing perspective) to know what the most frequent and most valuable transactions in the product are. This information can be used to help prioritise testing efforts.

Test Phases and the Sprint Pattern

We expect that meeting the acceptance criteria defined for each user story is part of the Definition of Done. This correctly implies that story acceptance testing will take place during the same Sprint as the story is developed. Where the change is relatively small, it should be possible to conclude all necessary testing during a Sprint. The automated delivery pipeline assures this and uses packs of automated tests to allow software to be deployed at the touch of a button.

There are of course valid exceptions to this process. Many of the systems we work with require further manual testing or integration with non-Agile workstreams and legacy systems. In such scenarios, these test phases may occur in parallel to ongoing feature development or during a special purpose Release Sprint. **Figure 8-9** illustrates the test phases we recommend and how this is achieved across the delivery pattern.

Figure 8-9: Recommended Test Phases

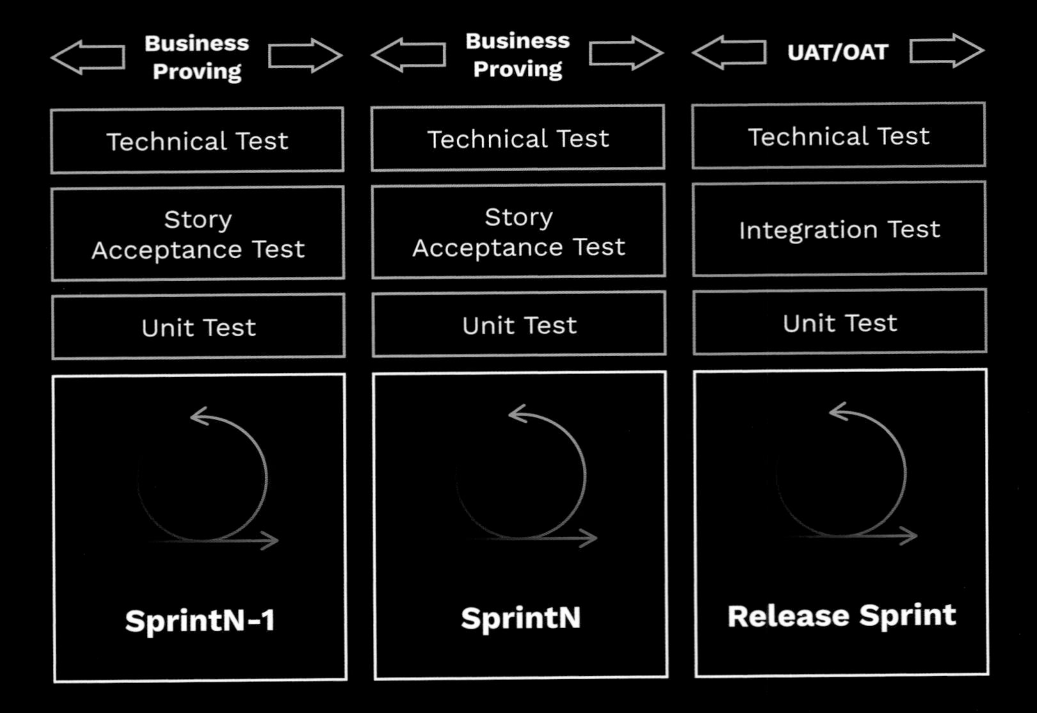

Dealing with Defects

No matter how extensive testing efforts are, defects and support incidents will arise. This should be a matter of routine and a large 'bow wave' of defects must not be allowed to accumulate near a release by watering down the Definition of Done or deferring testing. This is why we recommend as much testing occurs in-Sprint as possible and the full Product Increment is produced such that application, infrastructure and data change are aligned and fully working together.

Defects and support work will be added to the product backlog and brought into Sprint through the Sprint planning process and delivered alongside new stories. It is unlikely that all defects to be fixed in a Sprint are discussed at the planning meeting. A more common approach is to allow for some team capacity to address defects in priority order.

To ensure that defects are properly understood and assigned the correct severity rating, teams should run a regular defect triage meeting with the Product Owner. This session not only ensures that defects are categorised and dealt with correctly but also allows for the removal of duplicates and the identification of trends in particular types of defects.

Developing for the Cloud

Since the first edition of this book in 2008, the infrastructure world has changed considerably. We've seen a significant change from physical infrastructure, to private virtual infrastructure, to Cloud-based virtual infrastructure and now to global Cloud platforms. In the early days of Public Cloud, we used these Cloud services to mimic traditional on-premise architectures. This reduced the start-up time of a project. It is possible to use infrastructure automation tools to spin up a delivery pipeline and test environments in Sprint 0. It is possible to use the same scripts to build the production environments, minimising configuration drift and helping to reduce the time from development to release.

Recently we have seen containers and container platforms move from a developer platform to a reliable production platform. Containers are an ideal platform for microservices architectures and have brought new ways of thinking and a new vocabulary to the development and release of software. For example, the concept of 'pets' versus 'cattle' (where servers are either beloved, named 'pets' nursed back to health if they go down, or one of many numbered 'cattle' in a herd that are replaced if they go down) takes advantage of comprehensive automation to simplify fault handling and is one of the cornerstones of self-healing architectures.

Another advantage of containers is that it brings the configuration closer to the developer and puts the configuration code into the developer's domain. This is the same code repository as the application code and allows the images they create to be part of the continuous delivery pipeline. This ensures that the infrastructure can be proven earlier.

Now that the main Public Cloud vendors offer serverless computing, solutions no longer require virtual infrastructure or container platforms - although they are still available if required. As the name suggests, with serverless computing there is no server to manage. Code is deployed to the service and executed in response to events (such as RESTful API requests, messages arriving into a queue, or time-based schedules.) A complete system can be built using serverless computing or it can be combined with containers, virtual infrastructure or on-premise systems for a hybrid solution.

With each of the above options, the cycle time from define to operate (see 'Building the Delivery Pipeline') can be reduced significantly using Cloud technologies. For 'born in the Cloud' companies, this is their 'normal', and their ability to innovate, test their ideas, and keep moving forward far exceeds that of companies with legacy infrastructure and architectures. Companies with legacy systems and infrastructure looking to adopt Enterprise Agility must evaluate how Cloud technologies can be integrated into their current systems, architectures and processes to support them on their journey.

Delivery and Service Metrics

If you want to improve something - measure it. We are strong advocates of implementing metrics to understand the performance of the product and the delivery pipeline. There are typically three categories of metrics that arise from DevOps around a product; these are summarised in **Figure 8-10**.

The collection and distribution of metrics should be largely automated. We expect this to be part of the end-to-end toolchain. Getting data should not be a chore, but it does require a little support across the team. In particular, those responsible for delivering change will need to record the actual time spent on tasks and estimated time to completion. This enables the rate of delivery and estimation accuracy to be recorded and used as part of the feedback loop to adjust the forward plan and advise the Sprint planning process.

Figure 8-10: Categories of Product Metrics

The ultimate measure for the organisation is earned value and measuring the benefit gained for the effort expended on delivering new features.

Service metrics inform decisions about resource levels in Support Teams and highlight the quality of service being delivered to users. They also quantify how the platform has been scaling to user needs and the potential cost implications of that scaling.

Measuring product quality is important to ensure that customer expectations continue to be met and product quality remains high. This can be measured by examining defect levels and the stability/availability of the product.

We suggest that a metrics dashboard, transparent and visible to all team members, is produced dynamically from the pipeline tooling.

Measuring Change

A crucial element of achieving predictability is measuring progress towards the next release and any impediments to this. Many Agile methodologies have devised different ways of achieving this. Measuring velocity (the rate at which work is done) and Burn-down (or Burn-up) charts are common. The challenge is avoiding getting bound up in lots of metrics while having sufficient information to make decisions and interventions as required. It is also important the metrics tell a story, have an appropriate narrative and are not just raw data. Reporting to a senior executive that the team has a velocity of 27 isn't helpful.

Within a Sprint, we believe in recording progress using a Burn-down chart. This is because the content of a Sprint should be a fixed scope – the stories taken into Sprint during the planning session. An example Burn-down chart is provided in **Figure 8-11**. The Burn-down chart should be updated daily as a result of the Stand-up and a revised estimate to complete on tasks by engineers.

Figure 8-11: Example Sprint Burn-down Chart

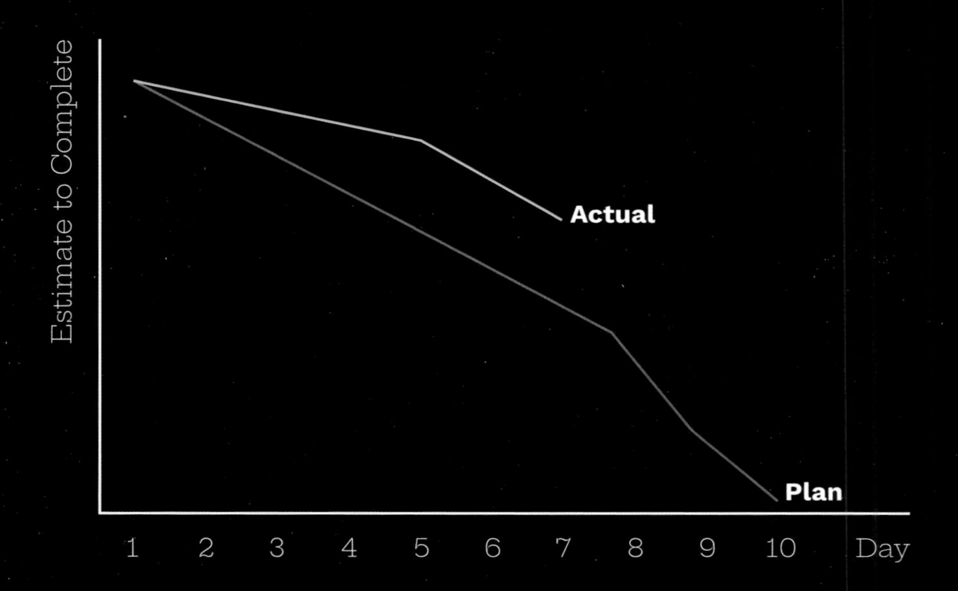

The Burn-down is calculated by plotting the estimate to complete for all the tasks in the Sprint. For tasks in progress, this is updated daily by engineers in the Delivery Team. For tasks not yet started, this is the estimate from the Sprint planning session. This actual Burn-down is compared to an ideal trend line that shows all tasks completing by the end of the Sprint. Note that the estimate for complete for a story should only reach zero when it meets the Definition of Done.

A release may occur after one or more Sprints. For a release, we recommend using a Burn-up chart because the scope of a release can change over time as stories move in or out of the release through the Sprint planning process. As can be seen in **Figure 8-12**, the Burn-up release chart clearly identifies a baseline scope for the release. In the case of an MVP, this will be the scope agreed during Discovery.

The Burn-up should reflect actual work completed to the Definition of Done. It might be useful to plot the Burn-up for each layer in the Definition of Done to be sure that a gap is not opening up between work completed by the team and being accepted by the user community.

Figure 8-12: Example Release Burn-up Chart

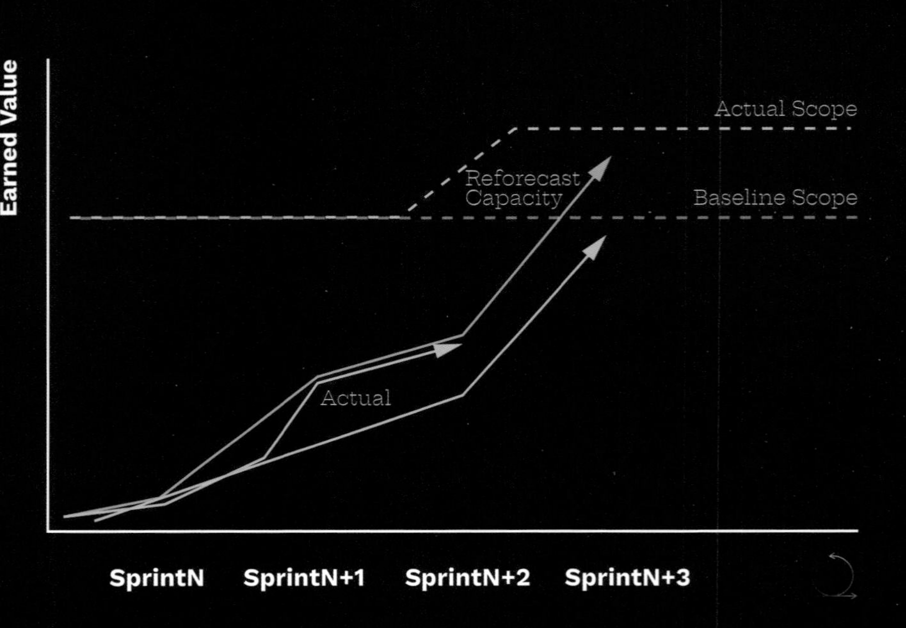

The concept of earned value is important here. Tracking effort, work done, velocity and so on is useful as an indicator and to aid planning, but most executive sponsors are interested in understanding progress towards goals. If the initiative needs to build 10 widgets to derive value for the organisation, then the only thing that matters is how many widgets are completed. In addition to monitoring completed stories against the baseline, we also suggest plotting the actual and planned resource capacity.

Inevitably, if progress deviates from the expectation, questions will rightly be asked. Often, the root cause is simply that less resource was available than expected due to unexpected urgent or critical faults that the Development Team needs to address, as well as factors like unforeseen holidays and sickness. It is best to make this easily visible, so that further analysis into potential issues is only required when the most probable cause of a resource issue is ruled out.

Measuring Service

Service metrics inform stakeholders about the performance of the product in live use and the level of support being provided. Much of our thinking on service metrics is informed by ITIL processes, combined with the application of a 'Necessary and Sufficient' filter. As a minimum, service metrics must cover:

1. **Usage of the product by the various user communities.**
   Often this is a non-functional requirement anyway and is certainly important in gaining insight into the interactions of users with the product to inform future enhancements

2. **Incidents arising from the usage of the system and how the resolution of these performs against any agreed service levels.**
   Incidents will typically be assigned severity levels and the investigation of these may lead to a defect being passed back to the Delivery Teams

3. **Capacity that is utilised to deliver the service.**
   This is important for forward planning and financial management and to some extent goes hand in hand with the usage metrics in point 1. These metrics are particularly important when not using elastic Cloud computing platforms.

As with delivery metrics relating to change, we would expect these metrics to be largely automated and derived from the tooling in the delivery pipeline and used by the Service Teams.

Measuring Quality

An important set of metrics are those referring to quality. During the execution of change and service, it is important to track the defects found and their path to resolution. We also believe that measuring system availability and unplanned outages is a good indicator of production quality. Many theories and convoluted metrics exist in the area of product quality. We prefer to keep things straightforward and put in place only the 'Necessary and Sufficient' metrics.

The number of defects alone does not tell a story or convey any meaningful information. Our recommended key defect metrics are the find and fix rates. These should be plotted over time to provide historical trends. The key question to address is 'Are more defects being found and is resolution keeping pace with Discovery?' Ensuring that a significant gap does not open up between the find and fix rate is key to ensuring a 'No surprises endgame' for the release of a Product Increment.

Figure 8-13: Example Defect Charts

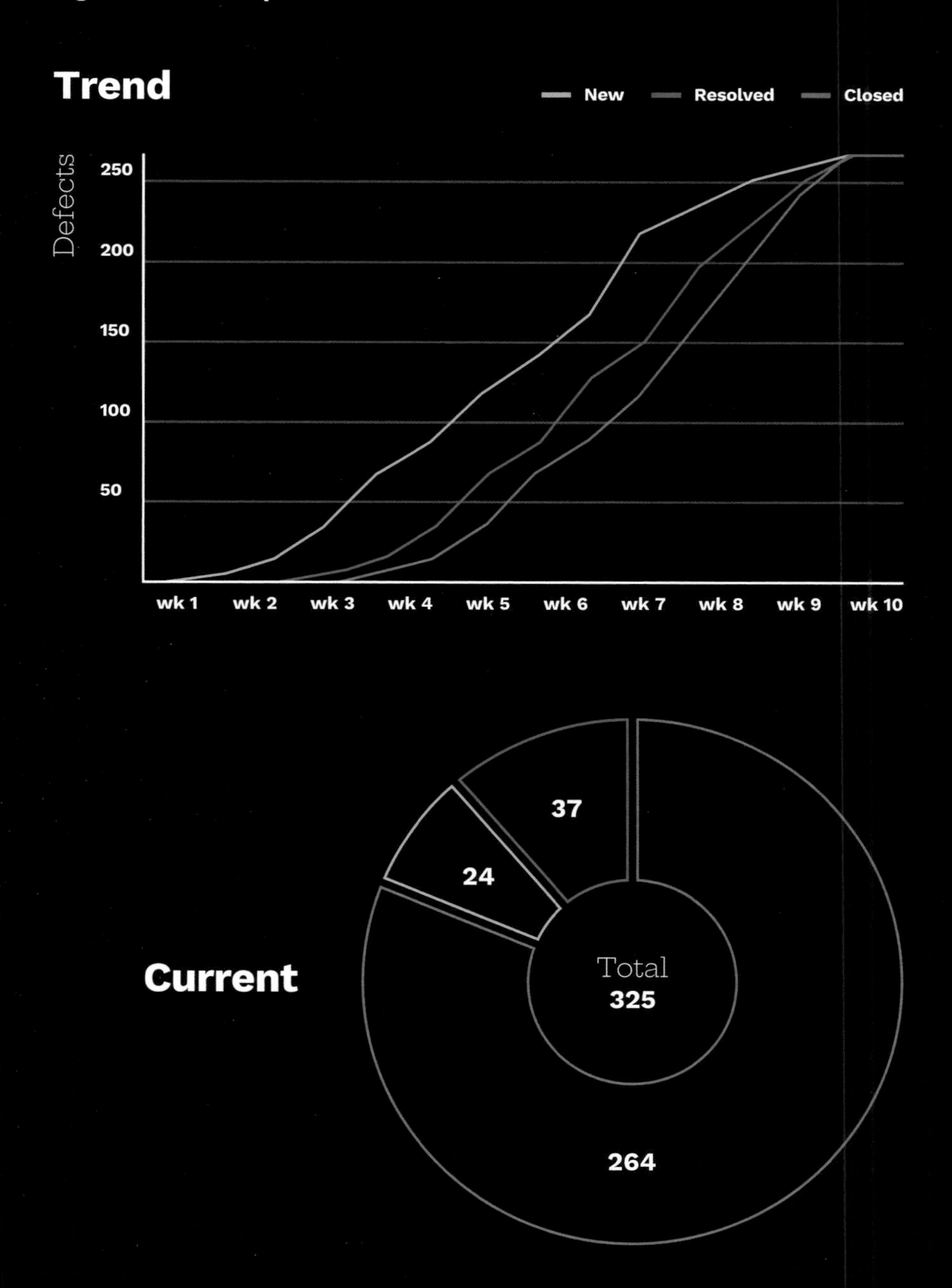

The sample defect charts in **Figure 8-13** illustrate the types of information we expect to see generated automatically from Agile lifecycle tooling and presented transparently for all stakeholders. Data on system availability should similarly be readily producible from the run time tooling in production.

Assuring Technical Quality

The Architect, with contribution from Technical Leads, will typically develop and implement a Technical Quality Plan (TQP) to underpin the quality of the engineering efforts. The purpose of this TQP is to ensure that all technical output meets the required quality standard. Its scope will include application software, infrastructure (software-defined and hardware), test assets and the full engineering stack.

The TQP should be considered a living artefact that evolves with the product. It is also important to recognise that the document or wiki that represents the TQP is not an end in itself, but a means to an end – high-quality technical output. The key areas covered by the TQP are:

1. **Delivery Pipeline Quality** - The section refers to the use of the delivery pipeline and how to manage the quality of setup and maintenance, including build, continuous integration, packaging and deployment
2. **Code Quality** - All aspects of managing the quality of code should be addressed. This will extend to peer code review, static analysis, coding standards, managing technical debt and documentation
3. **Product Quality** - This complements the test approach and determines from a technical perspective what 'Good' looks like and how to make effective use of the test tools and frameworks available. Typically, this will cover unit test and automated end-to-end tests

4. **Technical Risk Management** - This defines a process for identifying and managing technical risks associated with delivering and running the product. This will dovetail into the standard RAID log for overall product delivery

5. **Knowledge Management** - An approach is required for capturing, maintaining and sharing technical information relating to the product. This will include code comments, wikis and traditional documentation.

Do Everything Continuously

Do everything continuously to ensure quality is engineered-in and the risk of delivery failure is low. If you have to do it more than once, automate it and run it regularly. As a minimum, focus on ensuring the following are automated and run continuously:

1. **Build**
2. **Integration**
3. **Functional Tests**
4. **Non-functional (Technical) Tests**
5. **Data Migration**
6. **Deployments**
7. **Environment Provisioning**
8. **Health monitoring and repair.**

Key Points

1. Good engineering starts with strong architecture. Drive out NFRs during Discovery and prove out that architecture early through continuous technical testing.

2. Build and maintain an automated delivery pipeline for the production of high-quality software. If the pipeline fails at any point, stop all delivery and fix the problem.

3. Implement a well thought through Test Strategy that identifies the right balance of automation and manual testing, test phases and tooling.

4. Create and use a Technical Quality Plan to manage the code quality process such as code reviews, static analysis, technical debt and associated tooling.

5. Put appropriate tests around software-defined infrastructure and ensure that all software assets are subject to the same source code control.

Chapter 09
Service Agility

Service management comprises the activities, processes, and procedures that an organisation adopts to align IT services with the needs of the business.

We outlined the concept of a Service Wrap in **Chapter 8**. In this chapter, we explore service management concepts in more detail and how organisations can develop and refine a Service Wrap appropriate to their situation. We show how traditional structured approaches can be combined with Agile delivery to provide the level of support required in an Agile delivery pipeline.

Concepts

Service Maturity

Most organisations of any scale operate some type of service function to provide support for products or services. These functions operate at different levels of maturity. A simple service Maturity Model is shown in **Figure 9-1**.

Each maturity level carries a different risk profile and scope to support an Agile approach.

Figure 9-1: Service Maturity Model

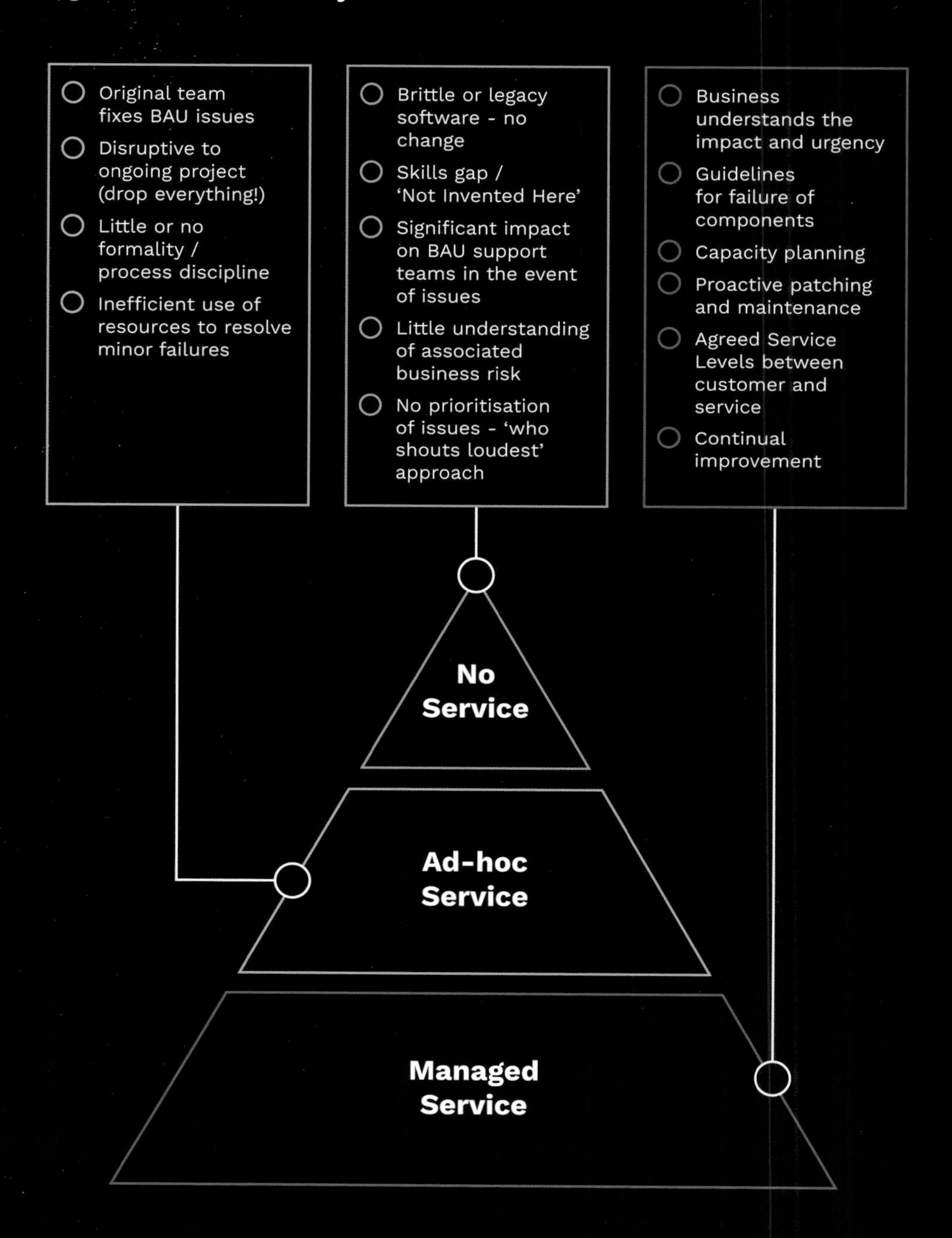

No Service

The notion of a product having no service is illusory – if an organisation is using software to conduct elements of its business then a service is being provided. Whilst this scenario may seem unlikely in a modern delivery environment, in our experience it is surprisingly common, particularly in the less mainstream areas of a portfolio. It is not uncommon for key production systems to be well defined and managed, whilst other services, perhaps dependencies of that key system, are largely ignored. As a result, 'no service' services may be responsible for significant business risk.

A legacy system may be in constant use and have experienced no issues for long periods. Nevertheless, a failure would have significant consequences. A common scenario we see is a small number of people managing high-value transactions using extremely complex spreadsheet solutions. In many cases, these solutions, now operating as key services within the business, have been created by Subject Matter Expert (SME) staff who have long since moved on. A faulty formula, a regulatory or business change, unforeseen circumstances in the data or technical changes to an unseen dependency can have a significant impact (real or reported).

Ad-hoc Services

In an ad-hoc services approach, the delivery organisation recognises that a service is being provided, but the ways of working are poorly defined.

A common scenario is that of a project never quite closing down - an otherwise well-managed and well-defined delivery project with poorly defined or non-existent terms of reference for the production system. This often means that the original Engineering Team that built the solution (the people best placed to support it) remains responsible for resolving any issues, even after the project has disbanded.

This approach works well in mitigating risk, particularly in the early stages of a new service, but it must be a conscious strategy, managed carefully.

It's often the case that the Engineers able to support the new service are planned into their next delivery. Diverting them to address second and third line support issues, which usually attract higher priority than project delivery, is disruptive. This unplanned competition for resources creates barriers between teams, friction between colleagues and demotivates the people involved.

Despite these issues, small Engineering Teams with a clear delineation of responsibility and an 'eyes open' approach to planning and estimation can operate this model quite successfully. It is often effective where there is a single point of responsibility able to address any intra-team tensions. For example, a single Delivery Manager responsible for Service A and Project B can set direction between the two without recourse to committee decision making.

Operating a service like this at scale is more difficult. Services of this type tend to over-emphasise the team's project domain knowledge, which naturally erodes over time as the team evolves due to attrition or reorganisation. This approach can breed single points of failure, allowing key person dependencies within the project to extend to the service regime with the attendant risks that this brings.

Managed Service

Mature service organisations typically employ a service management framework of some kind. Many standards and frameworks exist, including the Information Technology Infrastructure Library (ITIL), the international standard ISO/IEC 20000, the IT governance framework Control Objectives for Information and Related Technologies (COBIT) and elements of The Open Group Architecture Framework (TOGAF).

The most widely used service management framework is ITIL, first developed in the 1980s by the CCTA. The concepts are split into several core areas, as summarised in **Figure 9-2**.

Figure 9-2: Service Management Concepts in ITIL

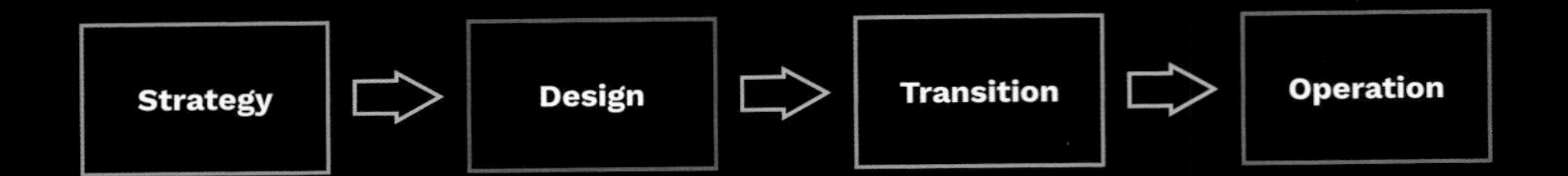

IT service management best practices are the activities, processes and procedures that an organisation adopts to align IT services with the needs of the business. The key elements are:

Service Strategy

Service strategy includes, but isn't limited to, Service Portfolio Management, Financial Management for IT Services, Demand Management, and Business Relationship Management.

Service Design

Service design considers Service Catalogue Management, Service Level Management, Availability Management, Capacity Management, IT Service Continuity Management, Security Management, and Supplier Management.

Using these broad concepts as dimensions, comprehensive service processes can be designed (including supporting procedures), dependencies can be understood, and a service design can be developed and communicated.

Service Transition

Service transition covers not only the transition of new services into a production setting but also ongoing changes to the live service, including release and deployment good practice. It includes Transition Planning and Support, Change, Service Asset and Configuration Management, Release and Deployment Management, Service Validation and Testing, Change Evaluation, and Knowledge Management.

Service Operation

Service operation covers the areas familiar to most organisations because these processes and functions are the ones they work with every day. These include Service Desk, Technical Management Application Management, and IT Operations Management. Service operation also covers the processes that deal with Event, Access, Request Fulfilment, Incident and Problem Management.

Continual Service Improvement

The final, overarching core area is Continual Service Improvement. This is an important aspect of any service management approach and ITIL's version covers, amongst other things, a seven-step improvement process to enable a service to change with the evolving needs of the business.

Like any framework, ITIL has strengths and weaknesses, but it is important to understand the basics. Many books have been written on the various versions of ITIL, and we don't propose to duplicate them here. However, the concepts are key to any structured approach to service management.

Figure 9-3: ITIL's Continual Service Improvement Approach

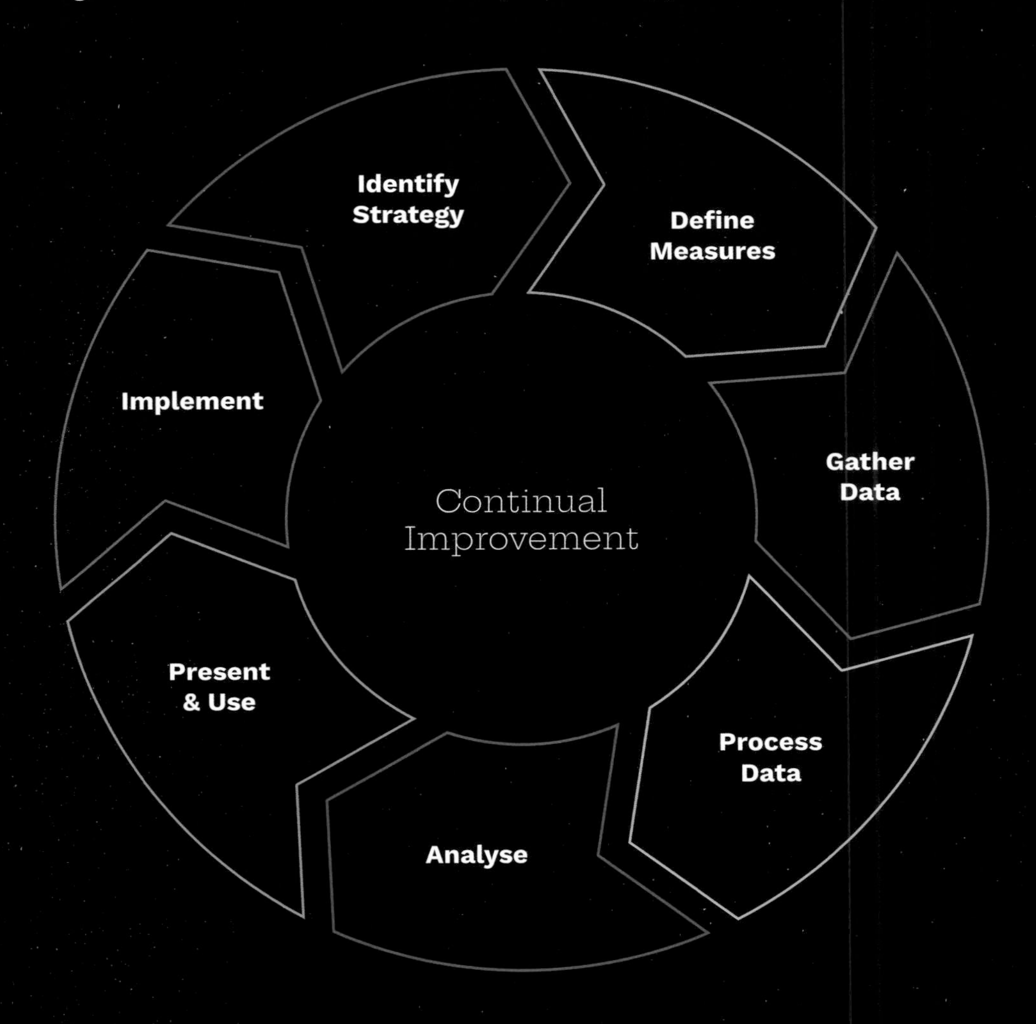

BJSS Opinion

A structured service management approach is sometimes seen by those who don't understand it as a hindrance in Agile environments. Often, it is perceived to be an unforgiving, unbending process. This is usually because the details of the service design are not fit for purpose. Many organisations implement what they believe to be best practice but do not take into account the needs of the organisation or the speed of change to which it aspires. Note that the design may well have been fit for purpose at the stage it was put in place, but evolving business needs have not been reflected or considered over time.

Service management should be at the heart of an Agile delivery from the outset. It is unlikely that the service representative will shape the product, but they can advise on potential service options that influence decision making before requirements are finalised.

Service design will be heavily influenced by the organisation's appetite for automation. If automation and quality are built-in as part of the development of the product and infrastructure, service processes can be more lightweight, and speed of delivery enhanced.

As with any other Agile process, once service processes are agreed upon and implemented, they should be refined and reviewed continually. What is relevant in an early life support stage may be irrelevant when the product has proved itself to be stable and resilient. For example, as confidence in the automation grows, along with service maturity, what would once be counted as a change requiring Change Advisory Board approval will become a standard change and be pre-approved.

A common misconception is that all best practice service management processes should be in place at go-live. In practice, this depends on the type of project and any external factors. In some circumstances it may be appropriate to design a Minimum Viable Service (MVS) that includes only:

- **Incident Management**
- **Change Management**
- **Release Management**
- **Event Management.**

Other processes can be implemented while the product is live and designed and enhanced in parallel to the product development.

Meeting the Challenge

Delivering an effective service is not straightforward. Challenges include:

- **Complex, evolving IT estates with multiple component parts**
- **Ageing technical infrastructure and legacy applications**
- **Legacy or niche technologies making it difficult (expensive!) to retain skilled staff**
- **No agreed to service levels (Operational Level Agreements) with an internal team or between teams**
- **No journey/plan to modernisation - service designed to 'keep the lights on'**
- **IT services failing to meet the need of the organisation.**

In our experience, these obstacles can exist even in organisations with a mature approach to service delivery and a clear understanding of their end goal.

Improvements can always be made, regardless of where an organisation fits on the maturity scale. An Agile approach will help with an incremental migration to a more mature approach.

Engineering Good Customer Service

ITIL processes typically dominate the service space and, although ITIL is still relevant, modern engineering techniques built on software-defined infrastructure and Cloud computing should be used to automate many of these processes.

Service Design

Service Catalogue Management

Likely, the product can automatically register its services to maintain a catalogue.

Service Level Management

The Agile DevOps delivery process described throughout this book includes this process. Consideration should be given to service levels when using public Cloud platforms, as they may not offer guaranteed "classic" service levels such as availability and performance. When it comes to Agile and Cloud development, the service level should be considered as part of the initial design, and techniques such as automated horizontal and vertical scaling should be explored.

Capacity Management

Whilst it is useful to understand underlying platform constraints and costs, we would expect the delivered product to automatically scale network, compute, and storage as required using Cloud technologies. The shift towards Cloud technologies may reduce the significance of capacity management, but the greater emphasis should be given to budget management and commercial offerings of the Cloud suppliers.

Availability Management

Using serverless computing, scalable microservices, automated provisioning, monitoring, and self-healing should allow for a product to be almost always available. The near-limitless availability of Cloud services also provides the ability to test this availability using manual or automated test techniques. The use of automated techniques largely reduces the need for manual approaches.

Service Continuity Management

Disaster recovery and service continuity is designed during Discovery, and should be fully automated within the product delivery.

Information Security Management

A secure coding lifecycle should be adopted to ensure compliance with information security standards. When using Cloud services, the possibility of using hosted security management tools should also be explored.

Supplier Management

Safeguarding the commercial interests of the organisation and ensuring that suppliers are aligned to project goals is the responsibility of the Product Team.

Service Transition

Knowledge Management

Product information should be maintained by the team as part of the ongoing service of the product.

Change Management

The rollout of change is completely automated, as is the generation of information allowing complete traceability of the contents of the change. In most organisations, a Developer check-in will not automatically deploy to live, and a final manual Go/No-go decision is made by the Change Advisory Board. As the organisation matures in its ability to deploy changes more frequently, the governance around change management should also evolve.

Asset and Configuration Management

When using a software-defined infrastructure, the content management database (CMDB) can be automatically generated by inventory scanning tools. With immutable infrastructure and Cloud platform services, the maintenance of a traditional CMDB can become a considerable overhead, and Leaner approaches to Asset and Configuration management should be explored as part of the delivery phase. Where possible, all configuration, infrastructure, documentation, and application code, should be stored centrally in the source code control repository.

Release and Deployment

It is expected that the release and deployment process is fully automated by the delivery pipeline. This removes one of the biggest headaches of implementing change, where often manual, error-prone steps are used to install software products.

Transition Planning

In a large change, such as the implementation of a new product, some manual transition planning work is still required.

Service Validation and Testing

A suite of automated tests should be used to ensure that the product operates effectively and that automated health checks and healing services operate correctly. Some work will be required to check the results of this process and align any remaining manual tests.

Evaluation

The process evaluation category is still potentially useful. We would expect the service to mature through the Agile change process outlined in this book. This will be supplemented by audits of the remaining manual processes.

Service Operations

Incident Management

Incident management and dealing with end-users will still require human intervention. The investment in an approach to meeting user needs and user-centred design will mean that user queries are reduced. In addition, the focus on automated testing and self-healing infrastructure should mean that reported failures decline as product reliability increases.

Problem Management

Problem management will still require work from the Support Teams. These are the challenges that go beyond the automated repair mechanisms of the product.

Access Management

This security-enforcing function likely remains manual.

Event Management

The end-to-end toolchain will include operational tools to monitor the health of the product. Events such as low free storage or node failures can be automatically fixed by a self-healing platform and automatically reported to the incident management tool.

Request Fulfilment

By using software-defined infrastructure in the Cloud, Engineers can provision the required infrastructure. Little manual work is required, but someone needs to keep an eye on the finances!

Continual Service Improvement

Service Measurement

It is recommended that service metrics are automatically generated by the platform.

Service Reporting

While service reporting can largely be automated, human interpretation of the reports is required to determine any intervention required.

Service Improvement

The service improvement step is still usefully a manual process but should be tied into the Sprint ceremonies.

The Enterprise Agile Approach

Implementing a Service Wrap is key to realising the benefits of good service management practice. The Enterprise Agile approach to delivering the Service Wrap is straightforward – treat it as a product to be delivered like any other.

Service Agility at 10,000 feet

The Enterprise Agile approach to service management embraces a DevOps philosophy. Continuous Delivery and cross-functional ways of working are key to delivering Agility in the Service Wrap. This way of working breaks the traditional 'Build' and 'Run' ways of thinking.

Figure 9-4 shows the traditional approach to service management, based on a 'complete' product being handed over to an Operations organisation to run the service. Future changes are bundled up into a notional 'Release 2' or series of releases.

Figure 9-4: Traditional Service Model

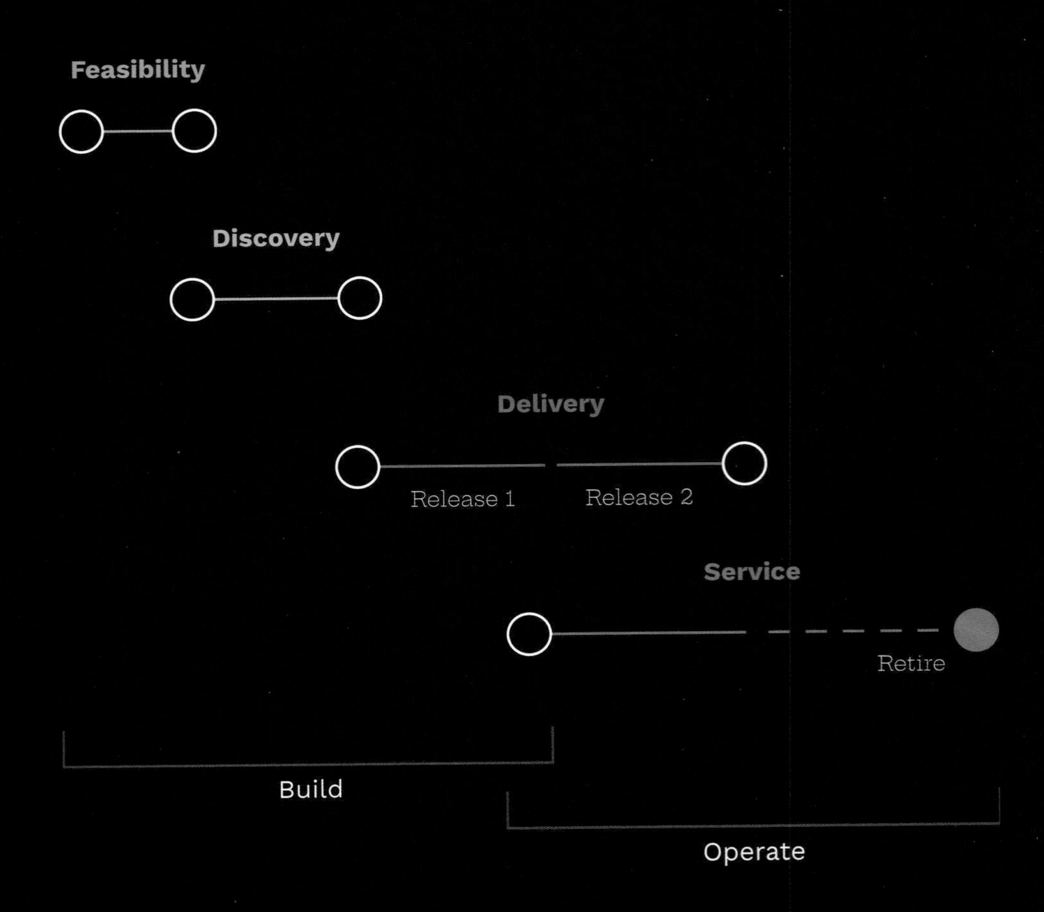

But how does this approach work with a Minimum Marketable Feature set (MFF)? What if the MFF has limited scope and could be earning value for the organisation very quickly, despite substantially more functionality remaining in the product backlog? The project is not finished, but the Product must be run.

Figure 9-5 illustrates the Enterprise Agile service model.

Figure 9-5: Enterprise Agile Service Model

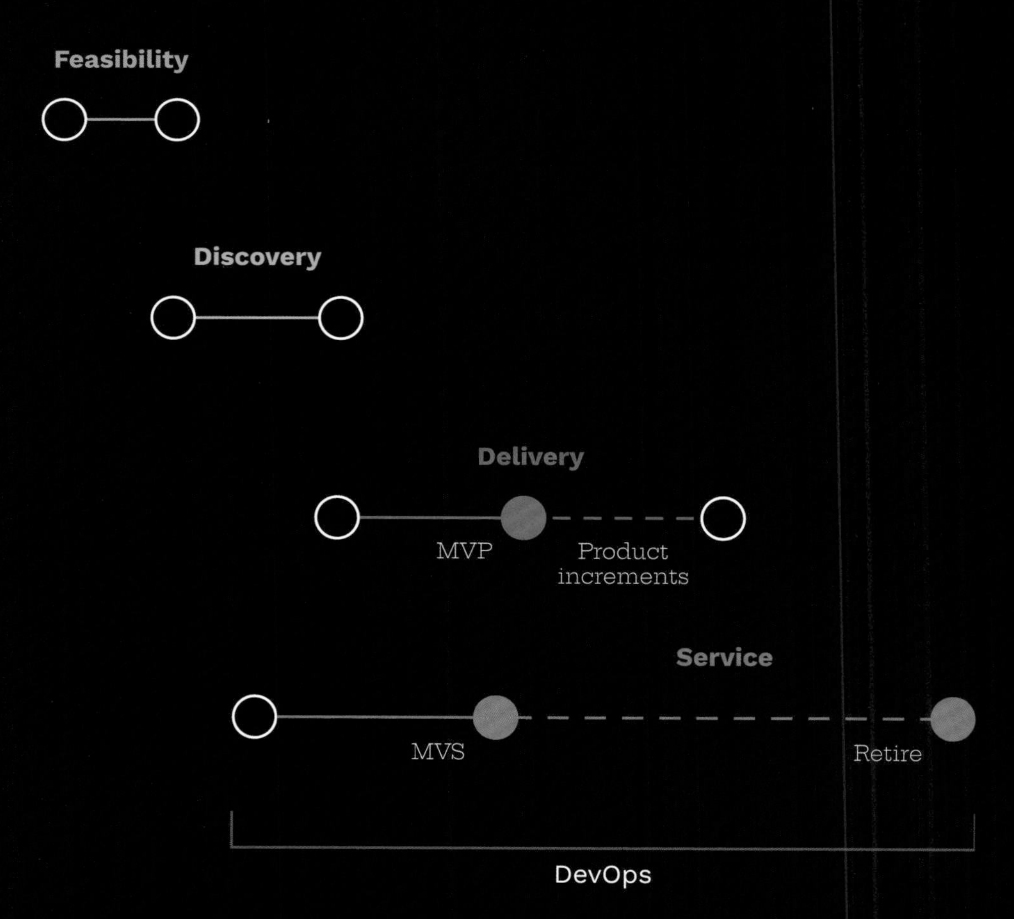

As soon as the MFF is launched into production, a service is being provided or value cannot be earned. This has several implications for the delivery. Service must be considered upfront, with a 'Necessary and Sufficient' Service Wrap in place. The key point here is 'Necessary and Sufficient' – just as a Minimum Marketable Feature set implements a subset of the product backlog, a Minimum Viable Service (MVS) approach can implement an appropriate subset of the Service Wrap.

Thinking about the core concepts, expected usage, and ways of working for the MFF helps inform the MVS. In particular, do not underestimate the challenge of managing a team to provide a production-quality Managed Service in parallel with the delivery of the next wave of features from the product backlog.

Embracing automation as part of the delivery of the MFF, and considering this as part of the strategy and design of the Service Wrap from Discovery onwards, provides the right platform for Agility in the service. The concept of 'Release 2' becomes irrelevant when changes to the product – and associated service – can be delivered on a Sprint-by-Sprint basis.

We believe that, wherever possible, the teams that build an MFF should provide the MVS. Using a DevOps way of working completely removes the 'us and them' of traditional Build and Run Teams.

Anatomy of a Service Wrap

The Enterprise Agile Service Wrap is a structured approach to good industry practice, drawing on ITIL, with Agility at its core.

The Service Wrap provides the people, skills, processes, and tooling required to allow the MFF and subsequent Product Increments to earn business value.

A Service Wrap typically comprises several key capabilities: Platform, Application Support and Maintenance, and New Business Services. The mix will vary for each Service Wrap depending on the unique needs of the underlying Product.

A basic Service Wrap is illustrated in **Figure 9-6**.

Figure 9-6: Enterprise Agile Service Wrap

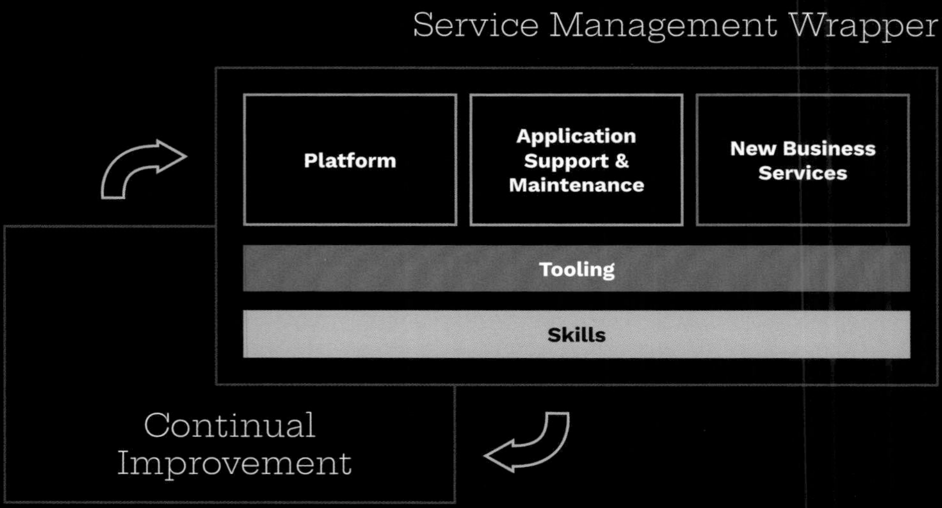

Service Management Wrapper

Platform

Application Support & Maintenance

New Business Services

Tooling

Skills

Continual Improvement

The Service Wrap is based on the following key elements:

- **Service Management Wrapper** - The fundamental processes that manage the service using an appropriate supporting toolchain, initially implementing the MVS and growing as required. The Managed Service Wrapper is based on a set of appropriate processes implemented by qualified Service Delivery Managers, Service Support and Process Analysts, and specialist teams
- **Platform** - The Service Wrap must manage the underlying infrastructure of the Product. This may be physical 'tin' on premises or in data centres, or Cloud-based infrastructure. Platform Engineering specialists will be required to deliver the Service Wrap. Platform-as-a-Service (PaaS), Software-as-a-Service (SaaS) and Infrastructure-as-a-Service (IaaS) components may all be relevant depending on the Product
- **Application Support and Maintenance** - By definition, an IT service is delivered by an existing application stack. Often the technology is dated, and technologists will lose interest when supporting it, leading to staff retention issues. This application will require support, together with any required changes and new product implementations. The Service Wrap should ensure that the Product can deliver value to the business. Incidents will arise, issues will be identified, and improvements will be required, all of which may impact the value earned. Incident and problem management processes are required, supported by resources to resolve any application issues that arise. It's worth considering the backlog of technical debt alongside user-driven support and maintenance items. Constant tactical solutions and 'quick fixes' may introduce technical debt and erode quality if not managed carefully

- **New Business Services** - The Service Wrap isn't just about keeping the infrastructure and application lights on. Product delivery doesn't stop with the MFF. Each Product Increment will transform the service in some way, and this must be supported by an appropriate change management approach. Some change will modify existing services, whilst others will introduce Service Wraps of their own. This area is often where new technology is introduced, providing challenges for staff.

Each aspect of the Service Wrap has Continuous Improvement at its core. Regular Service Wrap retrospectives will help identify gaps and areas for improvement, creating new backlog items to enhance and improve the MVS.

There is much more to the Service Wrap than process and tooling alone. As with any Agile transformation, there is a Culture and Values dimension. Having the right people, with the right skills and the right mindset, is fundamental.

Establishing the Service Wrap

The Enterprise Agile method provides a repeatable pattern for delivery that can be specialised to help navigate the creation and implementation of the Service Wrap by treating it as a Product like any other.

The specialised pattern is defined in **Figure 9-7**.

Figure 9-7: MVS Delivery Pattern

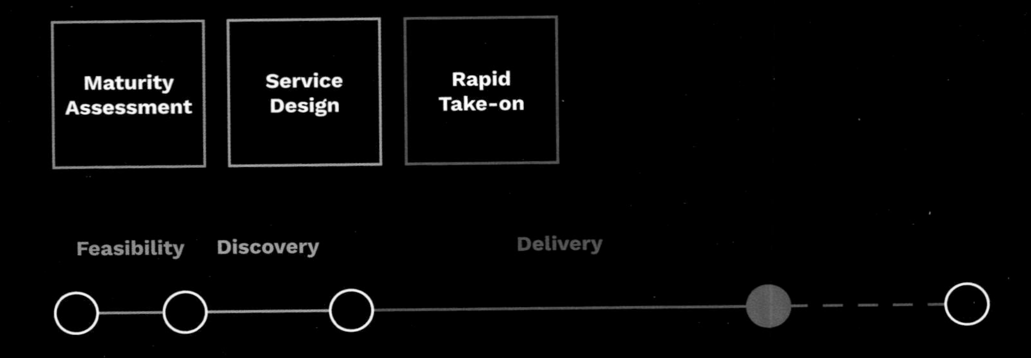

Each step should deliver value to the business:

Maturity Assessment

Take stock of the 'as-is' service. Undertake a 'state of the nation' review to understand what is currently in place, what works, what doesn't, and where the pain points are.

Service Design

Formulate a process backlog for the target service to address the gaps identified by the maturity assessment. Prioritise the backlog into an MVS view, identify any quick wins and establish a plan for delivering the MVS. Identify and address key Delivery risks and prioritise to achieve the 'No surprises endgame.'

Rapid Take-On

Implement the plan to deliver the MVS, including any knowledge transfer required and establishing any tooling. Refine the process backlog as you progress and capture lessons learned during the Delivery.

This is not an academic or box-ticking exercise. Each Service Wrap will have characteristics unique to the organisation. Identify the target Service Wrap, understand the appropriate MVS for the product and organisation, and then apply the pattern to implement it. Consider the Service Wrap from the outset of product delivery, and work toward the MVS in readiness for launching the MFF.

Don't try to 'boil the ocean'. Assess what is currently in place, understand the key areas of risk, and build a plan to address them with the MVS. Continue to review the service's product backlog and build Continuous Improvement into the way of working right from the start.

Key Points

1. The Service Wrap should not be a blocker to product development or speed of delivery but can be used as a control mechanism.

2. The Service Wrap should account for the ambitions of the organisation. If the perception is that it is a blocker, it should be re-evaluated and updated.

3. Don't try and boil the ocean. Assess what you have, identify the key risks and issues, and develop a plan to address them. Review frequently.

4. Continual Service Improvement should be embraced and embedded into the organisation's ways of working.

5. An effective Service Wrap isn't just about process. Ensure the right tools and skilled team members are in place to support it.

Chapter 10
The Journey to Agility

Following the first release of this book, we were often asked to talk to organisations about what Agile is, and what benefits it brings. More recently, we have been approached for advice on how to adopt it, or how to recover a failing adoption.

The key to success with Agile is understanding that it is not an end in itself, but rather it is a journey and a way of being. This may sound a little hippyish, but it is a key point - achieving greater organisational Agility can only come by adjusting thinking and embedding this into the culture.

In this chapter, we explore some of the lessons learned from working with organisations on their journey – what works, and what does not. It should be recognised that this is a long-term commitment and that benefits will not be realised overnight.

We strongly believe in a heavy dose of pragmatism around Agility - try things, fail fast and do not slavishly follow new ways of working that are not right for your organisation.

Concepts

The Rise of the Commercial Agile Framework

Recent years have seen the emergence of several Agile frameworks, all describing an approach that supports the adoption of Agile at scale:

- **Large-Scale Scrum (LeSS)** – Scaling of the familiar Scrum approach to Agile, developed in 2005
- **The Scaled Agile Framework (SAFe)** – Developed in 2011

- **Disciplined Agile Delivery (DAD)** – From the 2012 book
- **The 'Spotify Model'** – A description of Spotify's operating model from October 2012 that is frequently misinterpreted as a template for an Agile organisation
- **Nexus** – Created in 2015 by Ken Schwaber, one of the co-creators of Scrum
- **Scrum at Scale** – Developed by Jeff Sutherland (co-creator of Scrum) in collaboration with Alex Brown.

These frameworks have been influenced by experiences of delivering Agile within large organisations. They share common influences (Lean, Product Thinking, Scrum) and include some good practices and ideas.

Large scale organisations, envious of the pace of change that smaller start-up rivals achieve, often see the adoption of a commercial large scale Agile framework as a shortcut to increased Agility. These frameworks offer the comforting option to 'buy in' accreditation, a shared language for a big corporate, and what appears to be a process-driven approach to implementation and delivery. In this chapter, we explore the risks associated with the notion that one can implement 'Agile in a box'.

Change Management

Anyone who has been involved in a significant business change initiative will recognise the difficulties in making process and cultural changes.

Embracing Agile within an organisation is no different:

- **People are naturally resistant to having change imposed upon them** - Initiatives introduced without buy-in from the people who are engaged in the change are far less likely to be successful

- **The effects of change can't be predicted** - What works in one organisation is a poor indicator of what will work in another, which will be an entirely different collection of individuals, processes and environments.

Delivering change on the scale of Agile adoption requires a groundswell of support spanning the organisation at all levels, from the senior leadership outwards.

BJSS Opinion

Holistic Adoption

To be successful, Agile adoption must be holistic. It cannot be considered only as a feature of the system development lifecycle (SDLC) in the IT department. While a partial transition can add value, making Agile delivery work well impacts all aspects of the organisation.

Where this holistic approach is not taken, we have seen many anti-patterns, including 'Developer-only' Agile, where Waterfall requirements are 'delivered' using development Sprints, or Sprint-based release candidates only being released on a twice-yearly basis, reducing the benefits delivered in a holistic adoption.

One Size Does Not Fit All

Agile is not an end in itself, and not a desirable state of being in its own right. Agile practices, as we've seen, are helpful in accelerating innovation, reducing risk and improving delivery success. However, these outcomes can be achieved with a variety of very different practices, which all sit under the umbrella of Agile values and the principles described in the Agile Manifesto.

In practice, we have seen that aspiring to adopt a particular, fixed form of Agile is significantly more likely to fail when the characteristics of the organisation are not taken into account. Organisations should guard against engaging professional Agile coaches who attempt to impose a particular Agile variant that is not appropriate for the situation.

Large scale adoptions of commercial, off-the-shelf frameworks (LeSS, SAFE, DAD etc.) often fall foul of this approach. They attempt to proceduralise Agile practices into a universally applicable approach that doesn't recognise the cultural and structural complexities of real organisations.

Agile Transformational Models

We have seen several patterns in organisations attempting to foster Agile working practices:

'Big Bang'

The whole organisation makes a single, coordinated 'step change' to Agile – typically using a commercial framework as a base. As a result, the organisation will often be forced to be prescriptive in the application of Agile, effectively swapping one process-driven framework for another, and failing to embrace real Agility.

The Incubation Model

An extreme approach, in which a new, independent department is spun up, typically in a new creative environment, unconstrained by many of the 'old rules'. This approach engenders resentment and conflict from the 'old world', followed quickly by significant attrition.

Changing Key Positions

In this model, senior personnel are replaced, typically by external hires or consultants who bring in new ways of working. Cultural resistance from the 'old guard' is the predictable consequence.

We advocate a more adaptive, incremental approach to Agile transition:

- **Start small, deliver early and embrace a tight feedback loop**
- **Track progress and publicise success**
- **Fail fast and adapt less successful efforts**
- **Identify and specifically target any organisational blockers**
- **Encourage and guide rather than control and define.**

We explore these ideas further later in this chapter.

Example Barriers to Agility

Table 10-1: Barriers to Agility

Barrier	Approach	Benefit
Insufficient insight and information into user needs	Fast feedback from frequent release cycles and community input from social media	Increased flexibility to meet customer needs
Lack of understanding of Agile methods and principles across the organisation	Foster a learning organisation that encourages education and supports new working practices: **Read this book!**	Improved culture of delivery and customer focus. Teams bound by common goals, enhanced employee engagement
Resistance to change and attachment to existing organisational boundaries	Greater autonomy and empowerment for Agile Teams and individuals	Opportunity for greater visibility of the value of employee contribution
Existing supplier contracts and incentives not aligned to broader goals	Agile contracting based on outcomes and organisational goals	Suppliers can contribute more directly to the value delivered
Imperative to maximise existing investments in physical technology	Flexible on-demand infrastructure provisioning using Cloud technology	More flexible commercial models and reduced capital investment
Procurement and compliance processes limiting flexibility to introducing technology	Open Source technologies that can be downloaded and used immediately	Lower procurement and technology costs and teams are able to start delivering sooner

Table 10-1 continued: Barriers to Agility

Barrier	Approach	Benefit
Risk-averse culture and high overhead for technology releases and business change	Smaller, more frequent releases of changes that are inherently less risky	Greater flexibility to respond to evolving market needs
Funding and governance geared to big decisions vs several smaller ones	Value-based decisions made more often for smaller amounts by empowered teams	Ability to 'fail fast' and learn with minimal investment

A Culture of Innovation and Continuous Improvement

Teams will only embark on the transition to a more Agile mindset if the culture and values of the organisation support it.

Rather than coming from the top of the organisation, innovation frequently occurs in teams empowered to improve the way they work with the space to innovate and the freedom to make occasional mistakes.

This also means being Agile with organisational structures. Often, a team starting to adopt Agile processes highlights the problem that supporting or dependent teams are not Agile, hindering the delivery process.

Finally, it is important to recognise that the working environment plays a key part in working culture. Teams need space to collaborate, create and step out of their normal ways of working.

This doesn't mean you need table football and bean bags, but you should consider changing the focus from 'sit down' meeting rooms to Stand-up areas, providing whiteboards and collaborative team spaces.

Use Appropriate Funding and Commercial Models

Funding cycles can have a major impact on the ability of the organisation to deliver value.

An Agile IT and business function steered by a Waterfall governance cycle becomes an iterative rather than truly Agile organisation. The delivery organisation iterates towards an unchanging goal, and the true benefits of Agile are lost.

To gain the benefits of true Agility, organisations must adopt smaller, Leaner funding cycles, with initiative objectives set more as outcomes rather than presupposing fixed deliverables, months or even years ahead of time.

Funding and procurement strategies will also have an impact on the behaviour of suppliers. People generally want to do the right thing as an employee. The same is true of most suppliers. In our experience, whilst suppliers want to make a profit, they also care about repeat business, their brand reputation and the long-term relationship.

An organisation will likely want to ensure it gets good value from its suppliers. Various mechanisms exist to incentivise suppliers to deliver and behave in the right way. The substantive point is that incentives are used to drive behaviours - make sure you pick the right incentives such that they align with your organisation's goals. We have seen examples where this has gone awry. In one situation, a software partner was measured by the number of lines of code it delivered!

The Enterprise Agile Approach

Adopting Agility within the Organisation

Greater Agility is not achieved solely through training courses and implementing a new target operating model. Some organisations attempt a 'sheep dip' conversion process only for their people to arrive back in the office following the training course wondering where to begin. A 'big-bang' transformation of the entire organisation is unlikely to be successful.

The only time we advocate starting with a fully Agile model in mind is a greenfield scenario, for example, when bringing a previously outsourced service in-house, or launching a brand-new product. For most organisations, a fundamental cultural shift is required, which is typically only achieved through a concerted effort and with commitment from motivated, sponsored and engaged people.

We recommend taking an Agile approach to becoming more Agile:

1. **Plan the Agile journey in the same way as we have described for product delivery**
2. **Outline a set of goals for the organisation, develop a roadmap and then progressively move towards achieving these goals incrementally using a Sprint pattern**
3. **Measure success against outcomes, be realistic about where you have failed and adapt accordingly.** View failure as a useful output of the process and react to it positively
4. **Be mindful of toolset and terminology, but don't obsess over them.** Project collaboration toolsets, continuous delivery infrastructure and communication channels are helpful, but in themselves do not make the organisation Agile.

A suggested journey to Agility may look something like that shown in **Figure 10-1**.

Figure 10-1: Suggested Journey to Agility

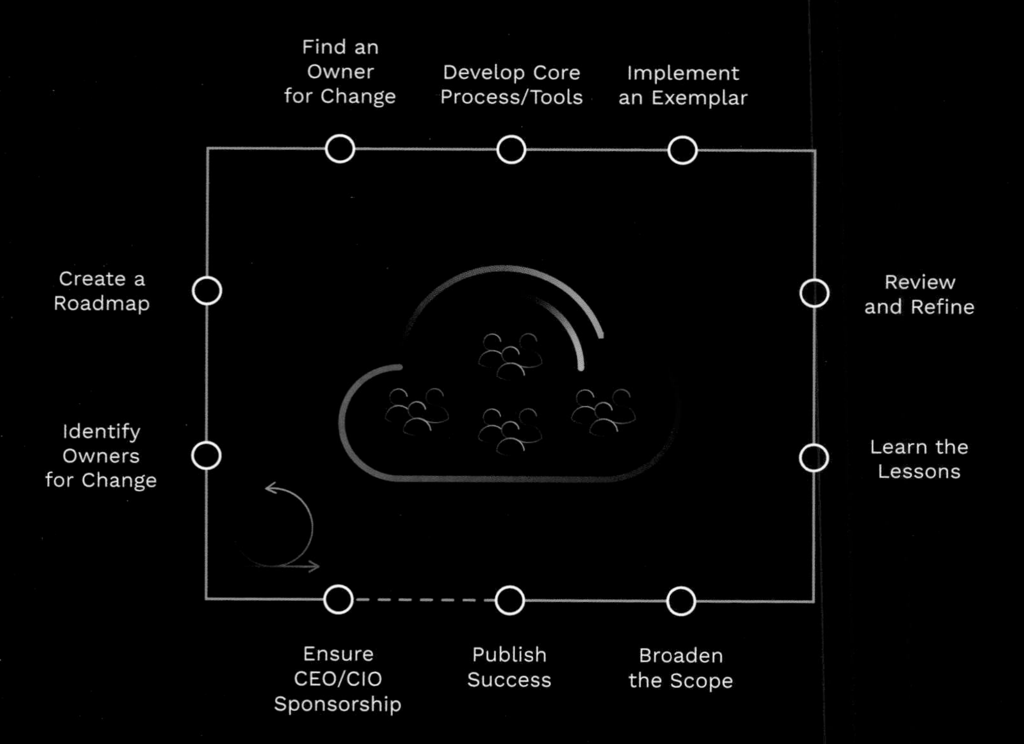

- **Ensure you have sufficient sponsorship to be successful – often the CEO or CDO**
- **Identify drivers for change and articulate them as organisational goals**
- **Create a roadmap for key initiatives and desired value**
- **Find an owner to lead the change and ambassadors to support them**
- **Develop the core processes and tools to support the transition**
- **Implement across a small number of exemplar products**
- **Constantly review and refine the approach using feedback for each increment**
- **Adjust the roadmap based on lessons learned from early adopters**
- **Broaden the scope to further products across the organisation**
- **Encourage knowledge sharing between teams and publish successes.**

In summary, there isn't a 'project' to become Agile. Identify goals, produce a roadmap and provide support to teams to help them achieve those goals. The journey to Agile requires ongoing support, not just formal training - identify individuals able to coach teams and help them to develop their skills.

Monitor Maturity

Useful tools to identify the progress being made on the Agile journey are those that track change or progress over time. We've seen some success through the use of carefully worded surveys, which are sufficiently lightweight to be repeated at regular intervals.

A more detailed approach involves the use of Maturity Models. These can be used to give a measurable demonstration of progress but must be carefully designed around 'outcomes' rather than to test conformity to a set of expected practices.

For example, the team should be assessed against a holistic measure of whether or not they achieved an objective, rather than simply if they implemented the required Scrum processes. Agile is a mechanism to help the team define, manage and work towards those objectives.

From a process perspective, there is value in assessing against the expectations you define whilst running Scrum - e.g., does the team regularly define proper objectives for a Sprint and meet them? This is an indication of their capability maturity and will help direct further support.

The key difference is that the team should be judged on whether they met their objectives. Any measurement of how they met their objectives is purely for assisting in their development and not for judgement.

When assessing an organisation against a Maturity Model, expect different Product Teams to be at different levels of maturity. Each team and product is different and their rate of progression will differ, often due to real-world constraints. A Maturity Model can help highlight which teams need additional coaching or support. Re-running the Maturity Model as a lightweight health check can demonstrate progress towards the company objectives.

The Maturity Model should also include the capabilities of the organisation. For example, a successful Agile Product Team will have a bias towards some skillsets over others compared with traditional delivery - for example, automation testers over manual, 'infrastructure as code' DevOps engineers over traditional infrastructure engineers.

Keep the model simple and supportive. Detailed audits are likely to create concern and are not necessary for an ability-led organisation where experienced Agile leaders work with Product Teams.

A typical Agile Maturity Model might include:

- **A series of assessments aligned to the different aspects of Agile product delivery (define, develop, assure, deploy, operate)**
- **A basic rating mechanism that identifies maturity against each category**
- **A method of positioning the different aspects of the team's work on a maturity scale**
- **A set of prioritised recommendations to take the team to the next stage of maturity.**

An example of a maturity assessment for a Technical Delivery Team is illustrated in **Figure 10-2**.

Figure 10-2: Example Maturity Assessment

Define	Develop	Deploy	Assure	Operate
Requirements Management	Source Control and Versioning	Server Provisioning	Peer Code Review	Configuration Management
Agile Planning and Task Management	Continuous Integration	Build Artefact Repository	Functional Test Automation	Metrics and Log Consolidation
Release Management	IDE Code Quality	Self Service Deployment	Non-Functional Test Automation	Monitoring and Alerting
Wiki / Project Pages	Central Code Quality	Deployment Testing	Defect Management	IT Service Management

Developing Maturing Completed

Foster Supplier Collaboration

A key aspect of achieving more rapid change and Agility is to ensure that all barriers are removed. No operational silos should exist and all contributing parties should be aligned with the same goal.

This is often why the organisations spearheading Agility are technology start-ups. They are not constrained by legacy systems and processes and have the brand (and finances) to attract and retain the skilled resources they need.

Most organisations do not retain all of the skills they need in-house and augment their numbers and capability by engaging external suppliers. Getting this relationship right requires effort. Long-term partnerships undoubtedly achieve more than a revolving door of different suppliers. The closer you get to making suppliers an extension of your organisation and motivated around common goals, the more likely you are to achieve results. This suggests a more collaborative approach than traditional procurement-driven relationships.

Funding for Success

Many factors play into the funding arrangements – either for internal teams, or external delivery partners. The organisation will naturally seek to incentivise all teams around its goals, but such outcome-based arrangements can be hard to broker.

Four elements require measurement and control:

- **Delivery** – Have the required outputs been produced?
- **Quality** – Are the outputs delivered to the required standard?
- **Collaboration** – Has the team worked collaboratively with other parts of the organisation?

- **Cost** – Have all objectives been met cost-effectively?

When working with external suppliers, the client organisation needs everyone to cooperate to deliver services to the appropriate quality standard. Several models can be used to drive the required behaviours and achieve the results. These exist on a spectrum from Time and Materials to Fixed Price.

All models have pros and cons, as outlined in **Table 10-2**.

Table 10-2: Commercial Models

Model	Characteristics	Advantages	Disadvantages
Time and Materials	o Supplier invoices for all work delivered	o Simple to administer	o Supplier not incentivised to deliver to budget
Target Pricing	o Both parties agree a price o Overrun charged at a reduced rate	o An element of risk transfer to the supplier o Outcome focus	o Requires both parties to agree a price upfront
Iterative Delivery	o Payments are based around incremental delivery	o Flexibility to fit Agile delivery o Penalty/bonus agreed Sprint by Sprint	o Assumes all parts make the whole o Risks focusing on iteration incentive vs final outcome

Continued overleaf

Table 10-2 continued: Commercial Models

Model	Characteristics	Advantages	Disadvantages
Service Levels	o Fee including bonus or penalties based on performance against SLA	o Requires a service that can be defined and measured	o Can miss broader organisation goals and outcomes
Productivity Based	o Supplier is rewarded based on items produced	o Assumes a price can be set for a unit of delivery	o No universally recognised sizing unit that is easy to implement
Fixed Price	o Both parties agree a firm price for the deliverables	o Notionally transfers risk from client to supplier	o Risk premium o Requires clear upfront scope definition o Change control challenges

No model is perfect for both parties. In our view, the best outcome is achieved when penalties and incentives are fair, balanced and based on straightforward performance measures.

Ideally, client and supplier will consider supplier contribution as an ongoing activity without constant reference to a contract. The more the vendor and supplier trust each other, the more value each will get from the relationship.

Key Points

1. Adopting Agile is not just about changing your SDLC, it often requires a holistic cultural shift within the organisation.

2. Avoid trying to move the whole organisation in one go. Focus on successes in smaller areas and build on these.

3. Be wary of 'Agile in a box' approaches and avoid obsessing about Agile as an end in itself.

4. Recognise that a lightweight audit process and Maturity Model can be invaluable to assess where you can improve the effectiveness of your ways of working and measuring progress.

5. When contracting suppliers, be sure to align any incentives and penalties with organisational and product delivery goals.

Chapter 11
Enterprise Data

Previous iterations of this book have focused on the application of Enterprise Agile to the delivery of software projects. In this new chapter, we look at how to apply some of the principles and values of Enterprise Agile to the delivery of data projects – a rapidly increasing proportion of the work we undertake with clients.

Agile is a word not commonly associated with the pace at which data projects move. They are well known for delivering slowly, being heavily IT-driven and lacking necessary levels of interaction with the rest of the business. Despite the way software delivery has progressed, it is only very recently that we are seeing the market start to adopt a more Agile culture and approach to data deliveries. There has been, and still is in many cases, a lack of value-driven thinking and results. It's reductive to assume that data itself is what brings value. Instead, it's how we use the data.

Data is a load bearing pillar of digital transformation, providing the information on which to make quick and effective business decisions, the foundations for automation and AI. It is critical that organisations are able to move quickly, responding to a fast-changing world and customer base. Unfortunately, technologies that underpin the delivery of value in data-driven projects have, until recently, reinforced 'big bang' IT delivery. Fortunately, those underpinning technologies are changing, as are approaches to data delivery - DataOps and MLOps are growing in their adoption.

This chapter details our recommended value-oriented approach to delivering results with data: nail it, then scale it. We suggest how you can implement a DataOps culture to deliver the technology that supports these results. By using these approaches, you can deliver the data you need, when you need it, in the way that you need – and then exploit it as you need it.

Concepts

Data Lake, Data Lakehouse, Data Mesh, Data Fabric

Some of the most popular and talked about architectural patterns for large scale and varied data today are architectures designed and evolved within the era of 'big data'.

The **data lake** was an early big data paradigm, a place to store data of many different types, allowing for the exploitation of unstructured, semi-structured and structured data, at scale, in a distributed manner. This architecture and the software that enabled it were a step change in capability and the foundation of today's data platforms. At the same time, the key technology was one of the primary reasons that projects saw such huge failure rates (one Gartner analyst claimed in 2017 that 85% of big data projects failed). While it may have started a data revolution, the technology was difficult to use effectively, with several cons that were often ignored or papered over in the rush to be big data driven.

Data technology and architecture has evolved quickly since then, as has our collective experience. As part of this evolution, and to resolve some of the downsides of the data lake paradigm, the data lake has developed into the **data lakehouse**, a combination of data lake and data warehouse. With many organisations feeding a downstream data warehouse with data in their lake, the lakehouse merges these popular yet quite different data architectures into one. The result is designed to maintain many of the benefits of each while avoiding some of the painful downsides experienced in separation. It aims to bridge the structured and curated natured of a warehouse with the less structured nature of a lake. This results in accelerated availability of data through a reduction in the data engineering required, as well as data that can be optimised on the fly for uses such as query, visualisation and analytics.

More recent still is the **data mesh** paradigm, mirroring a question experienced throughout IT - centralisation vs decentralisation. Where modern data architectures have attempted to centralise data, reducing silos through ingestion and management of data in a single enterprise data platform, data mesh looks to decentralise data ownership and management, with distributed data domains managed like data "products" with common self-serve components of data infrastructure provided as-a-platform to those managing domain datasets. This product-based approach to data is growing in popularity, and roles like Data Product Manager are starting to reach the mainstream.

Finally, the **data fabric**, one of Gartner's Top Strategic Technology trends for 2022. Whereas the other concepts covered in this section are architectures, data fabric is more conceptual. The "fabric" is a layer of data and information of all different forms (video, audio, text, structured tables, graphs, etc.), often using multiple technologies and architectural patterns for storage, processing and retrieval (e.g., a graph database, a search index, a data lake, and a relational database). Automation and machine learning are a part of the fabric itself – for example, extraction of structured entities and features from free text into a knowledge graph, or extraction of information from image and videos. This is clearly a very powerful concept; however, in our opinion, knowledge graphs would be a big step for many organisations currently struggling to develop approaches to basic data management.

Data Science

There is a lot of misinterpretation around data science; many assume it includes business intelligence (BI) or the descriptive analysis of data that analysts have been doing for many years.

Data science is a different discipline. It applies scientific methods and tools to extract knowledge from data. It focuses primarily on the upper end of the analytics spectrum – predictive or prescriptive analytics via machine learning – to predict what will happen and what action can be taken to make something happen.

Simply put, if data analytics seeks to understand data, data science seeks to make predictions with it.

Data scientists need to have skills in engineering, statistical modelling and business analysis – a hard combination to find. Therefore, the increased demand for data science and machine learning is rarely complemented by an increased understanding of data science and analytics. As a result, Data Science Teams are often formed without an appropriate level of business analysis, feasibility or design.

Many businesses struggle to set measurable goals for data science or machine learning initiatives. To overcome this, business functions and Data Science Teams must collaborate to meet customer requirements and create a supported and maintainable solution.

Due to the nature of the field, it's not unusual for data science to end up as a constant cycle of experiments. But data science should be so much more than experimental. Businesses need to get beyond this cycle and start generating real value from data science across the enterprise. We'll explore how to achieve this by conducting Agile data science in an enterprise context.

DataOps and MLOps

As mentioned, Agile is often not associated with data projects. The same could also be said about engineering and operational rigour.

DevOps has become the default mode for software delivery. A similar approach can be applied to data and machine learning. DataOps and MLOps are the data and machine learning versions of DevOps and they apply to the entire data and machine learning lifecycle.

The operation of data platforms has always been difficult, making the collaboration between business owners, data and operations professionals a necessity. Principles like repeatability, automation, metrics and monitoring, and the cultural approach to data delivery are all part of this. We will explore this in more detail later in the chapter.

Figure 11-1: The Data Lifecycle

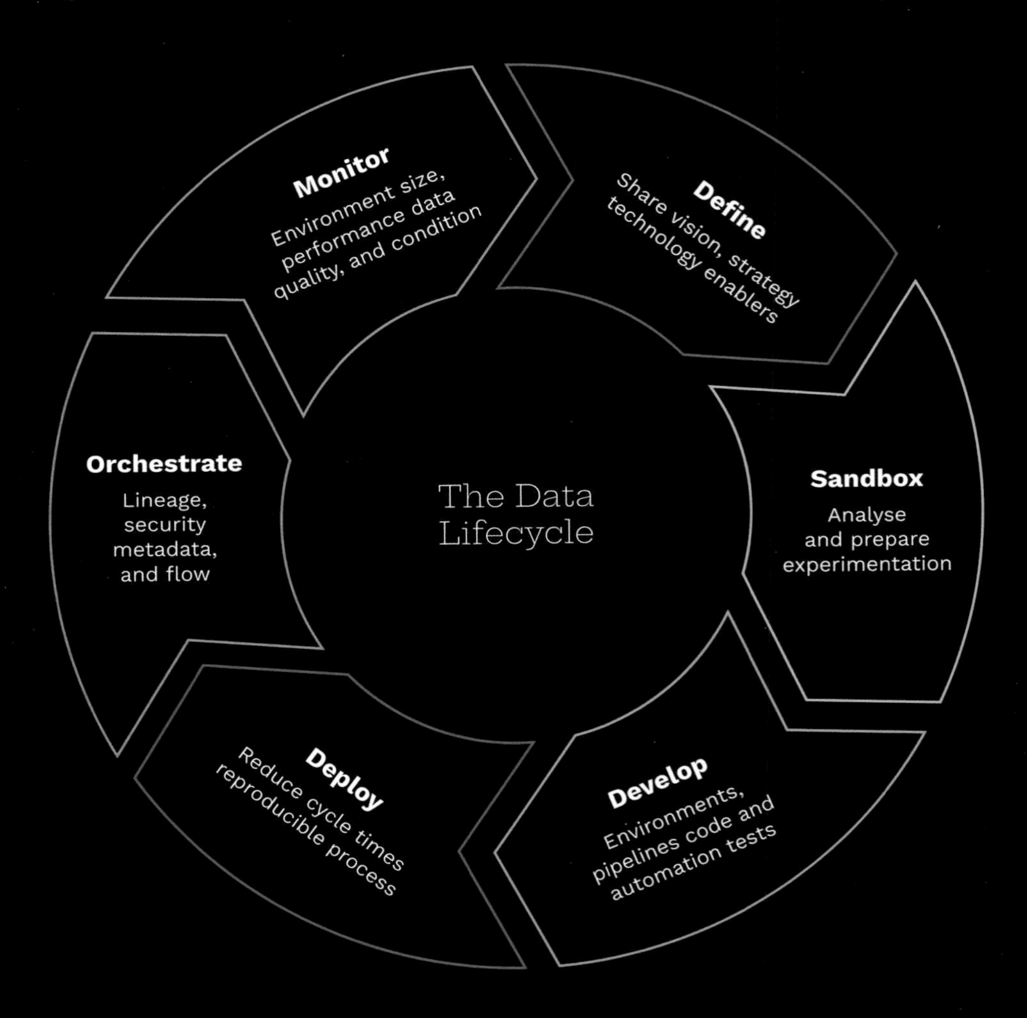

BJSS Opinion

Is Agile Data Difficult?

It's getting easier, but in our experience many organisations have found effective Agile delivery of data and data platforms to be challenging. Like software development, there are many benefits of taking an Agile approach to data, so it's worth facing up to the challenge.

Big data was a paradigm shift, one driven by the availability of technology that promised huge advances. Unfortunately, this technology brought a whole new level of complexity with a giant learning curve. Paired with a skills gulf in the talent market, people working on these projects simply learned as they went along. Naturally, this resulted in many missteps and a lot of bad practice was learned (and repeated) with the good.

And this is just one reason why Agile data has been difficult. What does a good data platform backlog look like? How do I test data? What comprises MVP for a data platform? How can I model the data incrementally? How do I accommodate a changing data model? Who are the users? What does the right team balance look like? What about Agile data governance? We could fill many pages with important questions for which the answers were unknown. And even once you've got the technology working effectively and in production, there's the data itself to consider. The platform is of no value until the data is in it and made available to people to use.

Even today, there isn't a lot of guidance on what Agile looks like in the context of data, and delivering Agile data is still challenging for most. For this reason, enterprise data programmes often still end up lacking effective formal software project management or revert to Waterfall instead. Trying to do Agile on something you know little about simply results in a Cowboy delivery approach.

Of course, development is not where data ends. It needs a great deal of operational care - the understanding of which you should not leave to the end or to an Operations Team alone. Operation of a data platform and the data within requires a different set of skills and roles to other software deliveries, as well as strong technical knowledge of the tools and capabilities that comprise a modern data platform.

We introduced the concept of DataOps earlier – DevOps for data. In our opinion, the principles of Agile and DevOps can be applied successfully to data, hence this new chapter. It does, however, require a level of expertise and experience that many organisations may still not have access to today, and a skills gap remains.

Centralisation vs Decentralisation

An important set of questions that appear throughout the implementation of IT, and no less in data, are: Should I centralise or decentralise? Is there a balance to be struck? Where is it? The big data movement came with the promise of the data lake, a central location for all your analytical data and the answer to those fragmented data silos many enterprises experienced. However, silos are hard to wrestle away from their owners, especially when the new promised land is outside of their control. Many have learned this on their journey.

In the concepts section of this chapter, we briefly introduced the data mesh paradigm, one which favours decentralisation over the centralised approach in the ascendancy today. In the last year or two, data mesh has received some interest, though adoption is currently low and there are few referenceable examples of enterprise adoption. With many organisations feeling the pain of implementing data programmes and the often-quoted stats for data project failure rates (although many of these are outdated now), an alternative approach is appealing. However, we find it hard to recommend the adoption of data mesh at time of writing. With limited real-world examples and a lack of best practice advice, we feel that a watching brief is the best recommendation. Instead of looking at wholesale paradigm shifts, organisations should focus on decentralising their approach to data exploitation while maintaining centralised enterprise data platforms.

While maintaining a central data platform as a shared business service is recommended, relying only on a central team to derive intelligence from data is not. Teams across the enterprise must be able to build and deploy their own machine learning, build their own dashboards, fuse their own data sources, and interpret their own data. A single Analytics Team is not Agile when scaling across an enterprise organisation; instead, it introduces a major bottleneck.

To enable Agile data-driven business at scale, exploitation of data should be decentralised through self-service capabilities in combination with fusion teams. These teams should have the skills necessary to take advantage of data quickly and effectively, as well as the understanding of the business problems faced. To ensure these teams don't eschew standards, security, privacy and all the other good things, they should be supported with patterns, good practice and time from experts – often through a Centre of Excellence or Hub in a Hub-and-Spoke organisational model.

The Enterprise Agile Approach

Align IT and the Business

One of the key issues in the delivery of IT has always been its alignment with the wider business. The same is true for data, yet its alignment is even further behind that of software delivery. As a result, we're starting to see patterns emerge where data programmes are treated like software programmes.

This misalignment used to be, at least in part, due to the complexity of the technology and a lack of skills. IT departments didn't want the business seeing or being involved in projects because they were scared they'd be found out. This led to more failure because, even if the technology worked, it was invariably late and not designed for users, so the business didn't want to use it.

This led to shadow IT, people working around data lakes, more data silos and a lot of wasted investment. Today, the profession has become better at aligning IT with the business and its users but we still see many enterprises getting it wrong.

Focusing on Value

Organisations invest time and attention in data because they want to generate value from it. The great potential benefit to the organisation often prompts teams to embark on large, slow initiatives aimed at producing perfect results. It's not unusual to see data platform deliveries go over a year without ever being made available to a user. This is a dangerous and unnecessary approach. You won't know how users will react to what you are building or learn from how they use it.

You also restrict your ability to generate immediate value in the business and force users to find alternative routes to their goals.

This is not to say that teams should abandon their professional standards and resort to quick and dirty solutions. Quicker and more frequent delivery can be balanced with data management rigour and effective, user-relevant data modelling. Access to data can be provided with incremental management, similar to incremental development of system features, thereby enabling the onboarding of users as early as possible.

There is often a tendency to delay or even block delivery of data science use cases until all the data has been fully managed into a data platform. In some use cases, this is a valid approach; for example, those which are sensitive to privacy concerns or require data sources with particularly poor quality. But there are often a wide range of use cases that can progress successfully and return great value and learning to your business without waiting for completion of the platform.

We believe you can and should support the undertaking of analytical projects outside of an in-development platform or managed data initiative where timelines and backlogs will not effectively align. This is especially important in the early stages of your data journey. The idea that you need to spend many months getting data into a fit state before you can reap the rewards of data science is a fallacy. Additionally, the discovered needs of your analysts and data scientists will help to inform the development of your data platform.

Focusing on delivering value in this way leads to a parallel approach to data management, data platform and data exploitation. Our experiences with this approach lead to a further recommendation: we suggest that enterprise-wide data science platforms are only put in place once several data science projects have been successfully implemented into production. This allows time to learn how the Data Science Team works best, what tools and technologies they see success with, and how you can best support them with platform components that improve their effectiveness. We call this approach **nail it, then scale it**.

Thinking Holistically

A successful data programme considers data holistically. The scope encompasses considering a technology platform for managing the data, the processes for managing and governing the data, information and cyber security, data valuation and condition, analytics, BI and visualisation. Critically, it also includes how you exploit the data to support your business strategy.

Unsuccessful data programmes can fail on any or all of these factors. Widely discussed reasons for failure include complicated technology, unrealistic expectations, lack of communication between IT and business, and skills gaps. We would also add operational complexity to this list.

With this in mind, we believe that it is key to success that data is delivered as a service to the business. It's not simply an IT project, which is how many data programmes are approached today. Rather, it's the combination of all these things wrapped in a set of services that are offered to those that use or interact with data within a business.

We call this data as a business service and have introduced service design into our data deliveries to help organisations implement data effectively. When you look at data through the lens of providing a service to the business, you can start to ask:

- **What questions are people in the business trying to answer? And why?**
- **What kind, quality, volume and frequency of data might people need to help them answer these questions?**

- **How will people turn data into information – that is, what context do they need around the data and how will this be provided and understood?**
- **How will people turn this information into action? How will it improve outcomes and impact?**

The key word in each of these questions is 'people'. If you're in the position of starting a data project from scratch, don't start with the technology, start with – and speak to – people. Ask questions, frame the problems you're trying to solve and capture user needs before exploring how to solve them.

Assuming a data platform is part of your solution, it's equally important to keep a human-centred, service-oriented lens on how you design, build, launch and operate it. This means you can ask questions such as:

- **How will people get data into the platform?**
- **How will people discover, access and use data in the platform?**
- **What kind of support will people need?**
- **How will the existence and value of the platform be communicated to people?**
- **Who will run and maintain the platform, and how?**

A tool we use to help answer these questions is the service blueprint. This captures the end-to-end user journeys of people interacting with the platform, expresses their user needs at each significant step, and maps out holistically what should be in place to meet those needs from the perspectives of people, technology, process, policy and partnerships.

When used as part of an Agile delivery, a service blueprint can act as a living document and focal point for keeping a human-centred perspective on what the team is building. It can evolve and flex as you continue to learn from users and the business, and help you respond to pivots along the way by highlighting gaps or new areas that might need to be addressed to ensure successful delivery.

Finally, when building a data platform, it can be tempting to try and boil the ocean, especially if you've done your user research and have identified lots of needs to cater to. We recommend a more measured approach. Aim to deliver value throughout, prioritise your backlog and consider your business objectives as well as the needs of your users. A helpful tool for this is a strategic roadmap. This allows you to plot out themed user needs, business goals and alignment with other initiatives so that you can plan your effort and budgets accordingly.

Delivering a Steel Thread

Many enterprise data programmes take a long time to start delivering value to the business, with a linear dependency between data platform delivery and exploitation of data for business value. This echoes the traditional, Waterfall approach to systems delivery which is being superseded by Agile approaches. However, just as functionality can be made redundant by changes in the environment, so data value is often dependent on timing. If value from data isn't delivered to the business when it can be exploited, opportunities are lost and the vision for data is tarnished. Interest in continued funding can quickly wane when return on investment is not forthcoming.

We have seen great success in delivering data programmes – including platform, data management, service design and data exploitation – through the adoption of steel threading. The steel thread is a software engineering concept that's popular in Agile development approaches. A system's main functionality is like a thread that runs through the system. Since all the other functionality is based on this thread, it needs to be very robust and reliable – as strong as steel. In the data programme context, we can define a steel thread of functionality, data, service and value running end-to-end, and deliver this into production first. Using this approach, you build some of the core aspects of the technology platform, onboard key initial data sources, deliver a use case which generates business value and thereby create a platform upon which to deliver further use cases iteratively, each time building out parts of another thread.

Agile principles are often not applied to the delivery of data platforms, aside from certain aspects of the Agile operating rhythm. We advocate taking more learnings from Agile and the wider field of software delivery into data delivery – the section on DataOps below goes into further detail on this.

Figure 11-2: Data Programme Steel Thread Approach

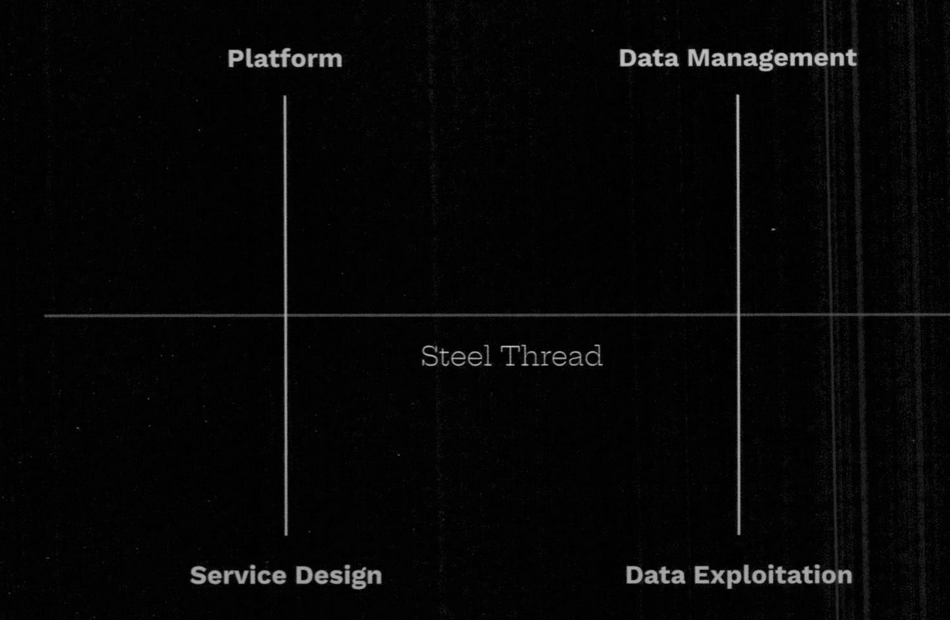

Technology in the big data space has been genuinely difficult for years. The invention of Hadoop was a turning point for data in the enterprise, but it was also a huge peak in complexity – one that many significantly underestimated.

Big data technologies can be hard to integrate, understand, deliver and operate. Implementing technology in this space has required specialist engineering skills and the skills gap has been significant. This has led to many organisations asking technical staff to learn as they go, adding uncertainty to the delivery timeline and risk to the initiative.

Figure 11-3: Hadoop Complexity

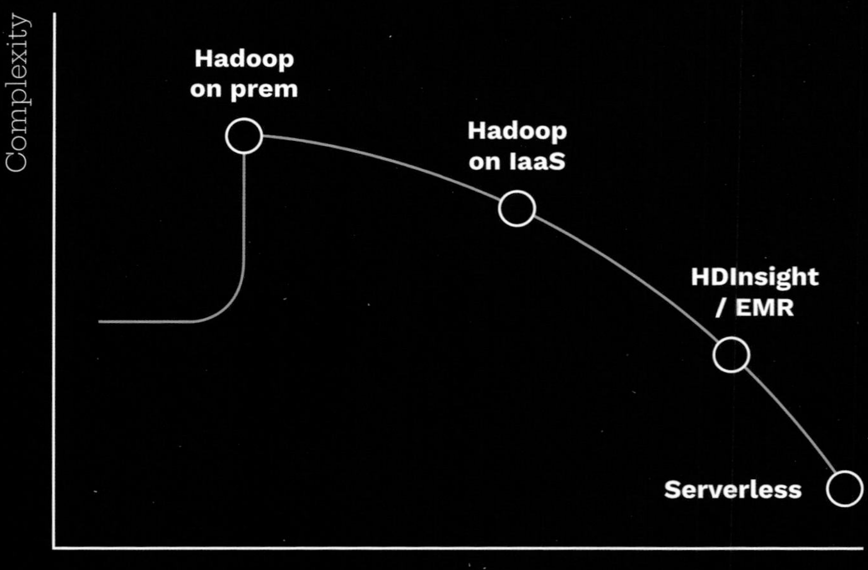

Ideally, organisations want to learn on small, low-risk projects. But in this case, much of the learning has been undertaken on expensive programmes and platforms that are potentially critical to business success. Clearly, this represents a huge risk and has had a large part to play in the failure of enterprise data strategy.

Recently, however, there has been a significant reduction in complexity through platform-as-a-service and serverless data services offered by the major public Cloud providers. These services are fully managed by the Cloud provider, with resources often dynamically managed and allocated, allowing the developer to focus on business logic and functionality over servers and infrastructure. This can make the technology part of the data equation significantly more straightforward.

The benefits of reduced complexity in data platforms cannot be stressed enough. While there is huge potential for value in an enterprise data platform, it is no use if you can't easily build upon it or operate it in production effectively – a trend we saw with on-premise Hadoop data lakes from vendors such as Cloudera and Hortonworks. While there are well-known tales of hugely successful big data solutions at organisations like Netflix and Uber, most enterprises do not have the engineering capability or investment needed to handle such highly complex software and data solutions. Nor, frankly, do they have requirements that demand such complexity.

There are trade-offs to be made in the use of serverless data capabilities. They often offer a reduced set of features or other compromises such as performance reductions in certain circumstances. Some organisations are wary of serverless data services because they don't support potential future requirements, one example being effective monitoring and workflow of data pipelines in AWS' serverless data services.

However, for the price, you'll get significantly reduced operational complexity, reduced engineering complexity, faster delivery times, and fewer bugs and operational issues. While decisions around technology and Cloud services should be made on a case-by-case basis with all considerations taken into account, we recommend weighting the benefits of serverless data services very heavily. We would also go so far as to recommend making any new data programme fully Cloud native by default.

Implementing a DataOps Culture

Automation

Automating data pipeline activity will increase velocity and repeatability, helping to overcome one of the common issues with data platforms: long lead times to onboard new data sources, resulting in unavailability of data when users need it. Patternised ingest with full automation, testing and monitoring will greatly simplify the task of ingestion. When implemented successfully, this can reduce data ingest from weeks or days to hours or minutes.

Automating testing, deployment and infrastructure will enable you to implement continuous integration and continuous delivery for your data platform. While this is similar to the approach taken in software development, there are some interesting quirks that can make this a challenge in data platforms – for example, automating testing and deployment of code contained in notebook form.

Security and Compliance

Data residing in data lakes and warehouses can be of high value to an attacker. We recommend that you implement security as early as possible in your SDLC and ensure your Data Engineering Team is well versed in common exploits and secure development approaches.

You should design the platform to be secure from the outset. Access issues are more easily overcome when defining the security model than when retrofitted to an existing model. Additionally, this allows your team to run effective, incremental threat modelling sessions, identifying security risk early and often. The outputs from this approach will aid implementation of appropriate security controls.

Finally, use Cloud native capabilities to ensure regulatory compliance. Develop blueprints, templates and compliance-as-code, which can transform one-time InfoSec sign-off into continually monitored, business-as-usual compliance. This provides an early warning system, saving you from potential data breaches.

Assurance

Availability of test data is paramount. Without enough high-quality test data, it is challenging to effectively test your pipelines, performance and analytics, increasing the risk of unexpected issues when switching to production workloads.

A testing strategy designed to work in production through isolation of data is an excellent investment. This will enable you to run high quality end-to-end testing with production data, significantly reducing the risk of unexpected outcomes in live operation.

Peer review, paired working and collaborative sessions including security and design should also be used to provide further quality assurance.

Operational Monitoring

Like DevOps, DataOps is as much about operating a data platform and data flows as it is about developing them. Identification of metrics required to operate the platform and KPIs required to operate the business will allow you to set up operational monitoring, logging and alerting early on. Information gained from trend analysis, combined with feedback from users, can form further backlog stories for improvements.

Data Science Enterprise Agility

We touched on conducting data science when we discussed MLOps, but data science doesn't have to be death by a thousand experiments. Doing lots of experiments isn't Agile. In fact, it's often wasteful. Extend your thinking beyond experimentation and look to how data science can make a sustainable difference to the business. Experimental phases should be regarded as preparatory to more widespread change. Some organisations ignore or forget their exploratory work when it is done and fund projects with little promise.

Business Teams sometimes invest in data science projects without considering the deployment and ongoing operational state of produced applications. This means that teams of Data Scientists create proofs of concept which need to be handed over to a traditional software operations environment which is unprepared to receive and operate them. A good way to avoid this divergence is to create hybrid Data Science Development Teams – although this will clearly require additional investment.

Machine learning originated as a research endeavour and the most experienced people in the field come from that world. But as the techniques of data science enter the mainstream, research culture needs to adapt to or blend with the business delivery environment. A practical way to do this is to balance research-led workloads with value-led ones. The two approaches have equal validity; it's not the case that blue-sky experiments must always take second place to projects considered more realistic in terms of current business goals. It can be hard to understand the potential use cases of something entirely new, such as graph databases. In such cases, well-designed experiments can suggest new paths for development or terminate unpromising paths before too much time or effort has been expended.

Effective data science models integrate with other software platforms and are therefore subject to enterprise governance and controls as other technologies evolve. It can be tempting to impose the same management formalities as you would on software delivery. But data science is characteristically distinct from traditional software delivery:

- **Activities are harder to predict and plan (because they are exploratory and research-driven)**
- **Instead of producing high-quality software with each iteration, the objective is to evaluate hypotheses as quickly as possible**
- **Early-stage data science focuses on the quality of the model rather than its code.**

Enterprise Agile data science prioritises early demonstration of working models alongside transparent and continuous sharing of results with the customer. Data Science Teams in an Enterprise Agile environment anticipate and address ambiguity and unknowns, using their close links with the intended beneficiaries to clarify and refine rather than generate multiple alternatives. They deliver models or model outputs frequently, breaking delivery down into iterations and running live demonstrations of each iteration with the sponsor for immediate detailed feedback. They hold regular planning sessions to determine approaches or enhancements. Weekly and even daily iterations are common.

The nature and speed of data science projects mean that formal written documentation is often inappropriate due to the rapid pace of change and the complexity of the underlying methods. It's therefore better to use face-to-face conversation as much as possible.

The problem spaces in data science are varied and the required business expertise is often to be found at the edge of the organisation rather than in the centre. For this reason, encourage co-operation between Subject Matter Experts (SMEs) and the Data Science Delivery Team.

Teams should direct their own work and feel responsible for the project and accountable for its success. Their attention should be trained on reaching a minimum viable algorithm rather than exploring every possible type of solution, catering for every variant of input or addressing every potential use case in the domain.

Plan the work so that it can be delivered at a predictable pace. Enterprise data science initiatives are likely to be accompanied by expectations about releasing value within a budget and are therefore subject to the same practical disciplines as other parts of the organisation. Work in iterations and plan on delivering work within allotted times so that delivery stays on track.

Although the primary aim in data science projects is to build great models rather than craft exemplary code, there's no doubt that good software engineering habits contribute to solutions that are more adaptable and usable as well as being more affordably integrated. Clean code with minimal dependencies improves the delivery of models intended to be iteratively enhanced. Data scientists from a purely experimental background may not have been exposed to professional software development practices. Helping them understand the benefits of clean code – to their own practice as well as to the organisation as a whole – will lead to greater productivity and satisfaction as well as better quality software.

Domesticating and professionalising data science in the enterprise setting ultimately means evolving a multi-disciplined capability that embraces analytical engineering, requirements definition, architecture and design work. The journey will include empirical retrospectives on the process and experience to date with adjustment of the team's methods to maximise efficiency and effectiveness.

Key Points

Align business and IT. Data is not an IT project or platform, it's a service that the business consumes to generate value.

Drive out business value early and often, and don't leave data science until after you've finished all the basics (they take a long time and there's lots you can do in the meantime).

Data is not just an asset to be managed, it underpins business-critical services. It has many users and stakeholders. It needs to be governed, protected, analysed and all the rest. Think about data holistically and design around it for the needs of the business.

Get to value quickly while still building strategically. Build out your data platform, management and exploitation through steel threads of value.

Choose your data technologies carefully – some can be cumbersome, complex and unsuitable for quick iteration without a lot of initial effort. Pick your technology well and use the Cloud.

Embed a DataOps culture (similar to DevOps) into your data delivery, from automation to operational monitoring of machine learning models.

Afterword

Enterprise Agile® is based on over 28 years' experience in delivering and supporting business-critical systems. We have helped many public and private sector clients adopt Enterprise Agile to improve the delivery of change initiatives within their organisations.

We hope you found the concepts and approach we presented in this book useful. If you would like to begin your journey towards greater Agility, you can find out more at **bjss.com/enterprise-agile**.

Get in Touch

BJSS **@BJSSLtd** **info@bjss.com**

Appendix A

Engineering Successful Change

We are often asked about the common pitfalls and lessons we have learned from running the hundreds of projects that we have undertaken over the last 28 years. In our experience the likelihood of enjoying a 'No surprises endgame' is dramatically improved by following these golden rules:

1. **Use a Product Lifecycle to define a pattern to de-risk delivery.** Use Feasibility, Discovery and Delivery phases to provide a 'ready, aim, fire' approach
2. **Implement structured and layered analysis to ensure that user needs always relate back to a business outcome**
3. **Account for all user needs and define non-functional requirements, including operational requirements during the Discovery phase**
4. **Employ routine Sprint events to plan, monitor, and control delivery.** Always use Planning, Stand-up, Show and Tell, and Retrospective sessions. Never delay or cancel them
5. **Only take stories into Sprints when they meet the Definition of Ready.** Stories are only counted as complete when they meet the Definition of Done
6. **Ensure Analysis, Development and Test are organised as cohesive activities working at the same rate towards common goals.** Never allow these activities to become separated or any one of them to fall behind or out of sync with the others
7. **Prove architecture early by using testing that can be automated and repeated continuously throughout delivery**

8. **Build a fully automated delivery pipeline during Sprint 0 that includes tooling for development and deployment.** If any part of the pipeline breaks, software production should stop until it is fixed. Never, for example, work around a failing build by ignoring tests

9. **Attend to data migration early and always test with migrated production data throughout delivery.** Only in cases where this is not possible due to security reasons, use synthetic or anonymised data which must still be production-like

10. **Create a transparent, 'visible to all', metrics dashboard that is fed automatically by the delivery pipeline tooling.** Ensure that progress and quality are measured.

Appendix B

Glossary

Agile

A software development approach involving the Discovery of requirements and development of solutions using collaborative, self-organising, and cross-functional teams which include end users.

AWS

Amazon Web Services. A provider of on-demand Cloud computing services.

Bimodal IT

A model for separating slow-changing systems of record from faster changing and more Agile systems of engagement.

Burn-down Chart

A graphical representation of work left to do versus time. Also known as a burn-up chart.

Capability

A logical grouping of individuals with the same role taken from several teams.

Cloud

Flexible compute, storage, and network capability that may be configured as software using defined APIs.

CMDB

Content Management Database. An inventory log of all the components parts of the underlying technology platform on which the product runs.

Cohort

A group of related users who undertake similar tasks using the product.

Community

A community is an interest group across a large Product Team or organisation, that looks at ways to share knowledge and improve ways of working in a particular technology or business domain.

Continuous Delivery

The process of technical automation for software build and deployment.

DA

Design Authority. Makes decisions on the functional and technical options for realising change.

DataOps

An automated, process-oriented methodology used to improve the quality and speed of data analytics.

Data Fabric

The concept of a layer of data and information of all different forms, using multiple technologies and architectural patterns for storage, processing, and retrieval.

Data Lake

A repository of data stored in a raw format.

Data Mesh

A decentralised approach to data ownership and management, in which distributed data domains are managed by dedicated teams as products.

Data Science

The use of scientific methods to extract knowledge and insights from structured and unstructured data.

Data Warehouse

A central repository of structured and integrated data sourced from one or more systems.

Delivery

A body responsible for ensuring that solution designs are fit for purpose and work within the enterprise architecture.

Delivery Manager

An individual who works as part of the product leadership function, and is responsible for the delivery of change and the service for the product.

Delivery Team

A group of individuals working towards a common goal and implementing change.

DevOps

The combination of software development and IT operations to shorten the system development lifecycle and provide continuous delivery with high software quality. Closely related to Agile software development.

Digital Transformation

A form of business strategy, management, operations, and culture that places digital technology at the core of every organisational concern.

Discovery

An intensive risk reduction phase in the Enterprise Agile product lifecycle used to establish a feature backlog for the MVP, prove solution architecture, refine the delivery approach, and establish assurance and governance controls.

Epic

A large user story that cannot be delivered in one iteration, or that is split into a series of stories.

Feasibility

The first phase of the Enterprise Agile product lifecycle used to establish goals and objectives.

Feature

A coarse-grained functional requirement, that performs a major step in a user journey. Features are decomposed into epics and stories.

Forming–storming–norming–performing

A staged model of group development first described by Bruce Tuckman in 1965.

Full Stack Engineer

A technologist who undertakes the full range of engineering tasks required to deliver change.

Governance

The processes of controlling and operating an organisation.

Hadoop

Open-source software that uses a network of multiple computers to solve problems that require massive amounts of data and computation.

Holacracy

A system of decentralised management and organisational governance in which authority and decision making are distributed amongst self-organising teams, rather than lodged with a management hierarchy.

Incremental Delivery

The process of delivering change in discrete chunks.

Innovation Lab

The combination of Lean thinking, processes and behaviours to generate new ideas for products.

INVEST

A widely accepted set of criteria, or checklist, to assess the quality of a user story. The checklist is: Independent, Negotiable, Valuable, Estimable, Small, Testable. If the story does not meet any of these criteria, the team are challenged to reword or rewrite it.

ITIL

The Information Technology Infrastructure Library. A standard set of processes for service management.

Java

A general-purpose, object-oriented programming language designed to have as few implementation dependencies as possible, so that application developers can write a single program that runs on multiple platform types.

Kanban

A Lean process for the delivery of change based on work-in-progress limits.

KDD

Key Design Decision log. Used to record the output of a design authority process.

Lean

Derived from the Toyota Production System, Lean manufacturing is a method of working aimed at improving flow, eliminating waste, and increasing quality. Lean principles have since been applied to fields beyond manufacturing, including service industries and government.

LeSS

Large Scale Scrum framework. A method for scaling Scrum.

Microservice

A microservice architecture is one where an application or system is developed as a group of smaller independent services.

MLOps

Machine Learning Ops. A collaborative practice for Data Scientists and Operations Teams to manage production.

MMF

Minimum Marketable Feature set. The smallest amount of functionality in a product that delivers recognisable value to customers/end users.

MVP

Minimum Viable Product. The version of a product that allows a team to collect the maximum amount of validated learning with the minimum amount of work.

MVS

Minimum Viable Service. The minimum number of service management processes that need be in place when a product goes live (usually incident management, change management, release management and event management). Additional processes outside of the MVS are expected to be implemented after the product is live.

Multi-speed IT

Encapsulates the principle of different levels of Agility in different types of systems, for example pace layering and Bimodal IT.

Nexus

A framework which enables multiple Scrum Teams to work on one project.

NFRs

Non-functional Requirements. System attributes such as security, reliability, performance, maintainability, scalability, and usability.

Organisation

The business or enterprise seeking to deliver change and run technology products.

Pace Layering

A model for separation of systems that change at different rates and levels of Agility. The common three layers are systems of innovation, systems of differentiation, and systems of record.

Pattern

A reusable solution to a commonly occurring problem within a set context.

Persona

A life-like description of an actual user of the product, used by the team to gain greater insight into user needs.

Portfolio

The organisation's collection of technology products and services.

Product

The combination of technology and manual processes required to deliver a service to users.

Product Backlog

The prioritised list of user stories to be delivered.

Product Board

Governance forum where decisions outside of the remit of the Product Team are taken.

Product Increment

One or more features that have been added to the product for a release.

Product Owner

In Agile approaches, the individual responsible for the value of the product being built by the team. The Product Owner is also responsible for managing the product backlog.

Product Roadmap

A statement of intent with broad milestones and features for product delivery.

Programme

A collection of several related change projects.

Project

A container for change to a product.

QA

Quality Assurance. The practice of monitoring software engineering processes and projects to ensure quality of the software. May include ensuring conformance to published standards.

RAG

Red, amber, green. A means of indicating the risk status of activities where green means on-track, amber indicates live issues, and red means serious issues.

Release Sprint

A special purpose Sprint used to integrate the product with non-Agile changes elsewhere in the portfolio.

SAFe

Scaled Agile Framework. A set of organisational and workflow patterns to help enterprises in scaling Agile practices.

Scrum

An Agile framework for developing, delivering, and sustaining complex products – originally for software products but latterly applied to other fields.

SDLC

System development lifecycle. A process for planning, creating, testing, and deploying an information system.

Service Blueprint

A process chart which shows the end-to-end journeys made by users of a service, including everything required to meet their needs at each step.

Service Team

A group of support analysts and engineers who resolve incidents in a live product.

Service Management

Management of the operational processes and support of a system typically in production.

Service Wrap

The set of manual processes, tools, and technology that are used to run the product in a production environment and support the user.

Shear Layering

An architectural principle that indicates that different aspects of a structure change at different rates.

Sprint

A timeboxed unit of development effort in Scrum, usually between one week and one month.

Sprint 0

A special purpose Sprint used at the start of the Delivery phase to build and prime the delivery pipeline.

Sprint Backlog

The list of user stories to be delivered in a given Sprint.

Story

A story or user story is an informal description of a feature of a system, usually written from the point of view of the user.

Story Point

A level of difficulty assigned to a story.

Stream

A group of teams working in a related functional or technical area.

TDA

Technical Design Authority. A body that meets to determine the best route forward for technical design decisions. It may be part of a generic design authority function.

TDD

Test Driven Development. A software engineering practice where tests are written ahead of the software performing the function.

Technical Debt

The implied cost of rework caused by choosing an easy approach rather than a better approach that would take longer.

'T-shaped' Individual

Someone who is an expert in at least one area and capable in many other areas.

TOGAF

The Open Group Architecture Framework. A framework for enterprise IT architecture that includes design, planning, implementation, and governance.

TQP

Technical Quality Plan. Defines the practices required to maintain a high-quality codebase.

User

An individual who uses the product.

Value

The benefit an organisation gains from implementing change and delivering a product to its customers.

XP

Stands for extreme Programming. A set of practices for Agile software development.

Notes

Notes